KIDS IN THE WILD

Cindy Ross &
Todd Gladfelter

THE
MOUNTAINEERS

Other Books by Cindy Ross

Journey on the Crest

A Hiker's Companion

*Hiking: A Celebration of the Sport
and the World's Best Places to Enjoy It*

A Woman's Journey on the Appalachian Trail

Published by
The Mountaineers
1001 SW Klickitat Way
Seattle, Washington 98134

9 8 7 6 5
5 4 3 2 1

Published simultaneously in Canada by Douglas & McIntyre, Ltd., 1615 Venables Street, Vancouver, B.C. V5L 2H1

Published simultaneously in Great Britain by Cordee, 3a DeMontfort Street, Leicester, England, LE1 7HD

Manufactured in the United States of America

Edited by Kris Fulsaas
Drawings by Cindy Ross
Cover design by The Mountaineers Books
Book design by Hargrave Design
Typography by The Mountaineers Books

Cover photographs: *Front:* Appalachian Trail to Little Rock Pond *(Cindy Ross)*, *Front inset:* Child proudly registers family for backpack *(Kirkendall/Spring)*, *Back:* Llama packing *(Cindy Ross)*, *Back inset:* Canoeing *(Cindy Ross)*

Library of Congress Cataloging-in-Publication Data
Ross, Cindy.
     Kids in the wild : a family guide to outdoor recreation / Cindy Ross & Todd Gladfelter.
        p.   cm.
     Includes bibliographical references and index.
     ISBN 0-89886-447-X
     1. Outdoor recreation for children—United States—Handbooks, manuals, etc.
2. Family recreation—United States—Handbooks, manuals, etc.   I. Gladfelter, Todd.
II. Title.
   GV191.63.R67   1995
   790.1'922—dc20   95–37429
                                                 CIP

For Sierra and Bryce,
our wild, wonderful kids, and for
Walkin' Jim Stoltz,
whose music and friendship
have been a great inspiration for us

Contents

PART I:
TENDING TO THEIR NEEDS

PART II:
ON THE JOURNEY

"A Kid for the Wild"

lyrics by Walkin' Jim Stoltz

Now when I was a babe just about knee high
How I loved all the worms and the butterflies
And I felt the need just to crawl through the weeds
Talkin' to the critters, all the bugs and the bees.
Mom says to Dad, "What's with this kid?"
Dad says to Mom, "Don't flip your lid. It's just his style. He's a kid for
the wild."

As I grew, well, I hit the woods
'Cause walkin' out there made me feel so good.
Just to be me, you know it felt so free.
I could wander here and there, or go climb a tree.
And I watched the deer and I chased the rabbits
And the chipmunks, too, and I learned their habits.
Mom says to Dad, "I'm afraid he's weird."
Dad says to Mom, "Oh, I think it's clear. It's just his style. He's a kid for
the wild."

I like things the way they are, not inside cages or in plastic jars.
You know, I like to see things running free
And I have the idea they were meant to be.
There's more to life than just TV,
There's the rivers and the mountains and the clouds and me.
It's just my style, I'm a kid for the wild.

I like critters like grizzly bears
And spotted owls and desert hares,
And I can't understand the big money, man,
Chase them from their homes and change the land.
They have a right to live for their own distinction,
There ain't no cause for their extinction.
Just my style, I'm a kid for the wild.

Yes, I like places where there ain't no roads.
You can listen to the crickets and the hoppin' toads.
It's all right there, even in the air.
The wilderness is something so precious and rare
You know to throw it away just don't seem fair.
Let's all get together, really try to care.
Just my style, I'm a kid for the wild.

I guess I'll always have this thirst—
Clean water and air, you know the earth comes first.
Let's save the seas and the mountains and trees,
Let's keep it wild and keep it free,
And when your parents tell you to go to bed
And they close the door and you nod your head,
They'll say, "It's just his style, we got a kid for the wild,
Yeah, it's just that style, we got a kid for the wild."
Be a kid for the wild, be a kid for the wild.

Preface

*T*here were times, while writing this book, when I feared our experiences were inadequate. Most of my knowledge in dealing with kids in the outdoors is with the youngsters, although I've consulted over a dozen other families whose children's ages cover the entire spectrum from infancy to teenagers. And I am not an expert at every sport that is included in this text, although I'd like to be.

We have an awful lot of experiences, though. We put in 1,100 long-distance miles with our daughter, Sierra, by the time she was four, and 600 with our son, Bryce, by the time he was two. If I waited ten, even five, more years to write this book, our children would be teenagers and the wealth of information I'd have would be daunting. And so, probably, would be the size of this book! Parents need this book now. The earlier you get your children out there, the better.

Part I gives you the basics on keeping your kids warm and dry, fed, clean, safe and healthy, and rested and (hopefully) entertained while in the wilderness. Part II describes the particulars for some outdoor activities, including camping, day hiking, backpacking, stock animal packing, bicycling, canoeing, and cross-country skiing. Throughout the book, I present age-specific information under the headings Babies (up to one year old), Young Children (one to five years old), Older Kids (six to twelve years old), and Adolescents (thirteen to nineteen years old).

You will need to consult good how-to guides on each individual sport before taking your children out, and will need to first become practiced at the sport yourself before taking your children with you. There's not enough space in this book to teach you that. The purpose of this book is to inspire. To make you believe that your children belong in the wilds and that it is up to you, their parents, to show them that world. It's imperative for the future of our planet that our young people feel comfortable and at home in the natural world. They can't feel responsible to care for something if it's foreign to them. They will only reach that point if we take them to it. Between the covers of this book, I hope to show you how.

Acknowledgments

*T*odd and I thank our contributors, who shared their stories and wisdom: Todd and Elizabeth Bauman, the Brown family, Dean Burroughs, Frank and Lila Fretz, Joe Gilbert, Ben Glo, Geoff Godfrey, Joe Kita, the MacAnaney family, Kathleen and David MacInnes, the Moline family, John Quimby, the Redwood family, the Rothenhoefer family, Bob Scheidt, Jim and Deb Schell, Cindy and Todd Taska, John and Marcia Vlah, Rob Wawrousek, and the Zimmer family.

We also thank our sponsors over the years for their support, which helped tremendously in gathering the knowledge for this book: Alpine Aire for freeze-dried food; Basic Designs for gravity-fed water purifier; Stan Ebel of Buckhorn Llamas for his llamas and gear; Columbia Sportswear for rain suits; "Country Inns Along the Trail" for our Vermont hike; Crazy Creek for camp chairs; Deckers for Teva Sandals; Family Clubhouse for diaper liners; Intermountain Trading Company for Bear Valley Bars; Kelty for children's sleeping bags and packs; Mad River for canoe and accessories; Merrell for boots; Moonstone Mountaineering for outerwear; Charlie Hackbarth of Mount Sopris Llamas for child's saddle and llama gear; Newport Kidsport for children's outerwear; Nike for boots and shoes; Patagonia for apparel and outerwear; Powerfood for PowerBars; Puddleduckers for rubber boots; the Rocky Mountain Llama Association, which moved mountains to see that we completed our hike; Sierra Designs for tent; Tough Traveler for child carriers and packs; and Wickers for long underwear.

For your empty, quiet house and a great place to write . . . Mik Charowsky, thanks.

And our sweet children, Sierra and Bryce, who did not have a choice in these adventures but who were darn good sports anyway.

Last but not least, I thank my wonderful publisher, The Mountaineers Books, for believing in what I have to share, especially Margaret Foster, my good editor and friend.

Introduction:

Why Take the Kids?

*A*bout the time we decided to become parents, we spoke on a panel discussion at an Appalachian Long-Distance Hikers' Gathering. The topic was why we love long-distance backpacking and how we manage to keep doing it in our lives. When it was my turn to speak, I surprised myself with my emotional outburst, blurting out tearfully, "Once we become parents, we don't know when or how we can possibly get back on the trail again and, oh, we are going to miss it terribly."

A few grandmother-type hikers came up to us later to reassure us that our children would be more joy than we could imagine and well worth the sacrifice of having to wait to hit the trails again. That wasn't what we needed to hear. What we needed was a book just like this to give us the confidence and the knowledge to go back out to the wilderness.

So we know where some of you are coming from. It sounds very scary. You wonder if the work involved will be daunting and, frankly, worth it. *But* you love it out there, you don't want to abandon your outdoor sports that you participated in before parenthood, and you really would like to know ways to share it with your children and have them come to love the outdoors too.

Take heart. We've worked out a lot of the kinks for you. We've gleaned all the information we've accumulated (from covering 2,000 miles just in the first three years of our children's lives), and gathered a ton from other families—in all different sports and age groups—and put it into this book to give you a great head start. We offer point-to-point practical information and illustrate some of these points with real-life stories of frustrations, discoveries, gained knowledge, and understanding. Hopefully you will come to see that to *not* take them along would be a tremendous loss for your children and you.

When our first child was three months old and the spring caused the sap to rise in our blood, we decided to just try it. We felt confident with our outdoor skills. We knew we had a lot to learn about parenthood, but we were willing to try. (We thought of the pioneer women, carrying their babies across the country in their arms, and we felt silly thinking we couldn't handle a hiking trip with such high-tech gear). It was a great first experience and we just kept building on it until it was second nature to bring them along.

The older they become, the easier they are to deal with in the wilds, and the more they contribute. Be especially careful with first-timers that you do not overwork them or have them carry too much weight (no more than 20 percent of their body weight if possible). You do not want them to focus on how they feel but, instead, to sense their surroundings: touch the trees, notice the clouds, smell the air, and admire the beauty. If they are feeling bad, they cannot focus on anything other than their feelings, which may lead to the conclusion that backpacking is hard. In time, backpacking not only strengthens one physically but also mentally, so it is important to explain to any first-time backpackers that the first trip is usually the hardest. Because of this, in order to do justice, you must take a child backpacking at least twice, or not at all.

But you must not wait until they are older to bring them out. Even the tiniest babies need the gifts the natural world has to offer. How do I know it's important to them and that anything we expose them to out there has any real positive effect on them? Sometimes they give you glimpses.

We were camped on a saddle in the San Juans between Middle and West Mineral Creeks on the Colorado Trail. I hadn't seen one-year-old Bryce for awhile and he hadn't answered my calls. I walked around the sloping meadow and found him sitting in a patch of sunlight in the green grass. He was holding a purple aster in his hand, very close to his face. The evening light was low and it shone golden on him. A caressing breeze blew his sun-bleached hair and the unusually long, feathery petals of the flower. He twirled it ever so slowly and watched, entranced, how the wind played with it, bending some petals up and bending some petals back, like long graceful fingers. He never heard me call, he never saw me approach him. He was lost in time with his purple aster, the wind, and a sunlit meadow. That was all he needed right then.

On our way home from Colorado, after our family had spent two months hiking across the Rocky Mountains, Sierra sat in the back seat of our pick-up, looking out the window at Nebraska speeding by, and began to whimper, "I miss. I miss." I couldn't get out of her right away what it was she missed and she, at three years old, had trouble putting her feelings into words. Finally she blurted out, "I miss Colorado!" Her father said, "Don't you want to go home and see your room and pet your kitty and jump on your trampoline and play with your toys?"

"I want the mountains," she replied. "I want to bring the mountains home."

Todd said, "We have mountains back home. We have the Appalachian Mountains in our backyard," and she, very profoundly, asked, *"Where?"*

Yes, exactly. Her idea of mountains and what they are had changed. Mountains are very high and grand, with passes and views and herds of elk and meadows of wildflowers and *wind!* She didn't remember any of those things about the mountains back home. It was interesting to see that a three-year-old can feel the same way as we adults after returning from a trip in the high mountains. These Appalachian Mountains are "hills" to her, or so they seem now. We told her we would return to the high mountains again and soon.

We created a need for the wilderness in her, already, at age three. That's why we bring them out there. To try to get it in their hearts. To try to have it grab hold of their souls. I believe, as Walt Whitman wrote, "Now I know the secret of making the best persons. It is to grow in the open air and eat and sleep with the earth." Nature has so much to teach us, and children's brains are like sponges—ready and waiting to absorb, even more so than our foggy, overloaded adult ones. For this reason, we want our children out in the wilderness with us.

I bring my children out there so they don't forget what is already in their hearts and souls—the beauty, the magic that can so easily get lost and forgotten as we grow older. These are the real reasons we bring them into the wilds. It is all the reason we need. It makes us close our eyes to all the work.

Pregnancy: A Good Place to Start

Pregnant or not, many of us don't exercise enough. But for women who aren't regular exercisers, the joyful news of a new life growing inside often has a magical way of encouraging them to begin. Pregnancy is the ultimate motivator for "cleaning up your act," and it should be, given the benefits for mother and baby.

If you want to go on an outdoor adventure of any length while you are pregnant, the second trimester may be the most ideal. You are often feeling your best because you are beyond the initial nausea and extreme fatigue that often accompany the first trimester.

The American College of Obstetricians and Gynecologists advises pregnant women to measure their heart rates during activity, and to exercise at least three times a week as opposed to intermittent activity. An additional 300 calories should be consumed for every twenty to thirty minutes of low-intensity aerobic exercise, and liquids should be drunk liberally before, during, and after exercise to prevent dehydration. In addition, vigorous exercise should not be performed in hot, humid weather or during an illness accompanied by a fever.

Finally, be sure to check with your doctor or midwife on your plans for an exercise program while pregnant. Remember that a pregnant woman's wind is greatly reduced as the baby grows and pushes against her diaphragm, and that she lacks resiliency. It can take a half day to recover from fatigue, whereas someone who isn't pregnant can bounce back after a half-hour nap. Use common sense and listen to what your body tells you.

Hints and Tips

- The second trimester, when you may be at your most energetic, may be your optimum time for an outdoor activity.
- Check with your doctor or midwife before undertaking any new activity or going on an adventure.
- Avoid hot, humid weather and consume additional calories and fluids when you exercise.
- Always listen to your body and never get close to your "limit."

Walking and the Pregnant Body

Walking is accessible to everyone, no matter where they live. A one- or two-mile walk daily or a few times a week is all that's necessary for good results. Regular exercise is one of the best ways to prevent hypertension (high blood pressure). Movement forces blood through your veins, which stretch and open up, thereby lowering blood pressure. The weight of the growing fetus places considerable pressure on the muscles, tendons, and ligaments that support it as they stretch, loosen, and soften to accommodate. A well-toned body will be spared much of the discomfort and backache that result from this and your body's shifting center of gravity. Stored calories that you might not need will be burned, keeping your weight down and helping fitness return after delivery.

Walking makes you feel good at a time in your life when you're likely to feel dumpy, clumsy, and fat. A toned and strong body will give you a positive body image and healthy mental state. Exercise also helps relieve the anxiety and stress that are common during the third trimester. While hundreds of new hormones surge through your body, often putting you on an emotional roller coaster, regular exercise can improve your mood and relax you. One study demonstrated that high fitness levels during pregnancy are associated with shorter labors.

Regular, rhythmic walking helps prevent varicose veins and hemorrhoids from developing by stimulating circulation and causing leg muscles to contract, which helps propel blood along the veins back to the heart. Walking helps relieve the normal swelling that occurs in the ankles and legs as fluid and blood pool and collect.

Walking helps prevent constipation that results from the slowed, squashed intestines and the increase in iron supplement. The rhythm of walking stimulates peristalsis—the wavelike movements of the intestines caused by rhythmic contractions of the intestinal muscles that help keep the bowels moving regularly.

Walking can help prevent muscle cramps in sides, legs, and feet. It can also alleviate morning sickness by not allowing the chemical by-products of the increased hormones to build up in the body.

When you decide to go on outings/adventures when you are pregnant, so much of what you are dealing with is unknown. Your pregnant body is far different than your normal one and every pregnancy is different. It is sometimes difficult to know your limits before you go. The best thing to do is liberally allow for adjustments in your plans and never feel bad if you must abandon your trip altogether.

Walking wasn't a new activity for me when I learned of my pregnancy. My body had already covered 6,000-plus miles of long-distance backpacking before conception, and I didn't relish the thought of being left behind on a lawn chair because I was pregnant while my husband and friends continued to enjoy the outdoors.

On a four-day backpacking trip during my first pregnancy, I was feeling spunky and my belly was still small enough to cinch a waist belt safely. My pack weighed forty pounds on Day 1 and I quickly learned that it was far too much for me to handle. We planned only eight-mile days but I got extremely fatigued during the last miles and hours of the first day. The next day my companions took fifteen pounds of my weight and we rested for an hour after every hour of hiking. I never felt overtired again. But I became very sleep-deprived after the four nights.

Early in my sixth month, I climbed 5,267-foot Mount Katahdin in Maine, the northern terminus of the Appalachian Trail, in celebration of the tenth anniversary of the completion of my first journey up the peak. The special people that I shared the hike with in 1979 were meeting again to retrace our steps up that sacred mountain. Because I had kept up my hiking all through my pregnancy and was so accustomed to the sport, my midwife agreed to let me try it, although she advised me to take my time, not exhaust myself, and be careful of my footing.

We chose to go on a 185-mile bike trip on the Chesapeake & Ohio Canal after discussing the plan with our midwife when I was five months pregnant with my second child. I was beyond the initial feeling-weary months but my tummy wasn't yet large enough to interfere with my pedal-pumping legs. I wasn't in top shape but felt fit enough to tackle a flat trail.

There was no heavy exertion involved because my twenty-one-speed mountain bike rolled nearly effortlessly on the smooth, packed riding surface, and we gave ourselves plenty of time to cover the

distance. Our one-year-old daughter needed frequent breaks (every five miles), which gave me plenty of opportunities to rest. I never grew winded and, at thirty miles a day, I never grew extremely fatigued either. Todd pulled the trailer with all the weight. I pulled the trailer for a mile just to experience it and it was far more than my body was capable of doing. If I had to have pulled it for any length of time, it would have been impossible. Here was my limit.

You must always listen very closely to what your body is saying and never hesitate to say when you've had enough. You shouldn't get anywhere near the "limit" of what your body can do when you are pregnant. It's not worth the risk. You should never get "too" anything: too tired, too hungry, too winded, etc., when you're pregnant and physically active. Moderation is the key. It is best to stick to the sport that is routine and familiar to you rather than start something altogether new, wherein you may be uncertain of how you will be able to perform. Of course, you will only be able to pull off an outdoor adventure if your partner or a friend is completely willing to perform like a work horse and shoulder much more of the weight and the chores, perhaps.

What About Baby?

With all these good things happening to mother, what about her growing baby? Does exercise cause any harm or stress?

In one study on fetal heart rate in response to maternal exertion, pregnant women exercised on a cycle ergometer while a Doppler ultrasound monitor recorded fetal heart rates. The results, published in the *Journal of the American Medical Association,* showed that if maternal exertion approached maximal aerobic capacity, the fetus may suffer from inadequate oxygen supply and have too slow a heartbeat. Chronic aerobic maternal exercise may be associated with reduced birthweight and increased incidence of pre-term deliveries.

Led by Dr. Stanley P. Sady and Dr. Marshall W. Carpenter, the researchers who conducted the study recommended that healthy women in low-risk pregnancies "limit their vigorous exercise to activities requiring heart rates of 150 beats per minute or less and conclude with a gentle and continuous slowing of effort during recovery."

Babies and Young Children

Just as parents need to understand their limitations during pregnancy, they need to understand the limits of children at various ages. And the older they become, the more fun and the easier the whole outdoor experience becomes. In many respects, it is more difficult to deal with children when they are young, but the seeds you are planting in their early years will really determine where their hearts lie in later years. As in other aspects of childhood development, the earliest years are the most important.

Use the outdoors early in their lives as an integral part of their development and upbringing. Walk babies outdoors to quiet them. Send quarreling children outdoors where the wide-open, natural world can distract them. Turn off the TV and send them outdoors for creative play. Walk places instead of using your car—fetching mail at your rural mailbox, strolling to the grocery store. Center social gatherings around outdoor activities. Make the outdoors and outdoor activities a normal part of their everyday life.

When Sierra was a baby, she had the occasional crying jag that makes a parent wonder if it is colic. We discovered a way to immediately quiet her and are using it still, years later. We took her outdoors, no matter what the hour, the temperature, or the weather. It wasn't even necessary for her to see the wind blowing or the light dancing to divert her attention—a pitch-black night worked the same miracle. There was simply something special about going outdoors that actually made her happy. We used this technique throughout her babyhood every time it was necessary. Now that we have two children, we use this technique whenever there is a conflict. "Let's go out," we say as soon as a power struggle begins, and soon all is forgotten. Outdoors is neutral ground, the peace place.

Walking needs to be part of children's lives if they are to come to love the outdoors and being physically fit. When children only walk from their parents' vehicle in the parking lot to the store entrance (and then it's the closest space mom or dad could find), using their legs to walk seems like a chore to them, instead of a privilege and a joy.

Our children walk a lot. They accompany us on feeding the llamas in the pasture, collecting firewood from the shed, and collecting the eggs from the chicken coop at the end of the day. Our mailbox is located a half mile down our stone driveway and, at two years old, Sierra could walk the round trip. I've taken my older nephews on the same walks and their legs invariably give out and they need to be carried, for whatever reason.

When you go to visit friends or family, turn off the TV, throw on their coats, and go for a walk. Holiday gatherings, when everyone feels lethargic from overeating and sitting still too long, are a great time to try this. Have the small children push doll carriages or kiddie grocery carts with buddies in them. I have been at my sister's home on numerous occasions when her three kids ran circles through the house, chasing one another and driving her up the wall. If they are sent or taken outdoors at times like this, they are more apt to play and work quietly and peacefully together when they are indoors.

Plan birthday parties (in the warmer months) at a park or a picnic grove, instead of indoors, where the children can discover nature and learn to love being outside. When you travel, plan your rest stops at parks that have trails instead of at highway rest stops where the only leg stretching is to the rest rooms and back to the car.

Todd and I like to plan get-togethers with our friends around an activity, instead of just sitting at someone's home. We'll throw our bikes and a trailer in our truck and meet our friends for a picnic and a ride after work. Memories are richer and more lasting when outings such as these are planned. They give the children a sense of adventure too. Remember, the small memories collect and turn into big influences as your children grow into adulthood. The earlier you start getting your kids out, the better. It will seem like a natural way of life and they won't resist.

Older Children

The five- to eight-year-old age group is when children are trying hard to keep up and be like adults. They want to try everything and want to see if they can accomplish a task alone. It's often slow going, for their bodies aren't strong enough to match an adult's pace, but they are willing to wear themselves out trying. Tremendous support and encouragement is needed. Children at these ages want to begin to feel like an equal, that their voice and decision matters, so include them in as much planning as you can. Explain the choices available in decision making. This is not the age to say, "Do it because I said so and I'm the parent." This age needs honest, solid reasons more than the younger ones. They are absorbing so much knowledge. These are the years where you can turn your child away from the sport you love, or help your children enjoy your company and have them come to love the sport too.

Some believe their kids are the most fun at between eight and twelve years old. They seem willing to cooperate the most, want to help, and truly want to go. But children know how to press their parents' buttons, to get the result that they want. They know that their parents truly want them to have a good time and will do a lot to see that come about.

No matter what their age, always include your older children in the planning of the trip. Just increase their input as their age increases. Someone might want to go to a particular spot to fish or someone else might want to climb a nearby peak. Give them the opportunity to have fun. Attempt to perhaps "sell" the trip ahead of time, but not once you get out there. It is then the kids' responsibility to find their own fun and entertainment.

Let the children do as much as they can—the planning, preparation, camp chores, etc. If you want your children to be willing to go with you when they are older, when there is a choice, they need to be made a part of the trip as early as possible. Children have to realize that the entire outing is a group effort. If one or two do it all, it isn't fair. When you live together as a community on the trail, all must help with the chores.

They must all be included and feel a part of it, but when they are young, especially, they must realize that their powers are limited. In the wilderness, there are certain rules, for there are real dangers and concerns (see Part I, Tending to Their Needs).

Pick your activities in accordance with your children's needs and desires. Pay attention to the season too. A bike ride is a good choice for a hot and humid summer trip. The constant movement keeps a nice breeze blowing, which cools you off. Converted rail-trails are usually fairly level, calling for little exertion on a hot day. They're often along waterways and enable you to combine the ride with the all-time favorite activity—swimming and wading—to make the trip more interesting and appealing.

Be flexible enough to change your plans if need be. An energy-draining heat wave could make climbing on an exposed peak in the heat of the day a poor choice, even if you planned it ahead of time. Don't set the kids up for a bad time by choosing an inappropriate activity or location for the weather conditions, their energy level, etc. Try to make the outing as foolproof and bound-for-success as possible. Adults can push themselves through uncomfortable conditions because their desire to reach their goal is stronger, but we should not subject our children to this. Flexibility and adaptation fortunately go hand-in-hand with parenthood anyway.

Hints and Tips

- Include your children in as many aspects of the planning as they are able to participate in.
- State your rules to avoid dangerous situations and make sure your children know them.
- Always remain flexible and adaptable in your plans.

Adolescents

The twelve- to fourteen-year-olds have a lot more going on within them, besides participating in the sport you have chosen for your outing. Their hormones are causing all sorts of upheavals in their emotions and this could be exaggerated during times of fatigue, stress, etc. Even more patience is required from the parents of children in puberty. Real challenges are necessary to keep them busy and help them find their new limits, for their boundaries are expanding daily.

Rob Frolek's relationship with his adolescent son, Chris, became closer because of their newly shared sport of backpacking. The men in this family—three generations of Germans with the same private, internal type of personality—are not ones to open up and not ones to pry. Communication of feelings does not happen frequently or easily. Second-generation Rob especially remembers a time in his life (adolescence) when he needed his father and the lines of communication appeared closed. Rob wanted things to be different with his own son.

In nature, something very relaxing seems to occur—putting the mind at ease, opening up the true person. The outdoors can teach lessons that are invaluable in life and it provided a stage where these two quiet males could find communion.

When Chris was twelve years old, Rob took him on his first overnighter. There was a lot of complaining, mostly over his pack, which didn't seem to fit his hips well. Rob was not discouraged, for he believed what they were sharing was a good thing.

A year went by and in that important time, Chris grew, gained weight, and became stronger in many ways. Rob waited until his son asked him two times before taking him back to the trail. This time, Chris showed no reluctance. He took an active role in planning and hiked much more assertively.

They have now been on a half dozen backpacking trips with just the two of them. On the trail, both continue to maintain their private space that is so true to their nature, but there is a subtle communication going on that feels magical to them. Looking out over a vista at the star-filled night as you lie in your sleeping bag next to your father is an experience a son will not soon forget. They sometimes talk when they hike. Chris opens up about school and his other interests. He expresses his feelings more, like exclaiming about the beauty of nature, so his dad knows it has become important to him too.

At home there is a difference too. He asks more questions in general. Chris asks his father how his day was and how work went. He makes an effort to go down into his father's office in the evening to say good-night. These may sound like minor things and are indeed subtle, but when it comes to such internal people, they are milestones. And Rob can see an increase in his son's interest from winter to the hiking season, when they share more from the trail.

Rob is trying to foster mutual respect. He wants his son to feel comfortable with him. He wants to let him know he's approachable so that Chris will come to him when and if he needs help. Taking the time to go out into the wilds with his son says, without a word, that he is important to him. At this extremely difficult time in a child's life, this is a very important message to successfully communicate. Rob hopes to lay the foundation for a lasting relationship, and times shared on the trail are some of the strongest building blocks there are.

Special-Needs Children

Special-needs children need the outdoor experiences as much, if not more, than other children. You can take your special-needs child camping, etc., but there are some questions you need to find the answers to before deciding on a place. Are there pathways that will be paved and smooth enough for a wheelchair to safely cruise along? Will the campground have an area flat enough to maneuver with assistance? Can you get to the marina to fish and boat?

Contacting campgrounds ahead of time for these answers will help you decide which ones are appropriate. These are simple logistical problems that can be solved. For experiences of families of special-needs children who hike, bike, canoe with their children, see the sections on special-needs children in chapter 7, Day Hiking; chapter 8, Backpacking; and chapter 9, Stock Animal Packing.

The handful of families I found who took their special-needs children out were incredibly inspiring to me. I found myself in awe of them and humbled by their extreme love and perseverance and belief. It made me ashamed that I sometimes thought my job out there was a hard one. After hearing their stories, what excuse could we parents with so-called "normal" children possibly have?

When Others Join You

You can never predict what will occur on a trip; so many variables are unknown—weather, trail conditions, levels of physical fitness. Everyone has their own tolerance level, too, of dealing with inclement weather, soreness, etc. The more people you involve in your group, the more complications that can arise, causing you to alter your plans. It is very important to remain flexible and have a good amount of independence so your decisions do not always drastically affect the entire party.

Having others join you on a day trip, overnighter, or even a long weekend is often more enjoyable for the children than going it alone with just the immediate family. But on family vacations and longer outings, you may want to consider keeping the outsiders at home so that your family can bond in the special way that families need. With children partaking in so many activities these days, it is rare to share intimate family time alone, but it is very healthy and necessary for the soul of the family.

Bringing another adult along as the parent's friend can introduce a unique set of human dynamics. That person could pull you away from your children if much of the conversation revolves around adult topics. For an outing of extended length, choose your hiking companions very carefully. Make them as aware as possible of what traveling with children is truly like and ask them if they are up to it.

We have a wonderful friend who accompanied us on part of a

llama hike whose presence only added to our family's enjoyment. First off, he truly loves our children and focused on them as much, if not more, than on us. He was very careful to give us our space—camping a good distance away, coming over to share a meal or visit at appropriate times, and allowing all logistics of the trip to revolve around our family's needs.

One outdoor activity where additional company is highly recommended is canoeing. Families I know who have been canoeing all their lives and who taught canoe safety for years believe that a family with young children should never go it alone. It is simply asking for trouble. Too many factors could come into play and cause a situation where assistance is needed. When an activity includes the element of water, the danger level shoots way up. It isn't always possible, or desirable, however, to include another canoe of people on an extended outing, so a family must be even more responsible in their decision making.

Kids' Friends

If your children have friends who think they would enjoy going on an outdoor excursion together with your family, their presence could possibly add to everyone's experience. Children (even those with siblings) enjoy other children, because it is a diversion for them. They get to share their wonder and their knowledge with a new person, the other children take the focus off of the parent to perform, entertain, and cater to them, and the children go off together kindling their own fun, setting their own pace, discovering the natural world from their perspective.

The outdoors often sets a stage where children can more easily include other children of varying ages (including their own siblings), because the activities one does and the interest in the natural world do not have as many age or skill limitations as other activities. Younger children seem to have more energy and drive to hike or climb a peak than older, more easily bored children. The natural world encourages equality, harmony, and acceptance.

Of course, whenever you bring other children or people along on an outing, it has the potential to increase the work load of compromising and tending to needs. Other children are raised differently in their families, have different ways of being disciplined, and have different eating habits and skill levels that you, who are not their parent, need to discover and learn to handle. It is best if the children you invite along have visited your family numerous times so everyone is comfortable with each other and knows how one another functions. If their parents are not coming along, you must take their place and this could be a sensitive thing if you don't know each other well. The guest children should be treated with respect, kindness, and patience, so that they feel included. At the same time, your own children's siblings should never be left out or made to feel like an outcast, or all the positiveness of bringing the friends is canceled out. The first importance should be the family unit.

Make sure the guest children know what to expect on the outing, and know what is expected of them, etc. The more they know and understand, the less of a burden and the more of an asset they become.

Hints and Tips

- Try to invite other children on your outings whom the family knows well and is comfortable with.
- Make sure the guest children know what to expect on the outing, how they need to behave, and what is expected of them.
- Guard against other adult companions pulling you from your children. Have them be a friend to everyone in the family, young and old.

Other Families

Joining with another family can mean less work and difficulties in some instances. More adults mean child-care responsibilities can be shared. Adults can take turns being with the children or leading them in an activity or camp chore, while other adults take a few hours to do an activity such as climbing a nearby peak or taking a quiet rest. This arrangement can also be good for single parents, for, by joining with others, there is help with the work load and the outing becomes much safer. If there is an emergency, a single adult would have a much more difficult time tending to all needs.

But an outing with another family can be twice as slow, for there are twice as many problems, nap times to coincide, breaks, etc. You often seem to get nowhere. The parents may be understanding, but it can still be very frustrating.

Parents handle their children differently—how they interact, how they discipline—and this can cause conflict. Physical fatigue can bring on stress and strain, making it even more difficult to communicate and compromise. The more people, the more children in the group, the more needs must be met. Every added person can contribute to slowing down progress.

But as long as you always keep in mind that your young children are there for the present, not the goal, you shouldn't have any trouble.

Organized Group Outings

Guided nature walks at parks and campgrounds can really add to your children's outdoor experiences if they are the right age (over six). They learn to see, hear, smell, and identify the natural world in aspects that you, their parents, might not be knowledgeable in. Special walks just for children can often be found at environmental education and nature centers, sanctuaries, etc., that are scaled down to their ages' attention span and understanding.

But if your children are under six or so, their presence in this type of organized program can be disturbing. The going is often slow with lots of stops for interpretation. Our very young children could never handle stopping for long periods of time, and often not even the short stops. Their impatience disturbed the others and prevented them from listening. We tried standing stationary and jostling their child carrier and even walking back and forth in a small area, but it never seemed to work for long. They often needed to nap, and constant movement was the only way this was accomplished. We were always forced to go ahead on our own.

There are so many reasons a family needs to stop while on a hike that to impose their needs onto a group is not only unfair but extremely aggravating for all involved. Potty breaks, diaper changes, hunger pangs, stopping to examine nature, rest stops, motivation problems are all part of a family's extremely radical schedule. A parent can seek out hiking clubs to gain knowledge of the sport from veteran hikers and to learn about trails and hikes in the area, but this is one type of outing you might want to refrain from bringing the younger kids. They are usually set up with a leader and a sweep in the rear who does not allow anyone to get behind him or her for safety reasons. Some clubs have a definite pace that is established by that particular leader, and it is impossible to make a family with small children adhere to it. Why, I've been on group hikes where designated "nature breaks" were announced. Can you imagine telling your young hikers that they must only eliminate at pre-determined times?

Organized hikes, canoe runs, etc., with a club can be a real bonus for your older children. The opportunity to be with others who are of varying ages, from all different walks of life, with unique personalities, can be a very broadening, opening experience for them . . . much different than an outing planned with comfortable friends. The potential for learning, including social interaction, increases. Your children can learn that wonderful gifts can be exchanged with others who are quite different from themselves.

PART

I

TENDING TO
THEIR NEEDS

▲ ▲ ▲ ▲ ▲ ▲ ▲ ▲ ▲

CHAPTER 1

Clothing and Equipment

▲ ▲ ▲ ▲ ▲ ▲ ▲ ▲ ▲

*R*egardless of how long in distance or duration your outing is planned to be, at the top of your list of necessary gear should be the Ten Essentials:

The Ten Essentials

1. Extra clothing
2. Extra food
3. Sunglasses
4. Knife
5. Firestarter
6. First-aid kit
7. Matches in a waterproof container
8. Flashlight
9. Map
10. Compass

Particulars on many of these items are covered later in this chapter and other chapters in Part I. Make sure you always carry the Ten Essentials and be sure you know how to use them.

Clothing

Babies

There is a definite limit of low temperatures at which you should not take your baby out for extended periods of time, for there is a limit to how many layers of clothing you can put on an infant. Our body temperature and insulation needs when we're exercising are far different from theirs, especially when we consider that they take naps and their body temperature dips down even lower.

Feel your baby's skin at every break (every hour or so), and occasionally during your activity. Check nose, hands, neck, and, sometimes, limbs. If limbs are cold, become a bit concerned. Warmth everywhere else assures baby is toasty.

Thin polyester sleepers for summer and assorted weights of "blanket" sleepers for cooler nights are the mainstay outdoors, adding and subtracting layers as needed. These are especially good in cold and wet weather because the feet are attached, preventing "gappage" and keeping in the warmth. In warm weather, the vinyl footies make children's feet sweat and so can be cut off then.

Synthetic socks, preferably polyester, are easy to find and these can be layered inside the sleeper feet. For extra warmth, you can also take adult socks and put them over their sleepers on the outside, pinned with safety pins if need be.

So much heat is lost through your neck, especially while you sleep. Cotton turtlenecks have great warmth-retaining power, but synthetics are far superior. Polypropylene and other synthetic fibers are the best insulators. A hooded sweater with a back zipper can be layered over sleepers. You'll need a size larger than normal, for it will need to go over other layers.

A hat is very important for babies, who have little hair and what hair they have is not thick and dense and capable of providing warmth. An acrylic balaclava—a pullover hat that covers your neck and has a hole cut out for your face—is much warmer than a pull-on hat. A sweater hood can be pulled over a hat, for added warmth. If it is exceptionally cold out, a poly-filled baby sack with legs works—the type with legs is necessary to get the child into child carrier leg holes. Another choice for outer warmth is a snowsuit. You can also get pile baby suits in specialty children's catalogs.

There is no reason why they cannot sleep right in these layers at night. Sometimes you have to layer your child up because he or she can wiggle the upper body out of the sack. It's difficult to test for and change a soiled diaper when they are dressed like this; it is nearly impossible to make a nighttime change without waking them up. But they must be kept warm.

In hot weather, to avoid sunburning your baby's skin, use a very thin, light-colored polyester sleeper with the feet cut out and no socks on. Lightweight cotton works well too. During hot, humid weather, put a cotton T-shirt on your baby and nothing else but a diaper and a sun bonnet.

If you are traveling on snow, in bright open areas, or on water, don't neglect your baby's eyes, for tiny sunglasses are made to fit them. They might not keep them on, but you can give it a try. A hat with a brim will help reduce exposure to glare.

Young Children

For young children, overalls protect their waist, and that extra layer on their vital organs really keeps them warm. A zipper on the inside of the legs makes it easier for them to go to the bathroom. If this isn't an option, put the overalls on top of all their shirts (except for their coat). Then they'll still have some protection from the elements on their tops when they take them off to go to the bathroom.

You can sew a pair of overalls because polarfleece fabric is readily available in fabric stores (at least during the cooler months of the year). Polarfleece fabric is not cheap, but there is still a considerable savings compared to buying it already manufactured. You could also sew outdoor clothing made of wool for your children if you are an adept seamstress. In selecting a pattern, choose one that has buttons on the shoulders so you can adjust it to your child's torso length. It is very important to be able to do this because the amount of layers your child has on underneath and the space they take up can vary, and a diaper or lack of one can affect the suit's torso length too. You can put in a separating zipper on the inside seams of the legs for ease in changing diapers.

You may have some trouble finding good outdoor socks for your toddler, for they are not sized down that low. The larger socks may not work well because there is too much width and they take up too much space in the boot. Look for synthetic socks (polyester/acrylic) in department stores and layer them accordingly. For liners, you can use dress-up nylon socks made for all children, for the outdoor companies don't make liner socks for small children. They really do add warmth to their feet, though, which are one of the first things to get cold on a child who is not moving around.

It's difficult to find wool mittens/gloves for the very young, but their socks can serve as a good standby. Any hand covering will present a problem for the thumb sucker.

Another piece of clothing for your young child for warmth whenever it is windy out but no precipitation threatens is a water-resistant, one-piece windsuit. It keeps wind from penetrating all the layers of insulation. They are cut generously for greater freedom and hooded for extra warmth. You can also put them on the children on fair mornings when the vegetation is wet from dew.

Older Children

Most of the outdoor clothing you purchase can be used for all the different outdoor sports and activities your child may be involved in.

To build your child's wardrobe, begin with lightweight, synthetic underwear like polypropylene or Capilene or Thermax. If the shirt is a light color, it can be worn even in warm weather with the sleeves pushed up. As the temperature drops, add more layers. Long underwear can be purchased in light, medium, and expedition weights. Turtlenecks made of these fabrics are worth their weight in gold. Nothing keeps your torso's heat in better than these. They are especially good for sleeping at night to prevent cold air from moving down into children's chests. Buy their outdoor gear on the large size, especially the outer layers (expedition top), because they will need to go over several other layers. Cuffs can be rolled up and the extra length will prevent their backs from being exposed when they bend over.

When it is warm, children can wear sturdy nylon shorts that repel water. You do not need any cotton pants, short or long. In the heat of the summer, you may want to bring some cotton pants for bug protection, etc., but still, be careful with cotton in the mountains, where you can have cold weather any month of the year.

As the temperature drops, older children can wear different weights of underwear as their pants until it gets cold enough to need "fleece" pants. Polyester pile or Polartec fleece clothing is superior because it's warmer than wool, it wicks moisture, and it provides superior insulation in cold weather.

Because polarfleece clothing has become popular, you can sometimes find jackets (select one with a hood for added warmth) and sweaters made from it in department stores. Outdoor companies' designs, however, are usually superior, for they know what details make life easier and warmer in the backcountry. Because of the jackets' availability in department stores, they are popping up in second-hand stores and outgrown shops. These shops are also a good place to find wool sweaters for your children. Adults sometimes shrink their wool sweaters to the point that they will fit a child.

Windbreakers are important, even though your children might also have rain suits. Avoid the kind of windbreaker that is lined with cotton. Some outdoor catalogs have fine nylon pullover windbreakers for children. Buy large because it will sometimes need to go over other layers. Cuffs can get rolled up and the extra torso length is desirable for warming their buns and for sitting on chilly rocks.

For good polypro/wool/nylon socks, go directly to an outdoor specialty shop or an outdoor catalog. The acrylic/polyester baby socks often do not come as large as your child's foot. Larger socks may not work well because there is too much width and they take up too much space in the boots. Bring four to five pairs of warm socks for each child for a one-week stretch. Always keep one pair totally dry for sleeping. Store them in their sleeping bag if you feel you might lose count or be tempted to use them during the day.

Warm wool mittens are another difficult item to find, but they're out there if you search the catalogs. Thin plastic bags (like the kind you find in the produce section of grocery stores) can be slipped on their hands if it is cold and their mittens or skin needs protection.

Never leave home without a hat for your child, even in the summer. In the cooler months, consider carrying two. Balaclavas do a superior job at keeping in heat. One catalog has a wool one which is lined to prevent itching. They can also be purchased in polyester pile. This is one place you can help children stay warm without trying to force on any more layers. Balaclavas are the best kind of hat to wear to sleep in, for they prevent heat loss from the head, neck, and chest; they turn when children turn their head instead of sliding over their faces like caps, and there is no tie pinching them under their necks like tie hats. When it's really cold you can use two hats for each child—a wool one tied under the neck and a skintight balaclava. The larger tied hat goes over the balaclava when it is very cold. Pile balaclavas provide ample room to put another hat underneath.

In warm weather, cotton short-sleeved shirts are not wise in the mountains in the summer (and in the other three seasons anywhere else). Very thin, polypro shirts with the sleeves pushed up make more sense. Comfortable cotton clothing is good for traveling in the car, but you'll need to dig out your pile and polypropylene for backcountry excursions if you're car camping.

Sunglasses can be very necessary for all children, even the very young, if you are traveling on snow, in bright open areas, or on water. They need glasses that fit their small faces and are UV protected. You can find children's sunglasses in some specialty catalogs, children's apparel catalogs, some toy stores, and even department stores, but check your area for "dollar" stores. If you can find good UV protected sunglasses in a store like this, buy multiple pairs, so you never have to do without. And at the rate that I break and lose my sunglasses, how can we expect any more from our kids? An eyeglass cord may be a good thing for your child to keep better track of them.

Adolescents

Fashion will be much more of a consideration when your adolescent children put together their outdoor wardrobe. Step in here if they are not bringing fabrics that will insure their safety in inclement weather. As competitive as the outdoor apparel industry is, a parent shouldn't have many problems choosing clothing that satisfies their child's tastes and protects their well-being. See the preceding section on Older Children for specific clothing information.

Hints and Tips

- Turtlenecks are the best style of shirt for immobile children to wear to keep in warmth.
- Avoid all cotton clothing except in the warmest summer weather and maybe not even then in the high mountains.
- Hats are important insulation for all children; always carry one. Balaclavas keep in the most heat.
- Layers of synthetics like polypro, polyester pile, etc., are the best way to build insulation.
- Buy kids' clothes one size larger. Cuffs can easily be rolled up, other clothing will have room underneath, and you'll get your money's worth.
- Buy personal gear from an outfitter where you can go and actually see and test out what you plan to purchase.

Rain Gear

On any longer trip, there is a good chance something will fall from the sky. You may experience the fear of the unknown—how you will handle the rain under certain conditions and for how long you can handle it. There are always so many questions and decisions out in the wilderness and every situation is different. Being prepared, with a plan of attack, relieves some anxiety, but by far the most important factor (next to your wisdom) contributing to your safety and comfort is your gear.

Some parents think garbage-bag rain gear is adequate for their children. Or the $1.99 plastic rain suit that comes in a pouch and rips on the first tree branch that they brush by. There is a big difference between needing rain gear to walk to the school bus stop and needing it for downpours or days of rain in the backcountry. This really is one place you cannot skimp. I shudder to think of what kind of misery and danger my child would be in on the trail if I did not get adequate rain gear for her. A wind suit is the wrong thing to wear for rain gear. It's not that the wind suit isn't a good piece of gear. It is excellent. Just don't try to make it perform past its capabilities. Truly waterproof rain gear is the only way to go.

I had trouble finding a rain suit made of a truly waterproof material for a small child. What I did find was a cute but inadequate poncho, with sleeves that ended at the elbows. Since I have sewn many articles of outer clothing and gear from kits, I thought it would be pretty simple to sew a waterproof rain suit. It caused me so many problems that I would not advise it unless you have experience doing this sort of thing. The suit did work in the rain, but I learned a big lesson. Some things are worth almost any amount of money when you weigh it against the sanity you lose over trying to do it yourself.

I later found an adequate rain suit—a fabulous two-piece rain suit that was an exact replica of an adult's. It had all the comfort features, including underarm vents, taped seams, snaps on the elasticized wrists and ankles, etc. When you search for your child's rain gear, think about what features you would want in your suit and select one like that for your child. They deserve and need nothing less.

Ponchos do not work well in wind, and wind often accompanies rain. Your child will not wear a poncho to school, either. Those rubberized slicker rain coats are too heavy and make you extremely hot if you are moving or exercising in the least.

Children do not like it when their hoods hang down over their faces, so a very important piece of rain gear for your children is a baseball hat or a visor. It keeps the rain off their faces and their hood up and back. We put it under their hoods, and if it is cold out it goes under their balaclava too. This way, it cannot shift when they move their heads up and down.

Hints and Tips

- Choose rain gear that is designed with the same high quality standards as rain gear for adults.

Rubber Boots

Since young children are not walking and warming their feet, and their tolerance for cold, wet feet is not very high, their feet must be kept warm and dry. Because children's hiking boots are not all leather but usually a combination of leather and fabric, it is even easier for their feet to get wet.

Super latex overshoes that stretch to fit over boots can prove to be a necessity. They should be high, should have cuffs, and should have non-skid soles for traction. If you carry your children when it rains, sometimes their legs extend beyond the protection of rain pant legs and the pack cover. To keep socks from getting soaked, slip thin plastic bags (such as those you find in the produce section of grocery stores) over the socks, and tuck them up inside the rain pants.

We devised a way to dry the socks of our very young children as we hiked. We hung them inside our rain pants, tops folded over the elastic waist, with the wet socks laying against our bare stomachs. (True parental love!) Sometimes we wore a half dozen each, but there were always plenty of dry socks to keep our kids happy.

Umbrellas

Child carriers often have a sun and rain awning that offers some protection, but it is minimal. Some babies throw their arms, or even their head, out into the rain and become soaked without you even being aware of it. If you need something else, it could be the humble umbrella!

Using an umbrella is especially nice for the carrier too because it enables you to not have to have your hood up or your rain jacket zippered or even on, if it is a light rain, so you do not get so overheated. If it is a cold rain, you can also wear gloves without getting them wet.

Slide the umbrella's rod under your pack's sternum strap to secure it, and hold the handle, if desired. A golf umbrella can be hooked over the back of the pack and rested on it. This way, you could use both your hands for a short amount of time if need be.

Umbrellas are great for taking breaks under, for they are instant, movable shelter. Even activities like changing diapers and nursing are not so uncomfortable in the rain.

They do not work so well when you are on a trail in the forest and there are low-hanging branches. A small, collapsible umbrella works better in forested areas. You may have to tilt your umbrella down as you walk to prevent trees from snagging it. If the wind is really blowing, they do not work well either. Umbrellas can be dangerous in lightning if you are in the open and are using an umbrella with a metal spike on the top. If lightning is anywhere near you, do not use your umbrella.

Pack Covers

If the wind is blowing rain and you are not able to keep an umbrella upright, a rain cover must be placed over your child in the child carrier to keep him or her dry. An external-pack rain cover that is boxed up at the top, and not gathered at the bottom like an internal-frame pack cover, works best for this. It becomes very dark in there, very conducive to sleeping, which is nice if your child is tired. You can use a clothespin to gather the cover and pin it to the pack to allow your child to see.

Stuff Sacks

A good way to store your child's clothes, diapers, etc., is in dry bags used for boating. These totally waterproof bags are made of vinyl with fold-down tops and fast-tex buckle closures. They can be left outside in the rain, if space is short in your tent or sleeping bag. It is disastrous to get gear such as clothing and diapers wet.

Tent

Next to your rain gear, the most important piece of equipment in the rain is your tent. You can set it up when the rain does not let up enough to allow for adequate breaks. When it comes to family-camping tents, there is a lot of junk on the market. Stick to a reputable brand and buy from a reputable hiking/camping store so if you have trouble with it tearing, etc., they can help you take steps on replacing or repairing it.

"Family-camping" type tents often incorporate fewer poles and less tie-downs in their design construction. They could be high—over six feet—which is nice for "walking" and jiggling crying babies in the night. But high ceilings and few poles could be dangerous in mountainous, above-treeline camping, where severe storms could collapse a less sturdy tent. A tent design incorporating three or four poles is more advantageous for the adventurous family.

Before we got our present tent, we had a six-foot-high "family-camping" tent. We thought the height would be nice when we had babies so we could stand up inside it and jostle a cranky baby to sleep. But one stormy night on Chincoteague Island in Virginia, an edge of a hurricane was teasing the shore and made the aluminum poles collapse. For such a large tent, there were only two poles to support it. I don't care what degree of camping your family wishes to participate in, you cannot always predict what your weather will be like where you are. Six feet seems too high and two poles seems too few.

Also, the rain fly design of "family-camping" type tents could inadequately cover the breathable nylon body of the tent, or not overlap the coated wrap-around bathtub floor by much. These features (or lack of them) may never pose a problem in the pull-up campground, but if your family plans on going any place more rugged, consider an expedition-type tent. The more rugged an outing your family is interested in going on, the further away from "family-camping" type tents you should move, and the closer to an expedition type tent.

You do not need an expedition tent unless you think you may be in severe weather or exposed to high winds, say above treeline camping or on the coast. We personally did not feel comfortable hiking through the Rockies without an expedition tent. You can never lose with a better-made tent, especially if your family has ceased to grow. It can be a near life-long investment.

If a family plans on backpacking, weight is an important consideration, even if the tent parts can be divided amongst hikers (tent body, fly, poles). Go as light as possible without sacrificing the space or the features that you need. Dome tents are nice for families, for they give greater head space and are more comfortable for sitting up to play cards or other rainy-day activities. I could not live without a tent vestibule either. Wet rain gear, boots, rubber boots, wet socks, cook kit, gas bottle, etc., can be stored out there. Without the vestibule, it would all be in the tent with you, taking up space. For mopping up the tent floor, a good rag is one of those backpacking towels (synthetic chamois). It absorbs water amazingly well and is very light.

Once the Lewistons were camping on Cape Hatteras in North Carolina when the high winds tore the parents' tent down. Ma Lewiston convinced Pa to go out into the driving rain to see how their son and his friend were faring. Their tent was entirely down but a peek under the canvas showed two peacefully sleeping kids—so sometimes we worry too much.

Babies and Young Children

When choosing a tent for your family, if weight is not a problem, try to buy a tent with a capacity that is one person greater than your actual family—a four-person tent for a family of three, for example. When it says four, it's usually a tight four. And it doesn't matter if the "persons" are small children. Their sleeping pads and bags are just as wide as an adult's and they do not respect your space like an adult would, but instead roll and extend their arms far beyond their border. If anything, a child consumes more tent space than an adult. Even a baby is capable of doing this. You will probably have to hole up in that tent with your family sometime, waiting out inclement weather. Then that extra room will be greatly appreciated.

We thought when our family got larger, we'd use two two-person tents instead of purchasing one for the whole family. We have quite a few two-person tents and a three-person tent already and thought we'd put the kids together some nights so Todd and I could enjoy a little time alone. We tried it on a bike trip—for only one night actually. Three-year-old Sierra began screaming for me when she woke in the middle of the night and found herself alone. We all ended up in the same tent anyway and never tried it again. We won't try it again until the kids are older, perhaps. We just enjoy being together so much.

Our children adore our tent. When we were on the Colorado Trail, they normally went right into the tent to play as soon as it was set up. It didn't matter if the day was beautiful and the sun was still up, the tent was their home, their symbol of security, one of the few unchanging, dependable things on that journey. It symbolized the end of fatigue for them and their parents' loving arms around them— no wonder they loved it so.

Older Children and Adolescents

The Lewiston family of eight always uses two-person tents, for they didn't begin to take their first children out until they were older. In this family, whoever was talking to each other at the time of the trip paired up in the tents.

Once children turn twelve to thirteen years old, they want to be separate from their parents and have their own tent. Splitting up like this can be a real added bonus for your older children, for it allows them some private time—to talk with their siblings or friends, away from their parents' hearing. They are more responsible for carrying the tent, putting it up and tearing it down, and caring for it once you return home (drying it, etc.). This takes some of the work load off the parents.

Hints and Tips

- Make sure the tent you're interested in buying suits your family's needs and is of good quality.
- If your children are already older, consider purchasing two-person tents as opposed to one large family tent. You'll get more use out of them and perhaps keep your kids happier.

Sleeping Gear

You can try to save on some things when you're taking your family out into the wilderness, but you should not try to "get by" with inferior sleeping bags. Young children never seem to mind sleeping on hard ground—they accept things the way they are because, in their inexperience, they think nothing can be done about it. Older children are much smarter.

Kids' bags often get very dirty, so pick a brand and model which recommends washing. There are some bags on the market that are made of synthetic fill that is one continuous layer of insulation laminated to a piece of fabric. This eliminates sewn baffles that hold loose fill, which can tear out if children are rough or if the bags get dirty and need to be washed frequently. Some bags have larger zippers, which is a plus for children's hands to manipulate.

If there is a leaky tent during a rainstorm or a bedwetting accident or other spillage, synthetic bags do not become soaked like the old, heavy, cotton-flannel-lined bags. Synthetic bags can usually be blotted dry and left to hang in the sun until you can get to a laundromat.

Babies

Babies can sleep in a baby sack—a tiny sleeping bag with legs. Their arms often come out, so make sure there are enough layers on top to keep baby warm. You can also cover baby with polyester blankets and sometimes a down jacket, depending on the temperature. We never took our baby into our sleeping bag with us, although we would have if we were afraid she was too cold and couldn't get warm. Most mummy sleeping bags are cut too narrowly to allow for an additional person of any size. I was afraid I'd get very little sleep with her in there, or have her get too low in the bag and not get enough oxygen, or even roll over on her and hurt her, but I know of some mothers who sleep this way with their babies. You might want to open your bag and use it as a blanket over both of you, making sure you have enough insulation below.

A rectangular bag or modified mummy would work even better. The Ricci family "tied off" their child's adult mummy sleeping bag so he could not go down into it. As he grew, his bag "grew" with him. They slept with their very young baby by putting him in between mom and dad in their zipped-togther sleeping bags.

A portable crib is a nice thing to bring along if you have a small baby and are camping by your car. If you can get them used to it before the trip, it could add much peace to your trip. A portable crib frees up *both* parents to conduct camp chores instead of one always needing to hold the baby. A portable crib gives you the use of your hands back and some time to take care of other things beside your baby.

Young Children

Some youth sleeping bags are designed with zippered sections that can be added on as your child grows. They are exceptional for young children because they are much narrower and do not have a lot of space that needs to be heated up. A kid's body is not going to be able to heat up an adult bag very well. What's wonderful about these is they weigh considerably less than adult bags. If a family is backpacking and weight conscious, it may be wise to invest in one. Choose a bag for your child with a built-in hood, if you anticipate being out in anything but very mild summer weather.

Our children's sleeping bags go down to fifteen degrees Fahrenheit. The night-time temperature on the Colorado Trail ranged from twenty-two to fifty-five degrees, and the kids were always comfortable. When it was cold, we put on their polypro turtlenecks and an expedition polypro shirt on top of it, and polypro long pants, socks, and their balaclavas. They were always warm.

We tightened the drawstrings on their bags to keep out drafts and put a stuff sack of clothes at their heads so they could not crawl out of their bags and get cold. Once children are a few years of age, you can teach them how to do isometrics, like pushing against their palms, to raise their body temperature. When Bryce got cold, he went down into his lower bag to get his face away from the cold air. I was always concerned that he wouldn't get enough oxygen and would be in too deep a sleep to realize it. On those nights, I slept fitfully myself, and continually awoke to check on him and pull him out. Sleeping on a slant can make the same thing happen. I ended up folding his sleeping bag in half and stuffed a sack of clothing under the foot to prevent him from moving down.

If they continually try to crawl out of their bags in the night, or if their arms are flung out and are above their heads, it may be a sign that they are too hot. When they are young, they may not actually sweat, but their brows may feel warm and a bit moist if they are sleeping too warmly.

Older Children and Adolescents

If your child is older, go right to an adult bag. If a twelve-year-old's father is quite tall, buy a long bag right off; it will not be long before the child fits into it. If the child's parents are of average height, a regular length is fine.

Miscellany

A head lamp is very bright and leaves your hands free to do whatever work needs to be done—setting up a collapsed tent in the rain, etc.

Another item worth its weight in gold is a gravity-fed water filter, for pumping water for a family can be the most time-sapping of camp chores. The bag is merely hung up and in an hour, your family has two or three gallons of effortlessly purified water. It is essential that you have a back-up system, either a hand-pumped filter or tablets. All precautions must be taken to insure that your children only receive pure water, for they are more sensitive to parasites, etc., and their smaller body mass stands to lose a lot more should they become infected.

Food

▲ ▲ ▲ ▲ ▲ ▲ ▲ ▲ ▲

*G*ood nutrition is important anywhere, but high-energy, filling foods are especially important in the outdoors. Balance is important and bringing too much non-fat or low-calorie food or too much fatty or low-salt food can be a problem. Take care of your body's needs for energy foods, fat, salt, and liquid, and avoid thinking about dieting.

Babies

When your children are infants, feeding them on the trail is simple—if you are breast-feeding. Their "pantry" is always with them and the "kitchen" is always open. I offered it at every break, just to top Sierra's tummy off and get us further down the trail once we got started. Because babies can only cry to communicate, I liked to have that need taken care of and eliminated when it came to our detective work of trying to figure out what was wrong.

When I nursed for any length of time, I needed to rest my back against something. If not, I slouched to get my breast to her mouth as she lay in my lap. Leaning against a tree works but the best way has to be sitting in one of those padded, fold-up camp chairs. They offer so much support and can even be used to rock your child in. Outside or in the tent, they revolutionize breast-feeding in the backcountry. Nursing/feeding in the rain is no problem if you have an umbrella. It covers you and your hungry baby nicely.

Once your baby begins to eat solid foods, there is an abundance of freeze-dried food crystals available in the grocery store. Besides the instant cereals, there are containers of fruit, vegetables, and complete dinners. You simply add water and stir. There is no waste because the unused crystals can be capped off until the next meal. They are extremely lightweight and hassle-free. Check your larger grocery stores for the greatest variety. Your baby can also sample much of your food out in the wilderness—bread, bits of juicy fruit, etc.

Good Foods for Babies

whole-grain crackers

unsweetened cereal

raisins and other dried fruit

sliced fresh fruit

dehydrated fruited yogurt roll-ups

cheese with a lower fat content

Young Children

No matter how short the excursion, snacks are as important as the roll of toilet paper. Even if you just had a large meal and there's no way your young children should be hungry, and you are only going out for a short time, bring something along for them to eat and drink. If they ask for something and you don't have it, they will suddenly have a ravenous appetite and continually tell you over and over how extremely hungry they are. If you have something to eat along, not only will they finally hush up about it, but it will occupy them for awhile. It doesn't matter if it's true hunger or boredom; once they get it into their heads that they want it, the drive behind it is insignificant.

When children are young, you can solve the problem of their desire for junk food by merely not bringing it along. As they get older and become more wise to this type of food, they may make more of an argument. You can meet halfway and get more nutritious "junk" food—for instance, granola bars that are chocolate covered—and this can also be their "treat." Don't deprive them of all sweets, but keep it to a minimum.

Explain the "sugar burn-out" concept to them. Educate them so they will want to feel good and choose the foods that will help their bodies meet the demands of the sport they are participating in. Anytime kids, no matter how young, are presented with a reason, they appreciate it and usually make some effort toward understanding and cooperating.

Don't expect to get away with eating food that you don't want your children to have (bags of chips, etc.). They think everyone is on equal ground, plus it's too much like torture for them. Do a really good job of hiding it, such as eating it while they are napping, or be prepared to share once they discover you.

Our kids do eat candy on the trail, but we bring it out after they've been eating a good amount of wholesome food. Saltwater taffy, red licorice (the kind found in health food stores), carmels or chocolate candies, small round lollipops (as opposed to the flat ones, because kids can have a hard time chewing them), and large suckers were brought out at the end of the day to get another mile out of the kids, or to help get us over a particularly difficult stretch, such as crossing a windy pass, traversing a snowfield, or during a hot road walk.

It is nice to have a few breakfast choices, such as a storebought, good-for-you toaster pastry that your young children can eat themselves. It occupies them while you pack up. Then about a mile down the trail, if they want to eat, get out the granola bars or dried apples and they can gnaw on them and be happy. Keep these handheld breakfast foods handy, say in your or your child's fanny pack. It is irritating to dig in your pack bags for something to feed them fifteen minutes after you break camp.

Let your children eat whenever they want. So what if they are sometimes only eating out of boredom, and not actually need? It makes them happy, and that's what you're aiming for. You can't deprive them of food if they are hungry, just because it is close to mealtime. They have enough stress being confined in a child carrier all day, much less being deprived of food. The only problem with this is that they are often not hungry at mealtime. We try to stop for the night early enough so they can run around, get some exercise, and work up an appetite.

If you don't have some sort of drink along to quench their thirst after they eat, you're better off not even bringing any food (unless it's moist food like fruit). Thirst is worse than hunger, I believe.

Crankiness, hunger, and sleepiness can be due to dehydration. Always offer water, and if your supply is low, deprive yourself before allowing your child to become dehydrated. Mild cases of dehydration often occur nearly every day in the backcountry simply because you don't always take the time to drink abundantly, nor is the supply always there. It's usually no problem for adults because their hydration level is replenished during the evening meal, etc. But greatly encourage your children throughout the day to take fluids to keep their smaller bodies healthy and functioning in top shape.

Toddlers are best off using a sippee cup. You can attach the sippee cup to the back of the child carrier with a shower hook. You need a cup with a handle to be able to do this. You can also carry the partially filled cup through your pack's sternum strap, so it is always available.

We anticipated problems with our kids "at the table" on a two-month hike. There are no "helps" out in the wilderness, such as rocking chairs for crying babies or high chairs and food troughs for active eaters. We could only carry so much food, so if it got spilled and dropped in the dirt, some sorry soul was out of a meal. Todd cut a three-foot circle out of a heavy poly-nylon tarp for each child. At mealtime, we plopped them in the middle of them, spread their legs apart, and put their bowls in between, and a terrycloth bib over their heads. If food was dropped onto the mat, it got scraped up and put back into their bowls. The mats got wiped off after every breakfast and supper and folded up tightly to fit into the "kitchen bag."

In the bag also went a plastic bowl for each child, a spoon and a fork for each, and their bibs. We used the kind of bib that is made from a terrycloth dish towel with a hole for their heads. They are very absorbent and large and can be used to wipe their faces if need be (although it usually got so dirty from their own spills that we used a separate bandanna or wash rag for face and hand wiping). Hang the bibs up to dry overnight so they don't have to be packed up wet. When you hang your food to prevent animals from getting it, hang the bibs with it. If you have to wash them out, they can be hung to dry on the back of your packs.

Older Children and Adolescents

Children six years and older are usually able to eat the same foods as adults. Follow the same considerations as for young children, especially regarding "junk" foods, and begin adding foods from the list below.

During the day, older kids can drink out of a water bottle, but they still might need to be reminded to drink water throughout the day. They shouldn't wait until they are very thirsty. Unless an older child learns this by experience, you may have a difficult time getting him or her to drink before it actually becomes a need. Having and keeping track of their own water bottle is a good idea. You will then be able to see how much water they are actually consuming. A sports water bottle instead of a backpacking water bottle may be more popular with older kids. You can get ones with drinking tops that push up or down to open or close, but beware: their lids/seals may not be totally waterproof. What sport you are participating in and how crucial it is that water does not leak all over your gear will decide what kind of water bottle you need. Run a test before bringing it out.

Good Foods for Older Kids

whole-grain muffins

cut-up veggies

popcorn

homemade jerky

nutritious bars

nut butters

pasta-based dinners

heavy breads that won't fall apart

cheese with a lower fat content

nuts

In the Car

It is more work to see that they are eating a balanced diet when you are on the road. For food during long car drives, keep a bag of non-refrigerated foods like dry cereal, trail mix, bread, bagels, wholesome cookies, popcorn, crackers, muffins, apples, bananas, pears. I pop organic popcorn before we leave, season it, and put it into bread bags after it cools. Each child gets an individual bag. When their individual bag is gone, they don't get more. It teaches them to ration or wish that they had the skill. A small zippered cooler bag can contain some cut-up celery and carrots, cheese, grapes, peaches and plums, and a plastic backpacking bottle of cold water. Anything that is messy to eat, such as yogurt, pudding, cottage cheese, etc., is better saved for a break and kept in a large cooler.

In the car, keep a bag with small plastic bowls, spoons, bibs, paper towels, a dish towel, cups, etc. Keep a pocket knife to cut up things. A large, quart-size thermos is a good thing to have along if you are traveling in the summer and especially if you don't have air conditioning. Get some ice when you stop and keep it in your thermos to keep your beverage cold. We also keep a quart of water on the floor for sticky hands and emergency drinking. When children eat salty foods, you will really need a lot of fluid to quench their thirst.

Encourage a lot of drinking to prevent constipation, a natural problem, especially initially, from the lack of movement while riding in the car. Offer liquids to your kids, don't wait until they ask. Bring snacks along that keep them regular—raisins, fruit (dried and fresh), cut-up veggies. Breadstuffs should have a lot of fiber and be accompanied with fluid. Avoid baked goods made with white flour to minimize constipation. Before a trip, I bake pumpkin, zucchini, or bran muffins with raisins to get more fiber and added vitamins into their diet.

If you are concerned with children not eating enough vegetables on the road, carry small cans of vegetables and beans. Canned vegetables may be bland, so though you may not normally salt and butter your children's vegetables at home, make an exception when you're traveling.

On long car trips, taking prescribed rest stops for bathroom breaks, to stretch legs, and perhaps to have a meal at a picnic table instead of in the car helps relieve everyone. Children have an excess of energy and need to run it off, get their blood pumping, and raise their blood sugar level, so stop frequently. Older children also need to get out for these reasons, but also because they may become more quickly bored.

When we are camping with our vehicle, we bring along a "portable high chair" that clamps to a table top. Young children have difficulty with the wide space between the usual picnic table and the table's bench. Both our children took more than one nose dive to the ground through that hole. With the chair in place, you don't have to keep a close eye on that child. A vinyl placemat put under the chair's handles on the table works well for kids whose food has a way of migrating out of their bowls. Keep in mind that the portable high chair is an easy thing to leave behind when you use it at a picnic table. The chair can also be clamped to a truck's tailgate for impromptu breaks where there is not a picnic table.

Remember to keep flexible on the road. There will be more harmony in the family.

In the Backcountry

When you're active in the outdoors, children can alarm you with how much they consume. Kids can eat at every break (every one and a half hours), and they can usually eat for the duration of each break (at least one hour). Eating can be their favorite daily entertainment.

Encourage your kids to drink at every break—every hour or two. This is especially important when it is cold, when all of us seem to forget to drink. It's best to avoid sugared beverages. You don't want them to derive their calories from these empty foods, or have them come to prefer it over plain water. You don't want to run the risk of having them refuse plain water because it's not flavored, or refuse it in hopes that you'll give them a drink mix, and perhaps become dehydrated because of it. For this reason, it is very important that the water tastes good—and that means pumping it through a filter to purify it instead of using strong-tasting iodine tablets or crystals.

If your trip is short, bring as much fresh food as possible—fruit, good bread, cheese, cut-up celery and carrots, wholesome cookies, etc. Refrain from bringing fresh meat unless the outdoor temperature is as cold as your refrigerator. Bring their favorite snack foods, as long as they are healthy and wholesome. Children of all ages are very active when they are outdoors and their bodies shouldn't have to struggle to eke nutrition out of junk food and refined sugars, if that is what is considered their "favorite."

If you are going off into the backcountry while living out of the car, it is better to pack your trail food separately from your car food. Otherwise you may end up bringing glass jars of peanut butter and jelly on your hikes, because that is what is in the car, instead of lighter, safer plastic containers.

On extended trips, you will have to resort to dried foods and foods with a longer "shelf life," such as peanut butter and crackers, raisins and dried fruit, nuts, jerky, nutritious bars, etc. It's good to try your food out with your children before a long trip. Then you'll know how much they like it and will be able to plan accordingly.

High-energy bars (the kind found in health food stores) are a popular item with kids, especially the hard chewy ones. When it is cold out, it takes kids a really long time to eat them, too. Mom and Dad like that. Many of these bars contain a lot of fiber and the manufacturers advise you to drink water with them. Encourage this because, without it or if they eat too many, the high fiber could upset their digestive system.

Dinner options include homemade dehydrated dinners, store-bought pasta combos, and freeze-dried dinners. The freeze-dried dinners are extremely handy when time is short and everyone is starving, or when you have had a very difficult day. Setting up camp can be very time-consuming, depending on how much of a help or a hindrance your children are. Sometimes boiling water is all I can handle for dinner preparations.

We've found that the mild noodle dinners are the most appealing to kids. Spicy chilis and bean dishes are not popular, although our children normally love beans and eat them if I pick them out of a spicy dish. If a packaged meal contains a separate spice packet, leave some of it out and sprinkle it in your own bowls, or add it to the entire dish later if it needs it. Carry some onion and garlic powder, etc., to make your own meal more appealing. One of our kids' favorite dinners was meat—either freeze-dried, dehydrated, or canned—added to a gravy mix and poured over instant potatoes.

Bread can be one of the hardest things to have enough of. Growing children seem to crave the starch and carbohydrates, so always carry along a few loaves of homemade bread. You can even bring a lightweight reflector oven to make drop biscuits and muffins.

Most youngsters do not enjoy instant non-fat dry milk. It may take some searching, but there is an instant milk on the market that has a touch of cream in it. The difference between it and the non-fat kind is amazing, and your children will drink it much more readily.

I wasn't too concerned that our children weren't always interested in supper or breakfast. Nearly all of the food that we had along was extremely nutritious and quite a few of the items (such as the bars) were complete meals. Sometimes they ate shortly before dinner if they were hungry, because I couldn't refuse them just because it was two hours before dinner. I wouldn't remain hungry either if I could help it.

They often got hungry right before they went to sleep, too, especially if they had eaten a few hours before. No one should go to sleep hungry, especially children with their small stomachs. You don't want them to become cold through the night because their bodies are low on fuel. Our children ate a plain piece of bread or a granola bar at bedtime, nothing real exciting—food you'd almost need to be hungry in order to eat. If they weren't truly hungry, the bread or the bar was refused.

Make sure there is enough drinking water handy throughout the night. It is easy to become a tad dehydrated during the day and in camp, and through the night is often when your body signals you to make it up. We put water in each of the kid's sippee cups and placed them in a secure spot, such as inside a pot or a lid, where it couldn't be spilled.

When we are away from civilization for an extended period of time, there is one thing we crave more than any other: real food. Food that is fresh and unadulterated. Our children are no different. Studies have shown that, in this situation, your body craves what it needs most. Our children must have needed fat. French fries, hot dogs, cheese crackers, etc., were always on the top of their list. We did have a lot of low- and non-fat foods on the trip. Consider bringing food that is higher in fat and calories for your children if you are out for an extended period of time. Our kids probably ate all the time because they had to in order to consume the calories that their bodies needed.

Their bodies aren't just maintaining, but growing besides. Perhaps it was the salt that they needed more of also.

Dry Your Own

I was concerned that our growing children would not get enough calcium on a two-month hiking trip we took when they were very young. One of our dehydrators has a special solid tray for drying liquids. We made our own plain yogurt and added our homemade strawberry preserves to it and dried it into yogurt leather. It was very tasty and we never grew tired of its sweet and tangy taste. You can easily buy store-bought yogurt and have a greater variety of flavors.

Venison jerky that we made in our dehydrator was perhaps the favorite trail food. We kept the marinade on the mild side and left out heavy-duty spices like cayenne pepper. The same dehydrator has a nifty contraption for making pressed jerky out of ground meat. It eliminates the work of cutting and de-fatting flank steak and it enables you to use other types of ground meat, such as turkey, etc. Jerky made from ground meat is much easier for children to chew, too. Making it yourself eliminates all the chemical additives that most commercial jerky contains—chemicals your child does not need in his or her growing body.

We also use the same contraption to make our own granola bars— apple butter and peanut butter. They dried into extremely hard bars which the children gnawed on while we hiked a lot of miles. Snacks like this are especially nice for children who are being carried because you never have to stop just because they are hungry.

Hints and Tips

- Make wholesome foods the rule with an occasional treat.
- Offer food and drink at every break. Don't wait until their desires become needs.
- Never leave home for even the shortest outing without something to eat and drink.
- Although pricier, health food stores may contain your best bets for nutritious snacks.

Sanitation

▲ ▲ ▲ ▲ ▲ ▲ ▲ ▲ ▲

Diapers

Lots of people would rather wait until their children are potty-trained before taking them on outdoor adventures. In the bush, there are no elevated, padded changing tables with high sides, no musical clowns to wind up to keep them occupied, no warm tap water to make them comfortable. And in the most awful weather conditions—pouring rain, blowing wind, raw cold—their diapers still fill up and need to be emptied. This is, perhaps, the most difficult part of outdoor adventures with your children, but don't let this deter you. Children are fun to have with you at this age and there are lots of ways to make this unpleasant job easier.

What to Take

Supplies you will need are clean diapers, diaper pants, wash rag, water, ointment, dirty diaper bag, and ground cover.

Cloth diapers make much more sense on the trail for environmental, monetary, and aesthetic reasons. There are many places that do not provide garbage receptacles so that you can dispose of disposable diapers; you should never assume that you will find them. Disposables might work on short trips or trips where weight is not an issue, but because they must never be burned, buried, or put down any outdoor toilet, whether a composting toilet or a pit toilet, they are not recommended in the wild.

The biggest advantage to cloth diapers is that so much of the bulk of dirty diapers are only urine soaked. If you had to carry out all that fluid, the weight would increase tremendously as the days wore on. With cloth diapers, you can air-dry them nightly and daily if conditions allow and keep your packing weight down considerably. This is possible even in the humid east, as well as the wonderfully dry west. Another advantage of cloth diapers is that if you need more diapers, you can take those unwashed, air-dried urine diapers and sandwich them between a clean diaper, using it as an absorbent layer. This gives you much more mileage out of your diaper supply. You could never do this with disposables.

Very thin, old-fashioned cloth diapers that open all the way up to one layer seem to dry in a moment and can be used very efficiently for urine diapers, if you are smart enough to figure out when your child will have a bowel movement and use these thin ones in between those times. Bring whatever diapers you have, though; most common are contoured, fitted diapers and rectangular pre-folded diapers whose centers are thicker. We did find, after four years of using cloth diapers, that the ones on which we splurged and spent the most money still look almost new. We wear out some of the others with every washing.

For a longer trip, figure out how many diapers you go through in a day at home, and then add at least three more changes per day. Sometimes you'll need an extra diaper to clean up an extra messy bowel movement. And sometimes there are changes in your child's eating habits (looser bowels from more fiber in the diet, more urinating from frequent drinking) that also necessitate more changes. Include the diapers needed to get to the trailhead and back to your home or a laundromat.

Velcroed, breathable diaper pants let poop seep out the sides if the bowel movement is at all loose. As a result, clothes can often be soiled and wet. With vinyl pants, the tighter legs keep the poop where you want it and clothes are nearly always dry, no matter how soaked the diapers become. However, vinyl pants get stiffer the lower the temperature drops. Coated nylon pants are difficult to find, but some major nationwide department stores and some baby catalogs carry them. They always stay soft and pliable. They are certainly worth the money, because they last a very long time. We found some amazing diaper liners from a children's/baby catalog that were made of a biodegradable material (looked like a cross between paper and a very thin cloth) that made cleaning up bowel movements incredibly easier. When figuring on how many diaper pants to bring, again, look at what you use in a day at home and bring quite a few more than that.

We do not use "chemical wipes" at home or on the trail. We use baby wash rags—a new one for each bowel movement, moistened with water. We carry six to ten wash rags, but they are small and weigh so little. And, yes, we use cold water. Children never get used to it and always complain, but that is part of being in the backcountry. When you are backpacking and carrying all of your water on your back, you must remember to allow enough water for changes. Keep your child's own drinking supply separate in a smaller water bottle, perhaps in the child carrier, to prevent contamination from diaper-changing water; keep a water bottle for diaper-changing water separate and never use it for drinking.

When traveling in or camping from the car, carry a five-gallon bucket with a tight snap lid for soiled diapers. On short trips, you can just leave them there until you arrive home. When in the backcountry, bring several heavy-duty garbage bags for dirty diapers and a large coated-nylon stuff sack for clean diapers. Use a five-gallon collapsible water carrier, cut off the top (and the handle), and use this as your rinsing bucket. You can use nylon webbing and duct tape wrapped underneath the bottom of the container (tape on top of webbing) to make carrying handles. Make them long enough so they can be folded down and out of the way.

Making the Change

It's best to not delay but to change diapers as soon as you discover they need changing. It often takes two persons to change little ones in the outdoors—one to distract and keep hands occupied and one to make the change.

Keep a ground cover close by to change your child on. We always carry a blanket in the car to use for diaper changes and to sit on during our breaks. It provides a clean and comfortable spot to relax on and it feels good to get horizontal after sitting on your buns for so long. When out in the wild, use a small foam pad. If the ground is dry and soft, we often do not bother to take a foam pad out to make the change, but just throw down one of our jackets or whatever article of clothing is not being used. First lay a clean diaper down to prevent the pad or clothing from becoming soiled.

When on the road, we sometimes use the hood of the car to change a diaper. We use the car seat if the weather is inclement, but you must pad the stick shift and fill in the hole between bucket seats, and be very careful that you don't soil the upholstery. When diapering in the bush, keep in mind the direction of the sun. If it shines right into your child's eyes, he or she will become very annoyed and can make your job even harder. Position your body, or your helper's—who is by the child's head—to make a shadow onto your child. When it rains, make diaper changes under the shelter of a large tree or an umbrella, preferably a larger golf umbrella.

Using a wash rag, genitals are cleaned first, then the hiney. Often you need to rinse out the wash rag partway through the change, and the easiest way to do this is to pour more water on; while you do this, you

never want to have that rag touch the opening of the water bottle. If you are doing the change yourself, it may be difficult to prevent this. Afterward, these wash rags are thrown into the bag with the dirty diapers. Then we usually double to triple diaper our kids, especially at night, and often change them halfway through the night if they are soaked.

I was afraid that my children would experience a marked increase in diaper rash eruptions on the trail because hygienic conditions seem remarkably poorer than at home. But we never had a rash that we couldn't get rid of in a couple of days—four at the most. During those times, we took extra caution to make sure our babies were kept dry (which uses even more diapers) and changed their diapers seconds after bowel movements were made. If the weather is warm, leave their diaper off while you are on break or in camp, especially if it's just after they moved their bowels. The air and sun will work wonders on diaper rash. Ointment usually clears it up completely overnight and sometimes even by the next diaper change. Of course, you can't take a half dozen tubes with you, so pick one that best suits your child's needs.

Cleaning Up

Rinsing out diapers can be a trick. If you choose to use cloth diapers while on the road, some method of pre-rinsing is necessary because they can't go into the laundromat "as is." Try to keep after the job on a daily basis, to prevent them from building up. When traveling in or camping from the car, look for public rest rooms at roadside rest areas that aren't heavily used. Or use a five-gallon bucket brought along for that purpose.

When you're in the backcountry, carry the urine diapers in their own separate, heavy-duty garbage bag, away from the poop diapers, which are best double bagged. Rinse out the diapers when you make camp for the night. Carry the clean diapers in a very large, coated-nylon stuff sack lined with a plastic garbage bag.

Don't wash out diapers in order to reuse them on the trail. Do rinse them out every evening if extra water is available. Don't rinse out in or near a water source.

Fill your container with water (by using a small, clean bucket or pot) and carry it at least 200 feet from the water source. Keep your contaminated bucket at least 200 feet away from the water source. Swish the urine diapers in the water and squeeze them out. For poopy diapers, first dig a hole at least 200 feet away from water sources, campsite, and trails. Dump all of the solids into it. Then swish out the diaper pants, which you can use until they are blown out by a bowel movement. Then dip, swish, and squeeze out the poop diapers. Oh, yuck! All the brown water and "chunks" must be dumped down the hole, too (or the outhouse hole if one is nearby). Hang urine diapers up onto bushes and branches to dry after one rinsing. If you need to use them, they could go back for a second rinsing, this time using soap.

Fill the bucket a second time. Use this to clean the diaper pants again, with soap this time, making them suitable for reuse. Then clean the poop diapers again.

Wash your hands well after cleaning the diapers, using a strong-smelling biodegradable soap to mask the stink. Have your partner dribble the soap liquid over your hands and pour the water so you don't have to touch a water bottle or container and risk the possibility of contaminating it. Clean the diapers *after* your evening meal and keep your fingernails short!

Complications arise if there are no water sources by your camp-site night after night, making your diapers pile up and your diaper pants dwindle. Then you must do this lovely chore during the day while on a break when you come to water. These diapers cannot be thrown into a washing machine "as is" without getting the solids out and neutralizing the uric acid, and the thought of doing them all once in town is daunting—a worse job than doing them nightly on the trail.

Freezing temperatures at night are a problem. When you are in the mountains, it can easily dip to freezing or below any month of the year. You cannot compact stiff boards of diapers and if you do try, you could easily damage the fibers and rip them apart. It is best to take them down before you go to bed and clump them into a ball in their bag, even though they're still wet.

Hints and Tips

- Cloth diapers may make the most sense in the wilds.
- Treat your babies' solid waste as you would your own—dig a hole at least 200 feet from water sources, campsites, and trails, and bury. Never bury, burn, flush, or leave behind disposable diapers.
- Change your babies as soon as you discover they have soiled their diaper.
- A small foam pad makes the most comfortable surface on which to make a diaper change.
- Never leave home without diaper rash ointment.
- Figure on needing more diapers rather than fewer.

Techniques for the Potty-Trained

The most-asked question and fear of parents who are considering taking their children into the wilds is, how do you deal with going to the bathroom in the outdoors? It's a little more inconvenient and messy than being at home, but it's certainly manageable. Never let this issue prevent your family from missing out on backcountry experiences.

When traveling in the car, carry a very small potty chair with its own lid. It's great for emergency potty-breaks when there isn't time to find a public bathroom. In some cars, the children can sit on it right on the floor of the car. It can be carried in a snug cardboard box in the trunk of the car or in the back of the truck to prevent sloshing, and be emptied when it is convenient and possible.

The potty is also great for using in the tent when you are car camping. Sierra is very groggy in the middle of the night and needs a lot of support to use her potty, and if we don't have to drag her outdoors, it makes the job much easier. (Mom has been known to use it too.)

If your young child is beginning to learn the ropes of toilet training, to make the process easier and less traumatic in the backcountry, bring along his or her potty seat top (taken off the potty itself).

All young, potty-trained children seem to need to be reminded to try to go. They get occupied and often put it off until it's very late, even too late. It's especially important to remind youngsters who have recently become potty trained. I usually make my daughter empty her bladder before getting back on the trail, to eliminate the need to stop again in ten minutes. She often insists that she doesn't need to, but nearly always does. Their lives are just too busy to want to take time out for that. The main reason you need to encourage them is because they only have so many changes of clothing along.

Bed-wetting can be another problem, especially if a child has not been potty trained for long. Keeping them warm at night can help to prevent accidents. If your child manages to crawl out of the sleeping bag and becomes cold in the night, he or she may have difficulty holding his or her bladder, especially if your child is a deep sleeper and not used to calling for help. Check throughout the night to see if your children are covered. (Place a parent who does not sleep so soundly next to this child so he or she can hear murmurings.) When your child stirs, ask if he or she has to urinate. If your child has an accident, all wet clothing will need to be stripped, so you need lots of extra clothing during this potty-training stage. Fortunately, synthetic sleeping bags do not become soaked like the old, heavy, cotton-flannel-lined ones, so the bag can usually be blotted dry and left to hang in the sun until you can get it to a laundromat.

When you're in the backcountry and can't carry the potty chair, it is up to you to teach environmentally sound bathroom habits in the bush. Little boys don't need much instruction when they need to urinate in the wilds. If they can pee into a toilet, they can pee on the ground. They just need to be directed where (200 feet away from water sources, trails, campsites, etc.)

Little girls have more trouble, because they must learn to grab their various pants and hold them together and away so they don't wet them. Your child can practice a lot—whenever you are outdoors at home, where it is easy to get a clean change of clothes. It takes them a while to get it down pat, and still there are accidents. If your child has a lot of layers on, help by holding them for her.

Bowel movements on the trail can be a production. Toddlers can have difficulty squatting to move their bowels. It can take forever, even if there is no constipation. Little girls may have to be older and stronger to be able to hold themselves up in the squat position for the amount of time that they need.

With our four-year-old daughter, we have to look for a log for her to sit on and then dig a hole six inches deep on the one side. The log has to be small enough that her legs can hang down and get her hiney safely sticking out over the back side. A nice, smooth-barked, dead tree is the best. Of course, they aren't always available and she usually doesn't give us much advance warning to conduct a good search.

I've hung her over large smooth rocks, but they aren't her favorite. If nothing else is available, Todd holds her in his arms, suspended above her hole, for however long it takes. If it's raining, she sits on her log with an umbrella and can take her good old time. If it's raining and Todd must hold her, I hold the umbrella. We make her help dig her hole (if conditions allow), we both cover it with soil and stamp it down, and she often finds a rock to cover it. This way, children learn very early the correct way to dispose of their bodily waste in the backcountry.

Children eat a tremendous amount of fiber and drink a lot of liquid when active outdoors—both practices that help keep you regular. However, occasionally when traveling and eating foods not normally in your diet, and when your child is doing a lot of sitting in a car or child carrier, constipation may strike. Consult your doctor before leaving on a trip for the best way to treat this.

Bathing

A bath is often out of the question in the mountains, so you might try "sponge baths" or "spot washes" instead. It can be sufficient for keeping your child clean. Two places to spot wash on babies are under

their arms, where an infection can grow in the warm folds, and behind their ears, where milk can run and get crusty and begin to smell bad.

While traveling in the car, real baths can be improvised in motels and in picnic ground utility sinks. Your child can also swim in creeks and lakes, but be sure to avoid contaminating water sources with any poop. On long trips, daily bathing is often whittled down to washing hands before supper and washing hands, face, and genitals before bed. Period.

CHAPTER 4

Health and Safety

▲ ▲ ▲ ▲ ▲ ▲ ▲ ▲ ▲

Risk Assessment

You are in total charge of your children's well-being and your decisions need to be the right ones. Sometimes there are decisions to be made all day long. It's a lot of responsibility to choose what is right and safe for another human being, so you, as the guardian, must have your act together.

Don't take your child out into the wilderness until you are a well-skilled outdoorsperson yourself. An inexperienced person could charge headfirst into a perilous situation without even being aware of it. Being educated to the ways of the wilds eliminates a lot of poor choices. Still, you will be forced to make decisions which are not only difficult but whose result may be very uncertain. How accurately you can determine the result of any given decision depends on how many times you have been in a particular situation. It is a very individual thing. All factors, all variables, need to be taken into consideration.

For instance, you may have these kinds of questions running through your mind: Should you keep going up the ridge if the weather is foul? Will the kids be able to deal with it? What if the wind is high? Do the kids have enough clothes under their rain gear to keep them warm? Should you go for it? How many miles remain to the campsite you hoped to make? Is there any place to camp near here or must you get to a flat spot on the ridge? But will that be too exposed?

Once all the variables are considered, your determining factor has to be how you feel inside. When you begin to feel uncomfortable and frightened, it is time to try to change the situation, work to eliminate the risk/danger, and get to the point where you are feeling safe again.

The fact that your children are in your care will make you much more conservative, and rightfully so, when risk-taking is involved.

I can remember camping in Death Hollow in the Escalante area of Utah with seven-month-old Sierra. The canyon walls were so steep that campsites were often limited to small patches of beach on the river. After we found a superb beach site, we noticed that the sky was getting increasingly darker up the river. The thought of a flash flood rushed through our minds. We sat on the beach a long time, totally packed up, trying to make a decision to camp at this lovely spot and risk a flash flood, or go in search of higher ground. We envisioned the storm coming at night, quickly and cracking and startling us from our sleep. Or would the water push against our tent and wake us that way? We needed to feel safe. If it were just Todd and I, we would be much more relaxed and daring when it came to making decisions. When the clouds dispersed and the sky changed from navy blue to baby blue, we decided to make camp.

People were shocked to see us backpacking with a small baby in the Grand Canyon. Even the shuttle bus driver told us story after story of trail-related mishaps. But it isn't like it's a jungle swarming with vicious wild animals. (The most dangerous creature was the scorpion—which we never saw—for their bite can be deadly to a baby whose small body cannot deal with the poison. All you have to do is sleep in a tent to cancel that nighttime danger out.) There will always be people who try to scare you out of doing something. They project their own fears into the situation. Know your stuff, know your limitations, and don't be afraid to turn a deaf ear to folks like this.

Another time during our southwest desert tour, we arrived at the Virgin River in Zion National Park. The hike up that steep-walled canyon was another where you walked directly in the water. At the end of the asphalt trail, where the water trail began, there was a sign alerting you to the "extreme" danger if a storm came up, but urged you to walk up the river a few paces and discover its fabulous world. The midday thunderheads were building and a raindrop or two had fallen, but the sun was still out overhead.

The canyon sucked us in. Each bend we turned, it was more exciting and more beautiful, with steep walls and muddy-flowing, knee-deep water. Three men were coming out and said only two more were ahead. When those two turned around, we knew we were the only ones up this far and no one would be passing us on their return. How far had we come? It was hard to tell. There wasn't anymore sunlight up above, nor blue sky. "The next bend," we said, "after that we'll turn around."

But it was difficult to stop. When we finally did turn around, we were surprised to see that the sky was very dark. Then the rain began.

We were suddenly very concerned. We couldn't hike fast because there were many round slippery rocks on the bed of the river. As we tramped out of the river, water overflowing from our leather boots, infant on our back, the tourists stared at us like we were from another planet. We were safe but so glad we took the chance, for it was an unforgettable experience. By the time we walked the mile back to our car, the rain was coming down in sheets. Surely, the Virgin River would be flooding soon.

On one hand, you might say what we did was foolish. But we did watch the sky and did not go up so far that it would have been a very long walk to get back. We weighed everything as we went and felt like the risk was small enough and our desire to experience it large enough to encourage us to go. It was also good timing. Sometimes that's the best you can do.

If you start your children early in the outdoors, they will learn their limits very early. They will recognize and understand what needs to be done in certain situations and will have the past knowledge that they survived and were not harmed.

Parents should be very cautious and not push the situation to dangerous levels. Parents should stretch their child's responsibilities to the next stage very gradually, and bite off small pieces. You will have a better idea of your child's capabilities and limits. Whenever conditions are risky, or there is a greater chance of children screwing up, refrain until they have more experience. Have them practice their skills (such as route finding) while they are in your presence for as long as it takes until you are comfortable having them do it on their own. Have them prove themselves before they try it on their own.

When times get hard, parents can use the situation to teach some positive values. Some stresses, however, may be too great for their capacity and they have to know it's okay to recognize this and not feel guilty. Children don't have the strength, stamina, and willpower to push themselves as adults do.

Older children can do a lot for themselves in the wilds, but "thinking for yourself" can be carried too far. One family learned this on a climb on Mount Katahdin in Maine. They sent the older two children (eight and ten years old) ahead to go to a cave they all wanted to see. There was an important fork in the trail, where one fork went to the Knife Edge; they were *not* to take that fork.

What happened when the parents and younger children reached the cave? You guessed it. The older kids weren't at the cave. Pa ran (as well as he was able) back to the fork and up the other trail. The kids had reached the Knife Edge and were about to cross it (although they had discussed the wisdom of this) when a grown couple reached them

and peremptorily turned them back. Kids are poor on directions, even assuming they listen in the first place. Parents can be too careless of the kids' lives.

Always stay on the safe side when setting boundaries with your children in the outdoors. The more wild the area (remote, higher mountains, lack of access, changeable weather, etc.), the more you should limit their risk-taking and their freedom to make decisions on their own. In conditions such as these, be crystal clear on what they are permitted and not permitted to do. Emphasize the reason for this—what could happen if they do not listen.

In all my years and miles of trail traveling, I've only felt unsafe or threatened one time when it came to people. We were biking on the C&O Canal and taking a break by a lock house, not too many miles outside of Washington, D.C., when a suspicious-looking man we had just passed going the other way turned around when he saw us. He seemed to just wait and watch us. I got nervous. He gave me the creeps. He had some sort of bag that hung over his arm that he held rather stiffly and his coat was awkwardly draped over it. He hung around a long time, doing nothing but sneakily watching us. I said to Todd, "Let's go. We can stop later. Let's put this guy behind us." I was a little freaked going past him so closely. As soon as we did, he got up and left and walked right into the woods on no trail.

Trust your senses. If you ever feel uncomfortable in a situation, pack up and leave, even if you've already set up camp.

Children need to have a certain protocol of behavior when encountering suspicious people or when finding themselves in these kinds of situations. Review with them the behavior you'd expect from them, whether in their daily lives or in the wilds. Certainly don't dwell on it, for your chances of something happening out in the wilds are incredibly rare and you don't want to frighten them unnecessarily. Sneak a subtle remark in sometime when it's appropriate.

Your older children, who may want to go out on their own, should know the rules on keeping themselves safe that apply to all backcountry travelers, such as not wearing provocative clothing. I once met a group of teenage girls on the trail, bra-less and wearing T-shirts with the sleeves cut off so the arm holes reached nearly to their waists. Anyone could easily see right inside their shirts, even if they weren't trying to look. I don't know if they were even aware of it. The wrong people could get the wrong impression.

The following safety guidelines from the Appalachian Trail Conference can give you a good background:

Backcountry Safety Guidelines

1. Do not travel alone. Traveling with at least one partner reduces the potential for harassment. It also provides security in case of accident or illness.
2. Inform others. Always leave your trip itinerary with family and friends.
3. Avoid provocation. Don't respond to taunts or attempts at intimidation.
4. Be friendly but cautious in your conversation with strangers you meet on the trail. Avoid people who act in a strange, provocative, hostile, or drunk manner.
5. Don't broadcast your itinerary to suspicious strangers, and avoid describing the whereabouts of your fellow travelers. If you are alone, claim to be part of, and ahead of, a larger group.
6. Camp away from roads and motor vehicles. Harassment is most likely in areas accessible to cars,

including four-wheel-drive trucks. If you are concerned because of an encounter earlier in the day, hide your camp.

7. Carrying firearms is strongly discouraged. They are illegal in most areas if carried without a license or if concealed, and the odds are good that an innocent person may be hurt.

8. Eliminate opportunities for theft. Don't leave your pack unattended. If you must leave it, hide it carefully. Don't leave cash, cameras, or expensive equipment in cars parked at remote trailheads.

9. If you are the witness to or a victim of harassment, promptly report the crime to local law-enforcement authorities (dial 911 or ask the operator to connect you to the closest state-police office) and also to the outdoors organization or club responsible for the area you are traveling in, so that steps can be taken to enforce laws and prevent recurrences.

10. Never underestimate the importance of trail registers. Sign entries with your real name as well as any trail name you may be using, and report any suspicious activity there too. If trail volunteers need to locate you, or if a serious crime has been committed and authorities need more information, the first place they turn to are the trail registers. These registers are a powerful tool and can be essential to safety.

Hazards in the Outdoors

When dealing with your children in the backcountry, always remember that if the danger appears obvious, don't take the chance.

Keeping Them from Falling

Before you get to a dangerous spot (an overlook or a riverbank, etc.), or immediately after you arrive, let your children know where their limits and boundaries are. The very young must hold your hand at all times to insure their safety. Don't let the "potential" danger inhibit them from experiencing a beautiful view, however, just because it is exposed. You, the parent, just take charge and control.

Don't let your young children run ahead too far in case of drop-offs, weather conditions that make areas slippery, trails across rock scree that may be difficult to negotiate, rain-slicked wooden board-walks, or bridges over streams and waterfalls. If you suspect there is a potential danger ahead, ask your kids to stick with you so you can negotiate through it together. Talk to them about how you are moving over the potentially dangerous area, as well as showing them by your physical example.

For older children who may be allowed to go on ahead, ask them to wait up for you before crossing something dangerous. They are not babies and don't need their hands held, but it is necessary to discuss and assess the situation. This is something adults should naturally do with each other, for one member may be off somewhere in thought and be unaware of potential dangers.

Riverbanks can be potentially dangerous, for the water often cuts back underneath, causing the bank to cave in if enough weight is put on top and conditions are right. Educate your children on this hazard and, as with everything else, explain what could happen and why. Have your kids negotiate these potentially dangerous situations while in your presence. The skill and knowledge they acquire will enable you both to feel confident to let them do it on their own. If your kids are unfamiliar with any of these conditions, no matter what their age (for we adults should know enough to stick together through dangerous situations too), have them stay with you.

Children of all ages love to climb trees—upright or fallen. Show them what dead limbs look like and tell them not to put weight on them. Mossy-covered branches could cause them to slip and fall too. Being aware of where your child is and what your child is doing can help you prevent an accident. Don't baby your children, but keep an eye on them.

I considered buying a harness for my one-and-a-half-year-old because I was afraid that if we were in an extremely dangerous situation, I would not be able to control him. When we got caught very late on the trail once and it was the only flat spot to place our tent, we had an emergency campsite perched on the edge of a cliff. Our daughter was young enough that we could put her in the zipped tent and keep her there. But a one-and-a-half-year-old could have been tough. Todd was really against the harness, though. He said we simply would not place ourselves in such a dangerous situation that we would feel that we needed one. I still thought about buying one anyway and hiding it in my pack, just in case.

Creek Crossings

It takes practice and experience for children to successfully negotiate a boulder hop across a stream. They need lots of advice on where to place their feet, etc., so it is wise for an adult to cross first and test it. Get them two sticks for greater stability. Offer your hand and if it is too dangerous or deep, carry them, preferably in a child carrier. Trails that necessitate crossing streams that are swollen from run-off or heavy rains should be avoided when you're traveling with children.

Children do not have the strength and experience and height to make substantial stream crossings safely.

Keeping Them from Getting Lost

Children who are old enough to know how to read a compass should be taught and should carry one. A child needs to be quite old before he or she can fully understand and use a map and compass (providing the parents are adept in this skill). More important is to teach children how to recognize landforms and develop a sense of direction by using their senses. Point out to them landmarks that you are traveling by. Have them become aware of the land you are moving through. Encourage them to turn around on occasion and look backwards. Point out what the trail is doing and will do further along, for instance, "We are traversing around this peak on its side (introduce those new terms to them), and will then drop down to the stream in the gorge between this mountain and the next."

Whenever possible, show them where the trail goes up ahead of where you came from—at a viewpoint, fire tower, etc., so they can have a concept of how the trail snakes over the land. Then you can draw a special map for your child, showing what the trail does in simple terms. Put road crossings in (and where they go off to), prominent features, where you're planning to stop or camp, and what the trail does along the way. This will get them used to converting three-dimensional sights to two-dimensional maps and prepare themselves for reading topo lines and visualizing the land.

Once they show an interest in topo maps, give them their own (a copy or otherwise) and frequently point out where you are, what the land looks like around you to your naked eye, and then how it is converted to topographic lines: steep mountainside—lines close together; open, broad valley—much space between lines, etc. Children at a young age can grasp basic landforms on a map, such as a saddle between two knobs, if they see it before them, walk it, and then identify the area on the map while they're there. Being there helps it become clear in their minds. Very basic instructions for learning to read a map and compass can be found in the Boy Scouts Handbook (see appendix C, Suggested Reading). As with anything, practice brings skill, and skill brings confidence to learn and try more.

Kids can hone their orienteering skills by playing a buried treasure hunt game in camp. To accompany their clues, they can draw up maps to direct the hunters and use their compasses to find it.

Young children should wear brightly colored clothes so that, in the event that they do wander away, you will be able to spot them much easier. They should also have a whistle, either on a cord around their neck or on a coiled wrist bracelet used for carrying a key. Instruct your children on when and how to use the whistle. The universal signal for help is three blows. If they have no whistle, the signal can be made using three of anything—three yells in a row, three bangs on a pot, etc. This universal signal will alert anyone within earshot that someone is in trouble. Teach your children how to blow the whistle loudly and teach them to only use it in an emergency. They should also stay put if they feel they are lost. Reassure them that even though they feel like they are doing nothing, their parents or the group will be working to find them and they'll be easier to find if they remain near the last place where they were known to be.

Each child should know his or her address, phone number, parents' names, etc. Depending on what outdoor activity you are doing and where you are traveling, it may be a good idea for your young toddlers who do not know this information to have it written and placed on their bodies somewhere.

Adverse Weather

There can be real magic in inclement weather, so don't refrain from taking your children out if the weather report predicts some adverse weather. Moving through seas of fog, seeing raindrops clinging to spider webs, thrilling at a sudden rainbow, even experiencing a storm away from the insulation of your home are all beneficial experiences for your children—if you are prepared.

Try to schedule trips or outings during fair weather—after a cold front has passed, for example—but this isn't always possible. Many times when bad weather is predicted, it often is not nearly so bad once you get out to where you want to be. On the other hand, the weather can deteriorate unexpectedly once you are there. Refrain from leaving when there is a 100 percent chance of an all-day rain. That is never fun. But don't let a "chance of showers" keep you home and run the risk of missing a really enjoyable outing.

When a storm comes and everything needs to be covered and protected quickly, your children need to cooperate. There is usually some anxiety in the air, which the children pick up on and seem to sense the need for them to listen. When the rain starts, throw on your own rain jackets first, because it takes only a few seconds. Then dress the kids. Then cover the gear. After the rain stops, you can leave the children in their rain gear to keep them warm and to be ready should it rain again. They can actually keep it on until the sun comes out and they become hot. We often put their rain gear on when the sky just looks threatening, to save time when it does come and to keep them warm in the meantime. You can do this when a child is not walking and will not be getting overheated from exercise.

Thirteen hundred lightning injuries occur annually, so anyone who is spending any kind of time in the outdoors needs to know how to minimize the danger of being hurt by it. It is sometimes difficult to determine if a storm is going to pass by. By counting the number of seconds between the flash and the bang (every five seconds equals one mile), you can sometimes determine the proximity of the storm. The typical thunderstorm, however, travels a mile every two to three minutes, so don't try to outrun a close storm, but seek shelter instead.

Avoid rocks, streams, damp crevices, mountain peaks and hilltops, lone or tall trees, large flat open areas, caves, and water. Find a clump of trees that is lower than the surrounding trees and remain there until the storm passes. Crouch on your feet (do not sit or lie down) and put some sort of insulation between you and the ground (foam pad, sleeping bag). Stay forty to fifty feet apart, so if one person is injured, someone else can administer first aid. Young children will most likely not want to be alone at this time, so *at least* put another adult or an older child not far away from them.

A problem that surfaces on cooler nights is dealing with temperature extremes during a baby's occasional crying jags. The more upset your child becomes, the hotter he or she becomes, making him or her more upset. Take off his or her hat, unzip the sleeper to expose his or her chest, and calm the baby down before he or she gets too overheated. But remember that even taking the hat off leaves his or her perspired bald head vulnerable to the cold. Try to put it right back on once your baby has calmed down, but before he or she drifts off to sleep.

Take precautions when traveling at the other end of the temperature scale as well. Children are not too good at sweating. Their sweat glands do not develop fully until they are adolescents. For this reason, heat exhaustion can be a real problem for young children. Do not go out in the middle of the day, and only travel in the mornings and evenings. During the heat of the day, spend your time at shaded picnic grounds or by water. Keep your baby in the shade at all times, either under your backpack's awning or under an umbrella. Frequently give baby water and do not worry if it slops down the front—the wet shirt keeps baby's body cool. When your child will be exposed to the sun, use sunscreen on exposed skin and thin cotton clothing to keep skin exposure to a minimum.

If your child is having problems keeping cool, put a baseball hat on him or her to protect face and head from the sun. Give a toddler

your bandanna dipped in cool water to dab face and neck. Soaking your head in water can help too—it is the next best thing to swimming. Take off their boots and socks to let more heat out.

Poisonous Plants

Children need to be aware of poison oak, ivy, and sumac and know how to identify them. Teach them the conditions or areas in which they could find them (when the trail crosses sunny power lines, for example) so they know to keep their eyes open for them. Point out the plants whenever you come across them so they learn by the repeated visual exposure.

Train younger children not to eat wild plants unless you are with them and you are adept at plant identification. Plants that look like garden produce must not be sampled, nor should children taste wild berries without your supervision, no matter how tempting. Wild mushrooms also must be properly identified to avoid serious poisoning. Make sure your children understand that only people with thorough training and experience can identify edible wild plants. Also point out any regulations on picking plant materials in the area you are traveling in.

Wild Animals

Teach your children to respect and keep their distance from all wild animals—even ones that don't look harmful, such as chipmunks in a campsite. Besides the fact that they could bite, wild animals are not helped by humans feeding them. Our food is not a good diet for any animal, it could prevent them from honing their skills to hunt and forage in their natural environment, and it could lead to their destruction—as with bears in national parks that have been conditioned to be less fearful of humans. Of course, parents must set the initial example. I heard a story about a father who smeared his child's face with honey in order to get a photograph of the bear licking it off. The child was killed and the father imprisoned for homicide.

Don't implant fear in your children over wild animals, but don't keep them ignorant either. When in mountain lion or grizzly bear country, teach young ones to stay close to you. Tell them why. Don't lie. It's good to have a healthy fear of wild animals that are capable of attacking humans. Children are especially vulnerable because of their size.

Teach your children that we are visitors in the animals' home. We need to conduct ourselves in a way which enables both humans and wild animals to stay safe. Tell them what to do and not to do should they encounter a potentially dangerous wild animal. They are never too young to rehearse what do if a potentially dangerous situation occurs, whether you are with them or not.

Children should be taught which animals are nocturnal and which are not, so if they see a raccoon out during the day, they know to get away from it immediately, since it might be rabid. If you are traveling in an area where there might be potentially dangerous animals, have children slow their pace and ask them to be more alert than usual, to watch the trail and the area more carefully. They need to know that it is dangerous to get between a mother bear (even the more passive black bear) and her cubs. If a bear approaches children while they are eating, they should leave the food and slowly and carefully vacate the area.

They must never take food to bed with them in these areas and must be very careful to remember where all their snacks are stashed (for example, in their backpacks or fanny packs), so they can be removed and included with the food, etc., that is being hung from a tree and bear-proofed.

When traveling in grizzly country have them wear bells. Never let them walk ahead. Teach them what to do if they encounter a bear.

Never make eye contact, roll up in a ball if the animal comes close, never run, etc. In areas with high concentrations of cougars, small children should not be allowed to wander, even in camp. Set up specific, close boundaries.

Campsite Hazards

Children adore fires, so they need to be taught proper handling, but you must be careful with children and fires. Younger kids can collect the wood; older kids can build the fire, keep it going, and be responsible for its safe extinguishing. When kids are given these responsibilities, they often behave very responsibly.

Kids love to play with sticks—poke them into things, etc. Depriving a child of this wonderful natural toy is not necessary, providing some rules are followed. They should keep a safe distance from each other when playing with sticks so nobody can be accidently hit, injured, or poked. No jousting games should be allowed. Try to curtail running with sticks in their hands.

Kids (especially boys) are naturally attracted to knives and axes and should be allowed to use them with proper instruction and guidance once they are around six to eight years old, depending on their maturity and dexterity. The six Lewiston children learned to use a pocket knife by the age of six or seven, giving them endless hours of whittling fun in camp. All six cut themselves as they learned correct skills, but none seriously.

Parents should first scout the area where their children are playing, to make sure there are no potential dangers around. The Newmans were setting up camp one time while the children played on a forty-foot-long by fifteen-foot-wide beach that was within their sight. They hadn't walked its length, however, to see what was at the far end. An evergreen tree downed on the beach had sharp branches sticking out dangerously. The kids got to horsing around and their son fell onto it, puncturing a hole one and a half inches into his life jacket, which he had fortunately left on and escaped injury, but it made his parents realize what could easily happen in the wilderness, far from medical help.

Boulder climbing/scrambling is another potentially dangerous activity. Have your young child learn basic skills and techniques of bouldering on low-to-the-ground boulders. Keep watch on their skill as they grow older and, if you are able, teach them techniques (using your toes and fingertips and keeping your body away from the rock, etc.). They tend to learn these naturally by just doing it and all kids are attracted to it. Play a role in what and how they are doing, and step in and judge if they are on or up something that is beyond their skill.

When your children are going through their putting-things-in-the-mouth-stage, keep on them almost constantly. Bryce managed to taste glass trash in Colorado and thought it hysterically funny when we got hysterical over it. Know the Heimlich maneuver by heart.

Children can be fond of discovering trash in popular camp and picnic spots. Pop tops from cans, six-pack plastic rings, aluminum cans—all of it intrigues them. We let our children discover it, keep a close watch on what it is and that no glass or sharp objects are in the area, and use the opportunity to teach them sound ecological back-country habits.

Dealing With Fright

Children can become frightened in unfamiliar situations and they should always be handled with extreme tenderness and understanding. There are some things you can do to help occupy their mind and keep it off their fears. Try to anticipate when they might get scared and begin to involve them in something before it occurs.

On a bike trip, we had to go through a half-mile-long tunnel. It was very dark and cool inside. The only light was a tiny arch at the tunnel's far end. Every now and then we'd catch glimpses of the water in the canal by our sides as it reflected the light. We couldn't see a thing in front of us and pushed our bikes along the narrow dirt passageway where the mules once walked many years ago. Sierra called, "Mama? Mama?" with a catch in her voice, just checking if I was still there. There was a wooden guard rail to our side with grooves rubbed into it by the mules' ropes as they pulled the canal boats through the tunnel. Back then, the children traveling in the boats would become frightened too and their mothers would sing them through the darkness. We did the same and felt very connected to those traveling families all those years ago.

It's a good idea to attempt to explain what is happening to your children so they understand your behavior. It isn't so much the danger itself that scares them, for they don't have enough experience to judge what is truly dangerous or not. It is the fact that their parents are behaving differently and they don't know how to read you or react. Even the smallest child will somehow know, just from the tone of your voice, that everything is okay. Tell them that you need them to cooperate. You need them to listen to what you are telling them to do, and to try to do it quickly. It didn't take long for our children to understand that when the sky rumbled, it was time to shape up. Commands like, "Come over here, put your arm in this sleeve," etc., were met without defiance or hesitation.

It's a difficult thing to hide your own anxiety and fear from your children when the level is high, but it's not necessarily a bad thing for them to see their parents frightened. It makes them understand that fear and insecurity are not something that should be associated merely with youth. When we get through scary times together, we feel much closer as a family.

To a great degree, kids take care of their fears themselves. In a magnificent Swiss Alps thunderstorm, Pa Lewiston yelled out to his sixteen-year-old daughter and four-year-old son in a nearby tent, "Are you two alright?"

"Yes, Dad," was the reply. "We're both in my bag."

When the children were frightened, say, in a tent in a thunderstorm, they would conjure up images of colorful butterflies in the sunlight. The children would lie with their eyes closed and take turns adding and changing the scenery. They need to believe they can get through the ordeal and they sometimes just need to feel that everything is alright in their world.

Be prepared for fears to surface in the middle of the night in young children, if they awaken and become disoriented. When the Lewistons were camping with their youngest—at one and a half years old—his small sleeping bag was lying crosswise in the tent near their heads. He settled down with a murmur, but later a small hand reached out and felt both of their heads and faces and then silently withdrew. All was well.

Dealing With Illness and Injury

Illness in your child out in the wilds can frighten parents. Outdoors can be a scary place for a child to run a fever or become ill. Fortunately, physical exercise, fresh air, and sound and adequate sleep will help to keep you healthy.

If your child becomes ill on an adventure, take the day off and try to get him or her comfortable. Very often, your child's body will heal itself very quickly (with the help of a little drugs, if necessary) and you'll be able to continue. If not, get out and into civilization where help is available.

The only illness we've encountered with our children was on a five-day drive. Bryce was not sleeping well and became run-down. He got a fever one night but was too sleepy to chew Tylenol tablets, so Todd had to run to a store to get drops. I realized how important both types of medication are, depending on the circumstance. I also got our doctor to prescribe an antibiotic to take along, just in case.

We did have some teething problems with our kids while they

were out in the wilds. We were backpacking with them when it occurred and they got much relief from gumming the top of their child carrier. It was at the right height, padded, yet firm for pressure. They were fussy but not nearly as bad as they were at home. There was so much more to look at out there, and that kept their minds off their misery. Our kids never went for that topical numbing medicine. It just made them angry. If your children respond favorably to it, by all means bring it along. Who could ever judge when a tooth will erupt and cause problems?

Always try to carry more water than what you think you'll need. If the water supply is low, it must be left for the children. Purifying enough water for an entire family is a laborious process, but it must be done. It's a good idea to have a back-up purifying system along, like iodine tablets, if your pump system fails. If there is a choice between tap water carried from town or obtained at a campground, store, or visitor center and water that you have purified yourselves, give the kids the municipal water. Filters sometimes foul up and you don't want to take any chances by risking dysentery or giardiasis with them. Dysentery can be more dangerous in their small bodies because it is easier for them to become dehydrated and they could be less cooperative about taking fluids.

A friend's seven-year-old daughter got very sick with a virus while they were out on the trail. She suddenly announced that she felt ill and before her dad could even get his glasses on, she began vomiting and having diarrhea at the same time. There was no time to grab a bucket or a plastic bag. Her sleeping bag, her dad's bag, and the tent were soiled. Bob took her out of the tent, changed her, and cleaned her. Then he emptied all the food out of their stuff sacks and put the soiled clothing and rags inside of them. He changed his clothes and wiped off the sleeping bags and the tent. He then dug a hole and buried the waste. Because they were only two miles from their car, they hiked out by flashlight and spent the rest of the night in a motel. Had they been in much farther, they could have stayed because Bob had done a very thorough job of cleaning up. It was to their advantage that they left, however, because her vomiting and diarrhea continued throughout the night. The next day it poured rain and it would have been a tough hike out.

Bob learned the importance of having extra clothes and things to mop with (bandannas, etc.) and he believes he will now always sleep with either an empty pot or a plastic bag close at hand. Bring along a diarrhea medicine from your doctor, just in case. Be careful that young children do not become dehydrated, a common problem with diarrhea.

Altitude sickness can be avoided by acclimating very slowly. Study the maps before departure, deciding on your itinerary, locating the national forest campgrounds to camp at, and noting the elevation of the town closest to it. Plan on gaining 1,000 feet maximum every night. Children's bodies are so small and their nervous system so delicate and immature. Besides that, they don't always know how to communicate what they are feeling. It is best to simply avoid situations such as high altitudes and to not take the chance, no matter how inconvenient the alternative appears.

Two other problems to be aware of are hypothermia and hyperthermia.

Hypothermia is a condition in which the body's core temperature gets so low (below 95 degrees) that it cannot be brought back up without outside help. It is often called "exposure" and results from a combination of air temperature, wind chill, wetness, fatigue, hunger, and exertion. It can occur at any time of the year, even in the summer.

You will need to recognize the initial symptoms in your child—uncontrollable shivering, stumbling, stuttering, difficulty with motor skills (buttoning their shirt)—and treat them accordingly. Strip off their wet clothes, get some hot fluids into them, set up camp regardless of the time of day or your location. Get them into their sleeping bag and if all else fails to warm them, get into the bag with them, preferably skin to skin.

Children should never even get to the initial stage of hypothermia if parents keep a hawk-eye on their condition and the weather conditions around them. Victims often do not know what is occurring and may think they are fine. Do everything before it becomes a need: rest before real fatigue sets in; eat before real hunger occurs; put on warm clothes before it gets really cold; and as a parent, take care of yourself so you can minister to your child, if need be.

Hyperthermia, or heat exhaustion, occurs when the body's cooling system becomes strained and cannot regulate itself. Symptoms may include nausea, headache, dizziness, pale skin, and shallow breathing. Vomiting may occur and the child's pupils may be dilated. Move victims to a cool shady spot, raise their feet, loosen their clothing, apply cool, wet cloths, and have them sip water.

To prevent hyperthermia, make sure your child drinks plenty of water. You can lose up to two quarts of body fluid on a hot day. Have children wear hats and have them pick their own hat out in the store so they like it enough to keep it on their heads. Dip your heads in cool water whenever possible. Wet a bandana and let them swab their necks and faces. Take a siesta during the heat of the day, preferably around water. Let children swim or slop in creeks when they come across them.

Watch their faces for redness and remember that children must reach puberty before they can efficiently rid their bodies of heat.

When children complain of heat or cold or any other uncomfortable condition, don't pass it off as idle complaining. Investigate all complaints and try to evaluate them realistically and compassionately.

The First-Aid Kit

Carry an extensive first-aid kit especially geared for children. Consult a general outdoor guide for a good list of basic contents, then begin adding necessities for traveling with kids.

The most important item for you and your children is likely to be bandages. Nothing stops tears and quiets moaning so quickly as a bandage. Splurge and buy the kind with juvenile characters and don't be stingy with them. They're worth the peace they're capable of producing.

Always carry children's Tylenol—both chewable and the liquid—and an anti-diarrhea medicine. Because most children's antibiotics are in liquid form and must be kept refrigerated, ask your doctor for a plastic bottle of powdered antibiotic with instructions on how to combine with water and the dosage. A two-week supply should suffice, and it needs to be tossed out after it is reconstituted. You can use it for topical infection such as an infected wound.

In addition, I always carry my herbal tinctures in my first-aid kit for times when illness comes creeping. One is an immunity booster containing extracts from the echinacea plant.

Young children love to climb, which can be dangerous, but I did not want to prevent them from exploring and having a good time. So we watched them closely and kept alert for potentially dangerous situations, and we had a good amount of butterfly bandages along, in a variety of sizes. They are capable of holding quite a large gash together. One of us is always up-to-date on our First Aid Course and we have the CPR cards handy for quick reference. If you are concerned about the pain and discomfort that could accompany a serious injury that necessitates evacuation, ask your doctor for a very strong pain killer and instructions on the dosage, and carry it in your first-aid kit.

Children need to know that many insect repellents are poisonous. The safest thing to do is to steer clear of any repellent containing diethyltoluamide (DEET). Check with health food stores for citronella-based repellents if your local outdoor store or favorite outdoor equipment catalog doesn't carry an alternative. Children should be instructed on how to handle insect repellents. It should never be applied to their faces. Their hands should be washed thoroughly if they apply it and boys need to be extremely careful when going to the bathroom. I heard of one little boy who sprayed himself down there, because the mosquitoes were thick around the latrine. The poisonous DEET is absorbed forty times greater in this sensitive area than on other areas of the body. If the bugs are extremely thick, use head nets and wear thin cotton clothing as an alternative.

Bring several strengths of sunscreen, or if you only want to carry one, choose one of the higher strengths, according to your child's sensitivity. Keep a kid-flavored chapstick in your or your child's fanny pack.

A very sharp needle and pointed tweezers for removing splinters should be included. Some children who climb and play on branches seem to attract splinters to themselves like magnets.

If your child is very young, bring along an anal thermometer, in addition to an oral one.

At the first sign of a cold, I start popping flavored zinc lozenges into my children's mouths; they seem to help them shake the cold right from the onset.

An ointment containing Vitamins A & D (traditionally used for diaper rash) should be carried. Some girls are susceptible to getting red and sore genitals since they don't always wipe completely in the outdoors or forego it completely. This should clear up any infection overnight.

Whenever you stay out for an extended amount of time (five to seven days or longer), carry a multiple vitamin with iron for your child. None of us gets a perfectly balanced diet out there and it is even more important that children have all their body's nutritional needs met.

Hints and Tips

- The safest, most responsible thing you can do as a parent of a kid in the wild is to be educated, experienced, and disciplined yourself in the sport you are participating in.
- Parents need to be cautious and not push their children close to dangerous limits. On the other hand, don't let others project their fears and prevent you from taking your children on new adventures or from trying new things.
- Never be careless of your children's lives. Don't dole out more responsibility than you're sure your kids can handle. Have them practice new skills in your presence until you're both comfortable.
- All people should wear a whistle and know how and when to use it. Children's whistles need to be easily accessible.
- Know the conditions that enable hypothermia and hyperthermia to occur more readily and be especially alert to symptoms at these times.
- Carry a well-stocked first-aid kit and know basic first aid.

CHAPTER 5

Awake and Asleep

▲ ▲ ▲ ▲ ▲ ▲ ▲ ▲ ▲

Keeping Them Entertained

This is by far your most difficult job—the most time-consuming, the most energy-sapping. But if it's working, peace and harmony prevail.

Keeping them entertained in the car is far harder than keeping them entertained in the wilds—for one big reason: they cannot move. All the stimulation and diversion must come to them. But with these hints and tips, it should go smoother for you.

Imagination is very important and environments like the out-of-doors encourage it. If you can get your children's imagination and creativity developed and have these remain strong through their school years, their adult life will be much richer, fuller, and satisfying because ot it.

One of the biggest sources of entertainment our children have is each other. The fact that they are close in age seems to help. In camp, they chase one another, wrestle, and often hold hands and walk around looking for and discovering things. Sierra likes to pretend and gets Bryce to play "house" and "family." She plays "mommie" and Bryce is the baby and they go off to the grocery store and such places together.

Singing

Traveling in the car, singing can be your most valued entertainment ally, second only to eating. You can sing your own animated songs, like "Itsy Bitsy Spider" and "Bear Hunt," and have your children participate.

Write the words down in a little notebook or bring along a song-book such as *Rise Up Singing* to avoid resorting to old, mind-destroying favorites such as "The Ants Go Marching One By One."

Stock up on kids' tapes. They can range from those for the very young, which incorporate finger games and very short little pieces for their short attention span, to "adult" music. Expose them to a wide variety of music—folk, ethnic, blues, gospel, reggae, jazz, etc. Older kids may enjoy listening to their own music with headphones, so they do not disturb anyone else.

Include both singing and story tapes (with or without accompanying books). If one of their favorite books is not on tape, you can make your own by reading the book slowly in an animated voice and recording it onto a blank tape. Use some sort of bell to indicate when to turn the page. We usually take turns with tapes—they select one, then us. We reserve their all-time favorite tapes for their more difficult moments—the end of the day, sitting in traffic, etc. See appendix C, Suggested Reading, for catalogs of children's tapes.

You might want to include some store-bought or homemade percussion instruments, so the children can join in and make music along with the tape and singing—shaking containers of raw beans or rice sounds great; a cook pot can be banged with a wooden spoon; two metal spoons can be hit together to play "spoons." Put on a jive tape (here's a good place to play your bluegrass, cajun, or Irish music) as long as it has a good beat. It will be fun for them to participate in the music instead of sitting stationary in their seats listening. It will make them feel like they are dancing.

If I had to pick one thing that helped the most while hiking, it would be singing songs. It doesn't matter where you are. You don't need anything from your outside surroundings, just a good memory or a notebook of lyrics and a willingness to do it. Lots of adults don't like to sing. I suppose it makes them feel self-conscious, as though they were displaying a secret part of themselves. But children love it, and if you give it half a chance and select some songs that entertain you as well, you should come to enjoy it. It really comes in handy and it does work. Your voice is always with you too.

Look in song books for ideas. Jot the verses down in a notebook and keep them handy. Next time your children are in need of a change, sing them a song. A song is a truly wonderful thing to share with other human beings, especially your children. If you search your memory, you will be amazed at what you can remember from your own youth. And kids don't mind if you repeat the same jingle ten times. They request it. You don't have to sing children's songs all the time either. Children appreciate a pretty song even if they don't

understand all that you're singing about. Sometimes I switch back and forth—one of their choice, then mine.

I wrote all of the words to some of the children's favorite lullabies in a tiny spiral-bound notebook and brought it along on our two-month hike in Colorado. One rainy day we were sitting under an umbrella under a big fir tree, waiting out the shower, and we passed a whole hour by singing. We all forgot our discomfort and the time flew by.

Since I became a mother, I discovered that you can teach your children things through song. You can help them understand their feelings and learn to put them into words. On clear, blue-sky mornings after a front has passed by, I like to belt out one particular John Denver song with the words "A part of everything is here in me." Sierra listened intently. Even at three years old, she knew what I was singing about. She felt it too and I gave words to the love she feels for the mountains and all of nature.

When we were on a pass and the wind was blowing, I sang Walkin' Jim Stoltz's words, "Don't turn your back on the wild wind, it's a gift that's so precious and rare. Don't turn your back on the wild wind, with a prayer it will always be there." Sierra came to understand that even though the wind is frightening sometimes, the opportunity to be up there experiencing the wind and the wilderness is very special.

Education

Another thing you can do to keep them entertained is to teach them about things. It doesn't have to interfere with what you're doing at all. You only need to look around you for ideas.

Take the trees, for instance. One day we talked about how trees grow, how they are able to stand upright, and how there are as many miles of roots underground holding them up as there are branches that we can see. We told our daughter to imagine tiny straws sucking up water to the leaves. We encouraged her to use her imagination and see images in her mind.

When we crossed a burned area, we told her about forest fires. We asked her what she thought all the animals did when it was burning and she pictured them running. We pointed out a ditch that was dug as a fire break and seedlings that were planted to help the forest return. We explained how pinecone seeds sprout naturally and showed her where young trees have sprouted up in the shadow of their parents. That night we had a campfire to teach her good fire-making habits and explained how it can get out of hand.

When we went past beaver activity, we showed her stumps that were gnawed by the beaver's teeth, and one particularly large tree that had to be abandoned. We pointed out the difference between an abandoned dam, where the silt was filled to the top of the dam and then diverted the water, and a newly built dam. The children looked for the beaver lodges and their entrance holes.

Because we are home-schooling (or schooling in the outdoors when we are on trips), we naturally think along these lines. But any parent can do it. It helps out with entertaining them, and it encourages them to use their imaginations—a skill that tends to atrophy as we grow older.

You can also look for things. In the early mornings or evenings, I sometimes get them to whisper or stop their chatter altogether as we search for deer in the open forests. As soon as they are successful and see one, they know it is not just a plot to keep them quiet. We look for squirrel nests in the trees when the leaves have fallen off. Along water's edge, look for ducks swimming and turtles sunning on rocks in the water. In your canoe, look for ospreys and fish moving beneath the water and ducks swimming up ahead. When biking, search for birds in thickets and briars.

On the trail, look for rocks with white quartz and sparkling mica or anything interesting at your feet. Look for flowers or particular colors that you take turns choosing. Scan alpine meadows for running marmots. In mountain lion country, search for trees that have strong horizontal limbs that are capable of supporting a large cat—hoping to see one and imagining that you did. In the mountain's scree slopes, we searched for squeaking picas and whistling marmots.

All you have to do is start their eyes looking. Teach them to begin to really see and they will never be bored. Explain the animals' habits and take some of the fear and ignorance away and replace it with some knowledge and understanding. Use these opportunities to teach your children things, such as explaining all the habits of a squirrel, where they get the nest material, what they use their nest for, why it's where it is, etc. Your children will learn to look closely and deeply and at details, instead of the whole broad picture, which might appear boring and stagnant. Your child begins to wonder why that farmer's barn is falling down or wonders what kind of accident caused that deer to get hit and die. Your child begins to think and use imagination, and is not just waiting for raw stimulation to entertain. Children naturally are inquisitive and want to learn, and with a little work, you can make road time into fun learning.

Parents can also entertain older children with spelling and geography bees, naming state capitols, and arithmetic quizzes and number games, etc.

In the car, keep a bag full of books—books that the children can look at themselves, i.e., chunky board books for young children and those that you can read to them. Older kids may have their own magazine subscriptions and can bring these along to browse through. Some children are susceptible to motion sickness when reading in the car, but this is something you will both find out very quickly when you travel.

Books can make up a lot of weight on the trail, but they will be read every morning and every night. When your child is small, the books in their age group have few words and often have heavy pages that don't give you a lot of mileage. There are some books which have no words but whose pages are filled with incredible detail. They depict

scenes and cultures from other countries and periods of time and every figure has their own story. It could take hours to get through a book like this. Our children really love the books where you must tell your own story. Small illustrations tell the story through their actions, but the parents bring the story to life with their own words. You can make reading these books last a long time too.

When you have more than one child who needs to be entertained or quieted at the same time, books that hold the interest of all are required. If the younger ones get bored because there is too much reading, they will demand your attention separately and defeat the whole purpose. Have a good idea what your youngest one is ready for. You can always compromise too and read only half of the text, just enough to tie the story together but make it faster moving. There are some small and very inexpensive books that are great for traveling. Reading really calms them down and gets their bodies thinking about sleep—especially since you are usually in a reclined position when you read in a tent.

Games

Once your children are old enough to communicate and think a little constructively, you can begin to play games with them. Even one-and-a-half-year-old Bryce was able to play our "Dog Game." We'd name a person or a family and the children had to say the name of their dog (or pet). If you compile a list just for reference, you may be surprised to find how many you know.

There are a few car games that you can play to help combat boredom—looking for particular-colored cars, finding things that begin with certain letters of the alphabet, etc. Look out of the car windows together and look for things—broken-down barn roofs, cows in pastures, toys in people's backyards, squirrel nests in leafless trees, chimneys made of different materials, etc.

One of Sierra's favorite games was the "Room Game." We would select a room in the house and I would describe an object in it—what it looks like, what it's used for, where it is located, etc., and she would have to guess it. We tried to include as many things in the room as we could, every knickknack, picture on the wall, cover on the dresser, and waste can by the door. Sometimes we'd move into the outdoors and include the porch and deck, or the surroundings around the house, or the garden/tractor shed. It was a favorite game when we were close to the end of a long trip and homesickness was starting to creep in. In one sense, it made her want her room and her home even more, but "seeing" it like this in her mind helped satisfy some of her need to be there.

Another game is one person thinking of a particular thing and listing all of the things you could do with it, and other players guessing what it is. For example, a tree: a home for birds and squirrels, fuel to burn to keep you warm, boards to saw to make furniture and homes. The younger the guesser, the more detailed and precise you need to be with your hints. Older children need more vague and difficult clues to keep them interested in the game. You could play it the other way too: name a thing and then have them list all of the things it can be used for. Children like the mystery of guessing answers, though.

Our most favorite descriptive game, though, when we are out for a long stretch and are getting close to town, is the "Food Game." One person describes a particular food—telling the color, size, texture, when you eat it, what you eat it with, etc. You can play this game with very young children and just give them more clues until they guess it. It's a good one for them to play back to you, for food is a very familiar thing. This game does tend to make you very hungry and crave culinary treats that are often impossible to get at the time. But it does help you appreciate it so much more and makes it taste so much better when you finally do get to eat what you're pining for.

We also play a more primitive version of "I'm Going to Grandmother's House and I'm Bringing," where you take turns listing items beginning with each letter of the alphabet. Everyone has to remember what was said before and repeat all of them. At three years old, Sierra didn't know her alphabet yet, so we just took turns naming things at random. It was amazing to see how much she did retain. Even when the list got very long, she remembered most of them.

One way we got the children's minds occupied on long road walks was to play the "Car Game." We each tried to guess the color of the next vehicle that might pass us. Three-year-old Sierra continually picked "pink," her favorite color, and didn't seem to mind that she never won. When we finally encouraged her to pick another color, she chose "yellow," not a real popular color in trucks and jeeps, which is what frequented those Rocky Mountain dirt roads, but what should come along but a converted school bus! She was thrilled.

One of the games the Lewiston kids play in camp is "Bushwhacking." One kid goes out fifteen minutes from camp and has to find the way back using compass, etc. On the trail, they play a game by sending one ahead to hide. The hider must be within the immediate corridor of the trail and must be visible, not covered up, but must hide by standing perfectly still. This only works if their clothes are inconspicuous. Cindy and Todd Harris sometimes get their child to hide behind trees and stumps and others have to look for the child as they pass.

I like to think they are getting something out of these games besides the little peace we parents are trying to attain. I believe they are exercising their minds and memories. Encouraging them to describe things and search for the right words to explain what they are trying to communicate is a very important skill that they will need throughout their lives. They are learning to express themselves. It helps if they win these games sometimes.

There are also many good manufactured travel games and activity sets that can help pass the hours. Some of the more popular traditional games come in mini sets.

Nature's Diversions

When out in the wilds, include anything that you can play with, both found in nature and manufactured by people. Both have their place when your child is in the wilds. Some parents are constantly on their children's backs, prohibiting them from doing anything fun if it involves getting dirty or, even worse, wet. We want our children to enjoy themselves out there and so we tend to close our eyes sometimes to the mess.

Both of our children have always been fond of getting one of our cook-kit pots and gathering nuts, pinecones, wild apples, etc., and bringing them back to camp to play with. They "cook" with them, stir it with spoons, put on lids to simmer. They've played this game with pine needles for close to an hour. Sierra was pretending to cook macaroni and cheese and Bryce was cooking grapes.

Often what is merely around the area is enough to keep them occupied, especially when they are traveling and at a different location every time you stop for a break. They climb on boulders, run toy cars down them, climb onto felled trees, and walk their horizontal trunks. We take their shoes and socks off and they simply enjoy walking on different surfaces. Sticks are great drawing tools in the dirt and one can always play being a mason and arrange rocks. They go for "rides" in "boat trees,"—trees whose bases are curved and create a seat.

There are bugs and insects to watch and play with. A small plastic magnified bug case is a great toy to bring along. The kids love to catch ants and put them in there. Mom and dad need to help capture flies, mosquitoes, etc. Another favorite is a small plastic hand lens. You can give it to your children and turn them loose in the outdoors with countless things for them to examine. Children's binoculars are also another great toy for helping them discover nature.

On our C&O Canal bike ride, gigantic, towering sycamores often lined our trail, strewing the ground with long pieces of curly bark. Sierra loved to crackle it apart and we'd toss pieces into her trailer as we rode—keeping her busy as she marveled at the sound and the feel.

Sierra sometimes likes to hike with a walking stick and searching for just the right one consumed a lot of time. Dad whittles off the bark and she watches intently. Then just the fun of using it occupies her for quite a distance.

The most favorite diversion found in the natural world, however, has to be water. As soon as we see water, we anticipate the children getting wet and take steps to keep the wetness manageable. Our only rules are that the weather must be warm enough to encourage slopping, that the water is shallow, and that their attire is either off or able to get wet.

Children don't need a lot of water to have a lot of fun. One evening on the Colorado Trail, we camped by a creeklet that was all dried up except for some tiny pools. After we dipped out what we needed for drinking water, we gave each child a pot, a spoon for digging gravel, and a cup to pour their "soup" from one container to the other. They were perfectly safe (except for the fact that Bryce found himself thirsty and dipped a drink out; we hoped he wouldn't get ill and he didn't) and it gave Todd and I some much-needed time away from their company.

Small children actually prefer small puddles and creeklets. They love to squish their toes in the sand and mud, dig stones out, stamp and splash with their feet. Our kids have chased minnows and hopping frogs in the water, trying to catch them.

Don't hesitate to hop in and join in the fun. Nothing pleases them more than having their parents participate in their play. Todd was always big on building dams. They race sticks under bridges and through culverts. It's great fun for them just to walk back and forth on a shallow bridge. When the weather is warm, we try to schedule a break by a creek crossing at least once a day. On the C&O Canal, there were water pumps every five miles. We took our breaks there and stripped Sierra naked so she could slop in the water. It was a grand thing for her to look forward to. They need to have fun doing their thing out there in the wilds too.

There is no finer entertainment on a hot day than swimming. We swam two to three times a day on our C&O Canal bike ride. That is the beauty of many canal and rail-trail paths—they often follow rivers. Sierra felt like she had to go in every time she spotted the water through the trees. On the Colorado Trail, Sierra discovered the joys of skinny-dipping in the wilds, after a five-mile dusty and hot road walk around Twin Lakes. We found a secluded campspot in the forest along the shore, quickly stripped our clothes off before we cooled off, and splashed and giggled and had a great time together.

Up on the Rocky Mountain passes, the kids played in a late-season snow patch. We let them take their boots and socks off and even though their feet got red and cold, it was good for them to experience such extreme sensations, as long as they didn't stay on the snow for long.

Toys

No matter how many wonderful found "toys" there are in nature, situations arise where you wish you had something more. For both travel in the car and in the outdoors, you may want to bring along children's toys—toys that you know have been favorites in the past and toys that they can do something with. Bryce brings an assortment of vehicles that roll—small toy cars and a few larger ones. Sierra brings her dolls with an assortment of outfits and accessories.

You can use an old tray, such as a high school cafeteria tray, for your child to use as a desk in the car, or cut out a piece of hardboard. Have crayons, colored pencils, markers, paper, stickers, scissors, etc., to do artwork with. Vinyl play sets are fun and they can be reused over and over. You can get those "magic pads" where you draw on the piece of acetatelike material with a pointed tool and then lift it up to erase it. Small plastic and metal hand puzzles are fun too.

Older kids also enjoy trading cards of all kinds (many more than just sports cards—animals, dinosaurs, etc.). And they can sort, review, and trade them.

Also consider the entertainment value of everyday objects. At eight months of age, Sierra kept herself occupied with cords and toggle switches from stuff sacks that were stacked around her in the car. She chewed her feet, made mouth sounds, and looked at big tractor trailers that passed by. Then we handed toys to her, one at a time, for her to examine and taste. Once she had gone through all of her conventional-type baby toys, we began handing her all sorts of objects: a small hairbrush, a comb, a piece of string, a metal spoon, a metal baby food jar lid, a harmonica (which she figured out how to play), a window beverage can holder, the ice scraper. We looked for a variety of textures, surfaces, shapes, and sizes. She got her sippee cup of water and a teething biscuit as a last resort. The water cup was great fun as she shook it to make the water splash all over herself.

We sometimes put on puppet shows from the front seat, using my headrest as a stage. You don't have to use actual puppets (finger or hand) but can just hold up a doll, a stuffed animal, or a plastic toy and make it talk. I like to have the puppet ask the children questions so that they can participate. Both children appear mesmerized, even though they know perfectly well that it is their parent. The only problem with this activity is that it gets mighty uncomfortable turning around in your seat like that with your seat-belt on.

Paper dolls are a good activity to share with your young children in the car. Bring along a small scissors with a very sharp point for cutting them out and puncturing the places that need to be cut out. You may ask your children to select which outfits they want you to cut out next, so they are actively participating and have a choice. It encourages them to wait patiently by playing with the outfits they already have. Get large dolls for smaller children so they can manipulate the tabs. If you have two paper dolls (of the same sex or opposite), your child can play at having conversations between the dolls, make them go imaginary places together, etc. You may have to suggest creative ways for your child to play with them to get them started. They all fit neatly and flatly in a large plastic bag. It is enjoyable work for the parent too, for it gives you some busy work to do with your hands, and yet you can still converse and look up for road signs and be navigator, etc.

If you only have one toy and it produces a problem over sharing, you might want to consider timing their turns, either with a watch or with a kitchen timer. You may want to keep their car toys separate from those they will be playing with on their outdoor adventure, to keep their interest fresh. They may want to include their most favorites, though, everywhere. Some modes of travel allow carrying extra weight, such as canoeing, stock packing, or cycling, and so weight is not the issue that it is in backpacking. The children's toy bag can be heftier.

We tried to pick toys that were small and fairly lightweight but could give us a lot of mileage. A die-cast metal tractor and wagon was brought along and some plastic farm animals. The kids set up fences with sticks and took the animals for rides in the wagon. We brought a toy dump truck and a bulldozer so Bryce could push dirt around in camp.

Sierra is in love with her dolls, so she brought two, a mommie and her daughter, and a half dozen outfits and accessories for each. Her aunt sewed the dolls some sleeping bags out of quilted fabric so they could sleep while Sierra did. The whole thing fit easily into a half-gallon resealable plastic bag.

Inflated balloons are a real favorite as a tent activity. We'd all lay on our backs and use our legs and feet to keep them from touching down. We didn't want to pop them every night so we carried some kite string and tied them to a pack to use the next night. They made us look like a traveling circus but it also made for colorful photos.

Sierra had a pink, plush teddy bear that she slept with and shoved into her day pack every day. In camp, she'd set him in a tree to watch over us, put him to bed with bandannas for blankets, and slide her sunglasses over his face.

We also had an assortment of toys like finger puppets, card games, a knit ball for batting around the tent, pop-it beads, crayons, colored pencils, scissors, and paper. You also might consider sticker books.

Because we hiked for two months in Colorado, we figured the few toys we had along would probably become tiresome, so at every re-supply point, we included small wrapped presents for the children—a few books, more balloons, a new doll outfit or card game. They really looked forward to them and it helped occupy them in town while Todd and I were busy regrouping, re-supplying, doing laundry, etc. We often stayed in motels or folks' homes who did not have children or child-proofed rooms, and this new entertainment helped keep the kids under control. Then, so the toy bag's weight did not get out of hand, it was gone through every week and any item that was not very popular was sent home.

I let them play with my "toys" too. Before we left for Colorado, Todd made me a portable flower press that measured eight inches across. The top and bottom were a very thin plywood and the layers of blotting paper and corrugated cardboard were held together with bolts and wing nuts. Sierra loved to wander the meadows with me, looking for flowers to put in our press. We were always careful to select flowers where they were in great abundance. We continued our shared pleasure by using them to make pressed-flower pictures for our loved ones for Christmas. It taught her that you can use found objects from nature and make them into beautiful presents as opposed

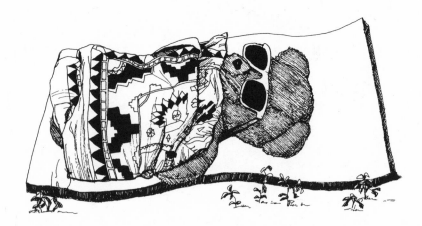

to store-bought gifts. Now we have lasting memories of those gorgeous, flower-filled alpine meadows.

The Lewiston children's toys consisted of a deck of cards, which was never left at home, a ball or frisbee, books, and whatever each child happened to be interested in at the time. It may be binoculars to see how many different species the bird lovers could find, a camera, or flower books. One child was into making molds of animal tracks and brought his plastic bag of plaster, rubberbands, etc. Their "toys" in camp had to do with their imaginations, and what they found from nature.

Camp Activities

Once you're in camp, the children can help with the many chores and can be occupied and entertained at the same time. The smallest children can carry gear over to the tent and gather sticks for fire making. At three years old, Sierra was capable of snapping tent pole sleeves together and clipping them onto the tent. She fed the llamas, arranged rocks in a fire ring when we had a fire, and laid out the sleeping pads in their designated spots and put the bags on top. Kids are good at "fetching" and can get out bowls, spoons, cups, bibs, and mats at mealtime. Be careful with them around the stove, however, and around the meal once it has the hot water added.

One of Bryce's favorite entertainments on the Colorado Trail was watching the vehicles that went by at the road crossings. We were in the wilderness much of the time and he was at the age when he was becoming completely enamored with rolling wheels. We planned to take our breaks at the roads so he could sit and watch them. The bigger and noisier the truck, the more excited the kids became. Sierra cried out, "There was a car pulling a motor home, and right behind it was a motor home pulling a car!"

We've always really enjoyed stopping at little snack bars that crossed our path. We never miss an opportunity. Food is such a big and important part of your outdoor traveling life, and really good food that is different from what you've been carrying is a treat beyond all treats.

Hints and Tips

- Encourage your children to use their imagination and develop their creativity. These skills and abilities will help them through and enrich their entire lives.
- Work on developing a song repertoire and memorize lyrics. Singing with your kids at an early age will establish this lifelong entertainment and way of sharing.

- Open yourself up and share what you know. Tell stories of your life and childhood. Teach them things that you know. Besides learning and being entertained, the closeness that you share during these exchanges will be some of their fondest life memories.

- Play word games to get their minds to stretch and think. An occupied mind can get you through the very slowest of times.

- Young children will naturally know how to play outdoors with natural objects. You may need to show children who are new to the wilds what to look for, discover, and wonder at if they have been used to spoon-fed entertainment. (Forget yourself and feel free and childlike.)

- One of the most valuable sources of entertainment is books . . . at any age. Nurturing a love of books early on will enable them to always travel and always entertain themselves.

When Your Efforts Fail

Remember that children are creatures of habit. When you are on a trip, their whole routine changes. New things are happening to them all the time. Try to not get angry with them over problems stemming from this. You are disrupting their lives in a major way and they are just seeking a little bit of a schedule. Try to help them cope.

If we simply cannot keep our kids happy in the car, our totally last resort is for an adult to sit with them. This isn't our favorite because the quarters are usually cramped. You can read them a story and hold the book up so all the children can see. You can do finger games with them or even manipulate their hands for them. You can roll cars and trucks down their bodies and the inside of the car. Their favorite part, though, is the fact that they can physically touch you. This is very comforting to them if they have been strapped in their car seats most of the day and are not getting their usual physical contact, but especially if they are tired. Sierra will often lay her head on my shoulder and both children will hold my hands. You can take off their shoes and play with their toes.

Things to Remember

- If all your efforts to entertain them fail, try to keep your patience and remember they are away from their routine and normal playthings. We are all creatures of habit.

- Try to find a discipline system that works for you in the wilds. Keep it as close to your procedure at home and always remain consistent.

Burn-out for Mom and Dad

So with all of this energy that you put into keeping your children entertained, where does that leave mom and dad? I sometimes felt brain-dead on the Colorado Trail. I passed by mountains and gorgeous scenery but I didn't quite feel "there" in the real sense of the word. Most of my day was spent chatting with a one-year-old and a three-year-old. Sierra loves to converse and I always felt it extremely rude and insensitive to ignore her, no matter how fatigued I was. Quiet Todd has little problem with it. Frankly, half the time he doesn't even hear her but is lost in his own thoughts. Sometimes I just said, "Honey, I need to be quiet for awhile. I'm going to stop talking." She always had a hard time cooperating.

I rarely thought "higher thoughts" on that trip or any trip that involved my children. My journal entries were busy and filled, but not with philosophical thinking. There was never any time for me to read before bed, either, because writing in my journal consumed my evening once the kids were asleep. I began to feel like I could barely converse in an intelligent manner. My vocabulary seemed to have shrunk. It was amazing. I wouldn't have wanted it any other way (without my children), but it certainly can take its toll on you. Because we were in each other's full-time company for three months, by the time we returned home I was craving just a few hours alone. And as far as intimacy and communing with my husband went, that was a total joke.

I think much of what we experienced was because our children were so very young and, hence, demanding. It is worth the little sacrifice of your own needs, I believe, because the children are getting so much out of the experience. The truth is, so are you. It's just a different kind of learning and growth. It has to do with parenthood, and these blessed children are ours for such a short amount of time.

Dealing with Kids' Fits

So what happens when all the entertainment and your diversion tricks do not work? What happens when they throw an all-out fit? How do you discipline out in the wilds? Todd and I perceive fits as extreme expressions of frustration. Something is definitely not right with their world. We don't feel it deserves punishment, and we usually try to ignore it and put them in a safe place, such as inside the tent.

When we drove to Maryland when Sierra was two, she decided to have a screaming fit in the car. There and then we made the rule that no screaming or loud yelling was allowed in the car, because it interferes with the driver's concentration, it mentally disturbs him, and he cannot hear if another driver is beeping the horn to alert him of something.

When we give a good reason for not allowing something, it makes sense to all but the youngest minds and is often accepted quicker. It didn't work in this particular case, because she never heard us speak a word. We had "time-out" instead. We pulled off the road and the entire family, except for Sierra, got out of the car. She remained in her car seat until she calmed down. She did not like the fact that her entire family was separated from her, and we never had to do it again.

The first time Bryce had a fit he was one and a half years old and we were on the Colorado Trail. It was over his boots, which he wanted to wear to bed. The next morning, he had a problem with his balaclava. He wanted it on, then off, then on, then off, and screamed and cried and flopped around like a fish. When I tried to hold him, he arched his back to get away. I put him into the safety of the tent with the sleeping bags and pads and let him get it all out. After awhile, he let me hold him and he sucked his thumb and it was over. I was worried this was a new pattern starting but it only lasted a few days. Again, I believe it was essentially fatigue.

Your children being mean to each other is not the same thing as a temper tantrum and warrants some sort of discipline and punishment. We made our children take a "time-out" on a stuff sack or something when this happened. The fact that they were not allowed to move, even though they were only fifteen feet away, was enough of a punishment. Our children were never very naughty out in the wilderness so it was never much of an issue. This environment seems to instill peace and harmony, so I don't think good behavior is that unusual.

Homesickness

I don't think it's a negative thing for children to experience feelings like want and loss. At their young age, they can be made to appreciate what they do not have and treat it as the gift that it is when it does re-enter their lives.

About a week from leaving home on our Colorado trip, Sierra asked when we were going to go back. I told her not for quite awhile. Knowing that, at three years old, she had little concept of time, I said that it didn't really matter, that as long as Mom and Dad and her brother are with her we can be at home on the road, and on the trail. It was enough for her.

After about a month and a half on the trail, Sierra began to say she missed her home and her bed again. One of the games we played on the trail was to name things in each room in detail and have the other guess what the object is, and so these images made her miss that other life. Todd and I thought it best to refrain from playing that game until the very end of the trip. Then, when it was raining and cold, home sounded like the most wonderful place in the world to be and we missed its comforts together.

Waning Interest in the Outdoors

Things change in our children's lives. As they grow, they draw closer to us and then pull away. If they are given the chance to search out their own way, with a little luck, they will return to the things we loved and shared together.

Bob saw a difference in his daughter Adrienne when she hit the eleven- or twelve-year mark. For seven years she had shared her father's love of hiking and backpacking, but now for the first time, things had changed. They were camping on the Black Forest Trail, a remote area in northwestern Pennsylvania, when he got his first sign. At nightfall, Adrienne got a faraway look in her eyes and was not interested in any conversation or reading her book, unlike usually. When her dad asked her what was wrong, she said she missed Mommie and her sister Amberely. Bob replied, "You've never missed Mommie and your sister before...all you do is fight when you are at home." Bob was suspicious. She closed the conversation by saying, "I don't want to go overnight again unless Mommie and Amberely come."

Bob was beginning to realize that his daughter's interest was somehow waning. Not a single school friend was even partway active in the outdoors, nor did they have even the slightest desire to try it. These were Adrienne's peers and their opinion meant a lot to her. Adrienne's friends were beginning to play a stronger role in her life and her father's company was losing points. Bob knew he would either have to find a compatible father with a compatible daughter who both enjoyed hiking, or he would have to return to the trails alone or, at the most, day hike with his daughter.

This sudden lack of interest in an outdoor sport (after spending years with their family participating in it) is not uncommon. All is not lost when the kids lose interest. They may pick it up later on as older teens when going out with church groups, scouts, or their friends. Give them the skills they need when they go out with you, and feel good that you've enhanced their childhood and family life at a young age.

Keeping Them Rested

Whenever my children act unreasonably contrary and uncharacteristically sour when we are on an outing, I give them the benefit of the doubt and blame fatigue. Entertainment only works for so long, then sleep is the only remedy.

Daytime Naps

If children are not comfortable, they will most likely not be able to fall asleep. Getting them comfortable enough to nap during the day can be an incredible challenge, especially if your child is used to certain rituals. You will need to do something different in order for them to get the rest they need.

My two-year-old is used to either being rocked to sleep, driven in a car, or carried in a pack to sleep. I could not tell him to lie down in a canoe by himself and take a nap. Either he'd skip, or we'd have to take a break on shore and go for a hike with him in his pack to get him to sleep, or just make him adjust to new conditions and put himself to sleep. The last option is miserable on all involved. It is best if your child can adapt to adverse and changing situations and still be able to sleep, but many young children are creatures of habit.

Both of our children slept well in their backpacks when we hiked. Bryce had some problems with strong wind though. And road walks were murder for him. Todd and I enjoyed walking side by side on those occasions because we get to talk. But the chatter stimulated his interest and kept him awake for hours beyond his need. Even on a single-file trail, I have to let Todd go ahead with Sierra so she will have quiet and nap, and Bryce too on my back. We meet up ten minutes later, each with our sleeping babe and ready to engage in some rare adult conversation.

When Sierra was eight months old, we took her on a long car ride to Utah. When she needed to take her first nap, nothing was the same as at home. There was no mommie to hold and nurse her, no rocking chair, no lullabies on the tape player, no darkened room. She got hysterical. After about five or ten minutes of listening to her scream, I made Todd pull the car off the turnpike to let me nurse her. When we put her back into her car seat, it started again. And again I made Todd pull over. After the third time, he said, "At this rate, we'll never get to Utah. We're not even out of Pennsylvania." We left her in her seat and let her scream herself to sleep. I watched the seconds tick by on the dashboard clock and put my fingers in my ears. I felt as though my heart were bleeding. It took twenty-five minutes of hell. From then on, she usually fell asleep much quicker, and cried less and less.

"Letting them cry" often does not work for some overtired children. What may work is stopping the car to get your tired child out, to walk, to play, to go to a restaurant. It changes the scenery and removes

your child from the problem. It changes his or her mood and enables him or her to relax and it tires him or her out just a little bit more. It is often better on the parents' nerves to take the time to stop, instead of passing the miles in tremendous tension. Once you all climb back into the car, your child will often easily fall to sleep in a matter of minutes, with very little resistance, if any.

In the car, children may be able to sleep with their heads bent over in all sorts of awkward positions, but I do not believe they sleep as well as they would with support. They tend to bob their heads, over and over—raising them up, then dropping them down. It is good to use a bed pillow and prop it up against the car door and their seat, and maybe shape it and wedge it a bit to fit well. They will be more likely to lay their heads on it when they become tired, go to sleep more easily, and sleep more soundly.

If children do not get their proper sleep on a car trip, they will become overly fatigued and perhaps have it interfere with their night-time sleep. This can result in them becoming rundown and, coupled with new places, new people, and new germs that they are coming in contact with, they can become ill.

You have to do what you need to do in order to take care of their needs. If you try to overlook or ignore them, you will only become miserable yourself. This is the kind of stuff that takes a lot of work on the parents' part. Nothing about an outdoor trip is normal (unless you remain out in the wilds for weeks), and although children are highly adaptable, their needs remain very strong and very important.

At Night

When you're trying to keep a child from sleeping during the day so he or she will be able to sleep at night, it is best to take a break when nap-time seems to be approaching. Riding in a backpack, riding on a bike, or sitting in a canoe can all encourage sleep, just from the relaxing and repeated movement. Get up, eat and drink something, walk and run around, play—all these activities will wake your children up and refresh them enough so they can continue for a few more miles in a more wakeful state.

We used to practice this on Sierra on the Colorado Trail. Every day, about 2:00 P.M., she'd grow fatigued. Either her eyelids would get heavy and she'd start to nod as she rode her llama, or she'd begin to get disagreeable and demanding. Then Todd handed Bryce over to me and I carried him in my child carrier and he took Sierra in his. Thirty-eight pounds of live weight is no picnic to carry anywhere, but especially not while climbing over 12,000-foot passes where the oxygen is wanting. We used this technique to delay her nap until we were on a downhill stretch, or to skip it entirely if we only had a few miles remaining to camp.

If your children are a little wound up after a day in the car, have them participate in a quiet activity to prepare for sleep. It's always difficult to go from full-speed-ahead to horizontal. Get cozy and read a few books. It will inevitably relax them to the point where they can close their eyes.

Something that's difficult is the fact that they may be sleeping in a different location every night and have different sounds to contend with, different levels of comfort, different sleeping arrangements, etc. Variety in their sleep habits is not the best thing in a traveling child's life, but it's impossible to prevent. Have some familiar items along to give them some consistency and security—a pillow from home, a special blanket or stuffed animal or doll. We bring along the children's lambskins that they've slept on since birth. Keep your bedtime ritual the same, whether you read books, sing, tell stories, cuddle, give back foot and rubs (or all of the above like we do).

Todd rarely pays attention to the kids' bedtime, but I think it is very important. If they're allowed to remain up later than usual on repeated occasions, it throws them off their schedule. They will become cranky the next day if they don't sleep later and make up for it. (Our children rarely do.) If it happens night after night, it will produce not only a miserable child, but a child who is on the way to becoming sick. Our children never compensate by sleeping late because they seem to have their own built-in alarm that goes off at daybreak. If you are camping, the rising sun will encourage it too. I put a lot of energy into getting them to bed at a decent hour and think it has paid off. The backcountry is not the ideal place to deal with a sick child. A parent must be flexible at all times, however, including the bedtime hour, but try to make their lost sleep up the very next night.

For instance, when we went canoeing and camping with our friends Frank and Lila Strauss and their grandson, Solomon, we kept the kids up a little later than usual for Frank's birthday because we wanted to wait until dark to surprise him with his lit birthday cake around the campfire. Besides a few-hour canoe ride, the kids had also hiked about three miles—a good chunk of trail for a three-year-old. The next morning, as we were carrying our gear to the cars (we were at a walk-in campsite), I asked Sierra if she'd help Mommie and pick up a paper plate that someone had dropped. She would not do it. She said that she couldn't, that it was too heavy! She began to cry and get all worked up. I told her we must all do our share and help out, but all she said was that she wanted her dad. Todd made her carry the plate anyway, and held her hand and guided her the long fifteen yards back to the car—with her crying all the while. It was 10:00 A.M. I really didn't consider fatigue to be the culprit, but stubbornness. Our car wasn't even out of the site's parking space and both children were sound asleep! And this was a three-year-old that never takes a nap! I was amazed and felt bad that I scolded her for not cooperating.

As we traveled west in the summer, we had some problems with the time change. Our children were used to a certain bedtime and their internal clocks were not adjusted to our watches when we crossed the time lines. When their bodies had enough and were ready to sleep, the sun was still up in the sky, brightening the interior of the tent and preventing them from sleeping. They were going to bed hours after their bedtime, but not sleeping later in the morning to make up for it. During times like this, you'll have to put extra effort into seeing that they get the sleep that they need.

Lack of Intimacy for Mom and Dad

We spent seven years of our married life with our sleeping bags zipped together. The benefits always outweighed the negative aspects of cold air bellowing out when the other person rolled over, smelling two times as much "bad air" after a night of freeze-dried beans, etc. But after the children, after pregnancy actually, I opted for my own space. There are so many interruptions in the night, between patting children, pulling up "covers" on all three of them, relieving my own bladder, that I want to get as much uninterrupted sleep as possible.

Todd misses the good old days. And after an extended period of time, night life as a couple in a family tent gets old. If you're going to be intimate, you've got to be incredibly quiet with a minimum amount of ripstop nylon rustling, but it can be done. We usually wait until the children are in a deep sleep (you can tell by how they are breathing), but even then they sometimes stir. We stop a few seconds and let them settle back to sleep. Sometimes they roll into the recreation area and have to be rolled back. The best is to put them to bed, and then drag your sleeping bags and pads outside to have your fun alone. Of course, it cannot be too cold or raining. These nights also have to be subtracted from all the nights when you are too fatigued or you fall asleep prematurely. The opportunities are not many. Be prepared for lean times.

Hints and Tips

- Lack of sleep and fatigue will be your largest enemies out in the wilds when it comes to maintaining their good mood. Make every effort to see that this need is met. Anything less isn't fair.
- Establish a bedtime ritual when on outdoor adventures, perhaps needing to be a bit different than the one at home. It will go far to create comfort, security, and stability in a changing environment.
- Remember to make time for yourself for you and your mate, even if it's a simple thing such as not putting your children between you at night, reserving fifteen minutes to talk about the day, or reading a few pages of a book before retiring. It will help prevent your children from monopolizing you.

Dealing with the Car Ride to the Trailhead

When it comes down to it, I was probably more concerned about the drive out to Colorado in the truck than I was about the two-month hike itself. The four of us would be in that enclosed space for much of two weeks—one week to drive from Pennsylvania to Colorado; another to drive around the state, picking up llamas, llama gear, attending orientations, workshops, etc. We really felt that if we could get through the truck ride and still enjoy each other's company, we would be fine.

Getting Them Comfortable

First eliminate all the physical factors that could make life in your vehicle miserable for your kids. Dress them in cotton knits that breathe and do not bind like other fabrics. There can be a big difference in the temperature from the front to the back of the vehicle. The air conditioning can be blowing on you and chilling you, while those in the back are still warm. Or the heat can be making you toasty but the kids can be chilled in the back. Somebody's got to compromise and it ought to be the parents. Carry a sweater or a blanket handy to keep warm in air conditioning. When the kids nap, throw a sweater or a blanket over their bare legs if they feel chilled.

If your car's interior gets hot, have a cotton towel or a pillow case to throw over their car seat and metal buckles so it doesn't burn them. Remember this when you stop for a break and leave the car sitting in the sun for awhile.

When the hot sun is shining on Bryce in the car, he is not happy. We sometimes give him a sippee cup so he can splash himself with water and drool it out of his mouth to keep cool, especially if it is at the end of the day and we didn't mind him getting soaked.

In colder months, we adults often take our coats off once the heat warms up the car. But are the poor kids still bundled up in the back? Just think about them and how you would feel if you were there. A better choice would be to warm up the car beforehand so everyone can take off their coats. Keeping the heat off and your coats on can result in cold feet or chills when they sleep. Plus you might be warmed by the sun coming through the windshield, and they might be sitting in the back in the shade.

A child can become totally miserable if the sun is low and is shining into their eyes. Some children are simply too young to keep sunglasses on. You can purchase sunshades that either stick to the window (supposedly), or the type that is a screen that you pull down and secure with a suction cup. We've never had any luck with the shades that stick to the windows, but then again, I think both the window and the shade need to be impeccably clean to work and ours are never in that state. The kind with the suction cups may just have to be moved from one side of the vehicle to the other or to the rear.

Very young children do not always have the verbal skills to put their feelings into words. It's important to not turn a deaf ear to their complaining, particularly if what they are saying is a little out of the ordinary. When we drove across Virginia, the mountainous roads were very curvy and twisted. Bryce bitterly complained that his booster car seat was too tight across the middle, which it wasn't. We figured it was a ploy to get us to stop and take a break. When he began violently throwing up, it became crystal clear that the problem was a tummy ache from car sickness. There is often a reason for their unhappiness, and as parents we owe it to them to try to discover what it is and try to help them.

The Strausses discovered that the leading motion sickness medicine can be divided down to a safe dose for a child as young as two years old. Neither of us are fond of administering drugs to our children, but in this case, which is the greater of the two evils? Many children, just like adults, never get car sick. If you have one that is sensitive to it, motion sickness medicine may be something to consider carrying in the glove box of your vehicle.

If you have to be on the road for many days at a time, you don't want to burn your kids out. We tried to keep it to around 350 miles a day, and sometimes went below 300 if we visited somebody or someplace special. When we need a break, which is usually every two to two and a half hours at the most, we try to look for playgrounds or parks. I look ahead on the map for a fairly large town in bolder print, but avoid those with multiple exits. You can spend too much time driving around trying to get to a spot. As soon as we exit off the highway, we go immediately to a gas station and inquire about a playground or park. A parent with children is also a good target. Nearly every town has a park or a playground or a ball diamond where the kids can run around safely.

Another place is an elementary school that is not in session. They almost always have a playground. Even roadside rest areas do not offer the recreation and peace of mind that parks do. They often have only a strip of grass with picnic tables and a parking lot on one side of it, and maybe even two lots, and you must be aware of where your children are at all times.

State parks within five miles of the highway provide places like lakes for rock skipping and creeks for slopping in. Some may have a day use fee which is usually nominal, but may not be worth it to you for a hour or so break. It doesn't seem like merely a road trip to get from one place to another with breaks like these. And when you take a really long break, the kids never mind hopping back into the car. It may be worth doing some research ahead of time. After your route is planned, contact some of the Departments of Recreation and Natural Resources in those states for referrals.

Some of the fast food restaurants have play areas and they are usually announced on the highway before the exit. Just be prepared to have them coax you into buying the food. When it's extremely hot or

rainy, and you need to take a break and stretch your legs, look for an air-conditioned mall. Crankiness peaks in hot weather.

Eating something cold like ice cream or frozen yogurt brightens spirits and offers some relief. Just the anticipation of getting it combats crankiness in the car. Children are always ready for a treat such as ice cream, and the peace and pleasure that this small diversion provides is worth the little bit of time and money. Children need the variety. Don't forget, you are very excited about where you are ultimately going, but your children live in the present.

Whenever we are traveling in mountainous areas, we look for a trail–road crossing and go for a short hike. We carry Charles Cook's *The Essential Guide to Hiking in the United States* in the car (see appendix C, Suggested Reading) and consult it whenever possible. You can still have a picnic at the trailhead, but also take a nice walk on the trail besides.

Always encourage the children to run around when you stop, climb rocks, try to catch falling leaves, etc. Bring out a ball to kick. They move so much less than we do when in the car and usually have an excess of energy to boot.

If you go near places that offer tours—such as Hershey's Chocolate World in Hershey, Pennsylvania, or Ben & Jerry's Ice Cream Factory in Waterbury, Vermont, places that children enjoy—stop and incorporate them into your trip schedule or rest stops. Diversion is the key to happiness.

It's hard to push kids past 5:00 or 6:00 P.M. if they've been in the car all day. It's the same level of tolerance that they have whether they're in a backpack, in a canoe, or on a bike. Anything after that is usually misery for all involved, or full-time, demanding entertainment.

Children who are strapped in most of the day often have excess energy come evening. Try to stop early enough for them to have a few hours of daylight to run around, stretch their legs, and get some fresh air. They always go to bed much easier then.

ON THE JOURNEY

▲ ▲ ▲ ▲ ▲ ▲ ▲ ▲ ▲

CHAPTER

Camping

▲ ▲ ▲ ▲ ▲ ▲ ▲ ▲ ▲

*I*t doesn't seem to matter which outdoor sport you do—all children enjoy camping the best. Try to quit early enough in the day so they have adequate time to explore the campsite. The longer your outing, the more comfortable your children will become and the greater their ability will be to entertain themselves while in camp.

No-Trace, Low-Impact Techniques

Children are attracted to things in nature that are interesting and different from their world at home. They like to discover things and handle things, and sometimes in their innocence, they can destroy them. At one campsite along the C&O Canal, Sierra found a huge rock covered with thick green moss. It was great fun for her to rip the moss off, to see the bare rock underneath and the undersides of the moss, and to see if there were any creeping creatures under it. But it would take a long time to restore itself and it was unsightly to look at, especially because it was in a designated campsite. We stopped her as soon as we discovered what she was doing, but she caused some damage in the meantime.

If your children have a need to discover things in this manner, remind them that we must leave flowers, rocks, and other natural features undisturbed. We should not squelch our children's wonder, but they may need a little direction with it. A big temptation for children is to want to pick flowers, mushrooms, etc. Tell them that, if they pick these things, the next person will not get to feel the joy that they now feel at seeing them. Be sure to explain and follow the regulations of the area you are traveling in; for instance, national parks often prohibit picking or taking any natural object, but national forests may allow picking small quantities of wild berries for immediate eating.

Try to teach your children to be sensitive to all of life in the natural world as early as possible. Really stress the philosophy of not marring or changing nature at all, leaving no trace behind. Use examples of those who were not sensitive to show your point. We always point out piles of toilet paper out in the open, on top of the ground, to our children. They see the negative impact for themselves, feel disgusted, and learn quickly why we practice low-impact techniques such as using established backcountry toilets when available, burying feces and disposing of waste water at least 200 feet from all water sources, and burning or packing out toilet paper rather than burying it.

Follow all low-impact, no-trace techniques when camping: Camp at least 200 feet from water sources. Stay out of fragile meadows. Visualize potential impacts when selecting a campsite; use existing campsites whenever possible to avoid creating unnecessary new ones. Never dig trenches around your tent; don't sweep the ground clean of natural debris with your foot when laying out your tent, but pick up large things like pine cones and sticks and remove them with your hands. Build campfires only in areas where they are permitted and conditions are safe; build only in existing fire rings and keep the fire small; use only dead or down wood from outside the campsite area. Consider using a stove even where wood fires are permitted, to minimize impact. Hang food four feet from the tree trunk and eight feet off the ground to keep it out of the reach of animals. Consider leaving pets at home so they do not disturb wildlife. Boil drinking water from a natural source for five minutes.

Consult a good outdoor book from appendix C, Suggested Reading (for example, *A Hiker's Companion*) and educate yourself so that you can educate your children. Children will only be as good stewards of the land as their parents are.

Children naturally go for the quickest way of traveling and may be tempted to cut switchbacks on the trail. It may simply look like fun to gain on the others and go down something steep. Explain why the switchback is there. Point out examples of trail erosion and show that a damaged trail is not fun or safe for anyone to walk on.

Littering is a very tempting thing for many kids, especially if their peers at school do it freely. They may not even be aware of doing it. One of the best ways to cure this is to have them participate in trail and creekside cleanups, so they learn to have a sense of pride in keeping the natural environment clean. Always point out trashed areas and exclaim how ugly it is and that we must keep the water and the air clean . . . not just for us, but also for the animals whose home it is. Even the very youngest will understand this.

Car Camping

Seeing the country in your vehicle . . . it sounds like a big adventure to some, perhaps a lifelong dream. A car camping trip can be the ideal method of traveling with an infant or very young child. Although we never traveled this way before we had a baby—we were used to leaving the vehicle behind and walking over this blessed earth for months—life seemed complicated enough as young parents, so taking all of the necessities and some luxuries into the car with us sounded like an ideal kind of trip.

You may miss what you were able to do before you were parents— being independent of the car. Be happy with what you can do, and that is day hikes and short overnighters. You can still see a lot. But as the trip progresses, you may feel married to the car. So what at first seemed like a help could also seem like a hindrance.

It is best if you have your trail food and clothing separate from your car gear. You need ample car space to allow for this. A van or mini-van or a king-cab truck would be comfortable and simple. Because we

did not have a vehicle that allowed us to store our packs loaded—they only fit if they were emptied and flattened—our greatest hassle was the packing and the unpacking that we had to do every day and sometimes a few times a day. Our VW diesel car had considerable storage space but our excessive gear filled up the normally large capacity.

One of the major causes of burn-out when traveling in your car is trying to do and see too much, trying to cover too much ground. A related problem is the near-constant moving, the sometimes daily task of setting up the tent and the portable crib (for use as a playpen), etc. You may find yourself much more relaxed if you stay put in one place for two or more nights. Leave your vehicle behind to go discover the land. Go slow. Don't make your vacation as fast-paced as your life back at home.

Where to Go

Most people would not think twice about staying in a motel, but the more time you spend in an area, the deeper will its beauty and essence become a part of your being. This can't happen if you spend your nights in a motel, or even in insulated public campgrounds, and not in a short amount of time.

One very nice thing about the west is the huge amount of public lands that you are allowed to camp on for free—all Bureau of Land Management (BLM) lands and National Forest (NF) lands are public lands open to free camping within their borders. It enables you to have a secluded camp, some privacy, a better taste of the wilderness, and your car still with you. Basically, any place you see by the road that looks like a good spot to camp (this will often be obvious from others that have come before you) is up for grabs, as well as land anywhere else within the jurisdiction's boundaries.

If you feel you need some facilities, national forest primitive campgrounds have pit toilets and picnic tables and do not usually have the crowds that the more modern ones do. What you are giving up is the lighted bathrooms, showers, and potable water at the commercial or pay campgrounds. A host usually resides in these campgrounds in season, which offers that bit of security or assistance should you prefer it.

You can obtain maps from these government agencies to learn where these public lands are located (see appendix B, Organizations). Often, secondary gravel or dirt roads, indicated on the maps, take you to the areas most suitable for camping. No permit is required for BLM or NF lands. The NF primitive campgrounds have a bulletin board where you enter that explains the pay procedure, which usually consists of inserting money in the envelope provided and depositing it into a box, depending on the season. The cost is very small. A host may stop and check whether you are registered, or it may be by the honor system.

Selecting a Campsite

Public campgrounds with rangers or residing hosts usually have quiet hours that campers are expected to comply with. Every campground has its own manner of enforcing these rules. The stricter ones have someone make the rounds in the evening to make the point that quiet hours must be observed and tell you how to report any violation. These campgrounds usually do not have the clientele who want to stay up late, make a lot of noise, and drink. (But you can find this type anywhere.) The more restricted and rigidly controlled the campground, the less problem you should have with this.

When staying in public campgrounds, cruise through the entire area first to find the most remote campsites if you are looking for privacy and quiet. These sites are often furthest away from the toilets and, because of this, are usually not the most popular with the normal car camper. You can also look for sites on the perimeters of the campground so you do not have neighbors on all sides. That way, you do not have to be concerned that your baby's middle-of-the-night crying is disturbing your neighbors.

Some folks are not the family type; they may not be sensitive to families that need to get some sleep at night or may not be understanding of crying babies. Sometimes the best you can do is stay remote and even warn other campers who are pulling in alongside of you that you have young babies who may be up in the night. If this will disturb them and there are many other sites available, they may appreciate being forewarned.

Dealing With Unruly Neighbors

Whenever possible, go on your outings during the week and avoid holiday weekends. Do not plan to camp in heavily used areas if you have a choice. Saturday night is party night, and if you are camping in a public campground within an hour of a large city or close to a road in public lands, it provides easy access for partyers. Evaluate the condition of the site to determine if you could get late-night company (lots of broken glass, trash, etc.). Extreme behavior can happen in primitive or open-use areas where there are no hosts or regulations, but these areas can also be the most private and secluded.

I am always quick to go over and ask a neighbor to keep it down. It is often done unintentionally on their part, for they aren't aware of how their voices are traveling. Sometimes your confrontations work in your favor, but they are always uncomfortable and sometimes downright scary. What you have to be afraid of are drunks. Sometimes it might be better to pack up and leave. You have to weigh the situation—where you are, the looks of your neighbors, their behavior, etc. When you are traveling with your children, there is more to be concerned about.

Todd gets nervous, and rightfully so, thinking about what our inconsiderate neighbors are capable of doing and about his wife shooting her mouth off and angering them. He calms me down to a polite level. I stir him up to an assertive level. You need to check each other and pre-plan what you're going to do and say in the event of a confrontation.

During a long cycling trip, we'd planned to stay at one of the non-car camping hiker/biker sites on the route. When we pulled in after a long day's ride, we found that a group of fishermen had already taken over the site for the weekend. The community picnic table was covered with their equipment; there were folding chairs and white gas lanterns, all brought in by canoe. They got off the river late, after we were already in bed. Their talking and laughter and the brilliantly illuminated woods kept me awake.

I pulled on my clothes and went out to talk. I explained that we were tired from riding all day (plus I was five months pregnant), and asked if they could perhaps use their candle lantern instead of their white gas lantern. They were polite and said, "We'll try that." It didn't seem like a lot to ask. But I could tell they were perturbed by the way they banged their pots and pans for the next hour, primed the very noisy water pump, and slammed the spring-loaded outhouse door numerous times. They finally took their light and went to the other side of the tent to shadow it. It was considerably better and I fell right to sleep.

Two nights later, when we arrived at our next planned hiker/biker site, we saw that some other cyclists were already there. Down by the river, we met our first neighbor standing in the river sucking on a bottle of beer. There was a pile of firewood collected and I was afraid they would blatantly disregard the posted quiet hours. I approached another member of the party and asked if they were planning on staying up late. He was very nice and said that he didn't think so. He asked when we were planning on going to bed, and I said, "At dark." He wondered if the children would enjoy the firecrackers they were going to set off. I told him the "children" consisted of a one-year-old who would be terrified of them. He promised he'd try to keep his buddies quiet.

When night fell and we were getting ready to turn in, I saw him loading up his arms with firewood to take down to the river, out of our earshot. His beer-drinking buddy was cursing loudly and throwing glass beer bottles into the metal trash can so they made a loud shattering sound. When I got up in the middle of the night, I heard them faintly through the woods and the party was still going strong. Come morning, when we were packing up, the polite one was up and about (the drunken ones could not yet face the day), and I told him how much I appreciated what he had done the night before.

Though both of these examples occurred during non-car camping trips and at supposedly less accessible campsites, they illustrate the types of conflicts that can occur out in the wilds. Gauge your willingness and ability to deal with these types of problems, and select your campsites accordingly. Even at well-regulated public campgrounds with rangers, you may have to exercise your people skills in negotiating with others using the area.

Camp Manners for Kids

It is just as important to keep your children under control so they do not disturb other people. Campgrounds can be a lot of fun for kids. The outdoors, for them, feels like a place where they can be unrestrained in their laughing and running around, but they need to understand that a public campground isn't really the same as a public city park during the daylight hours.

You may want to think about leaving your children's noisy toys, such as their plastic-wheeled tricycles which sound very noisy on asphalt drives, at home so they don't disturb other campers. Have them keep their yelling down. Think in terms of how others may view your children and their activities, and try to keep them in check. Remember, these kinds of restrictions may not be for you. If so, think about more primitive campgrounds or campsites, away from other people.

Don't think that your younger children are the only ones whose actions may need watching. Older children might go off on their own and behave in ways that are disturbing to other campers. Teach them how to be sensitive to other people (not talking loudly at night by lakes, for example, where sound travels far). The older and more independent they become, the more time they will be spending away from your watchful eye. Teach them manners when they are young and don't hesitate to remind and refresh them as they grow older.

Setting Up Camp

With a family, there are even more camp chores to do than for a single person or a couple—pitching the tent, making beds, washing out diapers, cooking, washing dishes, filtering water, changing diapers, brushing teeth, etc. If there is a baby in camp, one parent may have to dedicate all his or her attention to caring for the baby, especially if it is in a crawling stage and could get into trouble. Try to take turns and switch baby duty for camp duty, so no one feels burned out. Remind yourself that it will not be easy, but you are out there for other reasons besides a "vacation." You're there to share nature and the wilds with your little ones and that can be life-changing for them.

When your children are older, two parents can begin taking care of the camp business, instead of one just tending to the children. Children want to help at a very early age and can be included in camp chores as soon as they're able. They will not hasten progress for a few years, and will probably slow it down for awhile, but if they learn at an early age

that their participation is enjoyed and appreciated, they will continue through the years until they're old enough to actually be an asset.

Start them off by fetching or handing tent stakes to you, etc. Chores like clipping tent poles to their accompanying hooks and rolling out and positioning sleeping pads and sleeping bags in the tent is a good next step. As they grow older, more and more chores can be assigned, which they will more than likely find joy and take pride in doing. There is a marked feeling of unity and cooperation in outdoor activities, and the usual static that you receive at home over doing chores is usually not encountered.

Encourage individual children with individual skills, talents, and interests to embrace particular chores as their own—for example, cooking. Our daughter Sierra enjoys helping Todd stake out the llamas and feeding and watering them. As long as your children are actively participating somehow, they shouldn't have to do chores they hate.

Ending the Day

Babies

Babies can have a rough time during those initial nights in the tent. They can become frightened when they awake on the first night of their first trip. They might feel the nylon tent close to their face. There is no night light. It may be difficult to nurse in the dark. A candle for night feedings may fascinate them so much that it wakes them up thoroughly.

The most difficult part for me was the marathon nursing when my daughter was four months old. Up to seven times a night I needed to nurse her to put her back to sleep. I never knew if she was hungry or cold or thirsty and not just dependent on me to put her back to sleep. Sierra drained me. I used to feel like she was sucking blood, for surely there was no milk left. When we were camped in a public campground, I worked twice as hard to keep her quiet so she didn't disturb anybody.

Todd offered to take her outside to walk her, but I was afraid she would begin to demand it always and this would be terribly inconvenient, especially on cold and wet nights. I sat up and held her and rocked my body to calm her down. It was extremely hard on my back. Her crying lasted about twenty minutes the first night, went down to ten minutes the second, and a minute or two the third. We later got some collapsible, padded camp chairs which made rocking in the tent a dream with all the support they give. With my second child, I got smart. He sometimes only got pats in the night.

Young Children

Although young children often say they are tired early in the night, it can take at least an hour to get them to sleep. They may not be able to sleep until the sun has gone down and, unlike at home, you can't simulate darkness by pulling down shades or closing curtains.

We often go on very short walks around camp in the evening, sometimes carrying a hot drink to share. If children are carried all day long, this is a chance for them to stretch and explore. But mostly it is a wind-down, relaxing activity that we do as a part of our camping bedtime ritual.

I often sing to the children before bed, and they lie on either side of me so that I can have an arm around each one. Bedtime is a very special time for us and it can be the biggest joy of your camping experience as a family.

In the Lewiston family, most bedtime rituals seemed to cease after the children reached six or seven years old, but reading aloud knew no age boundaries. They never had any trouble with their children staying up late and talking or carrying on. They were tired after the day's adventure and knew well what consequences the following day would bring if they weren't well rested.

When your children are older, the nighttime part of camping is usually as restful as it is back home. It might take a little thought to figure out the family's sleeping arrangement in your tent. You might want to consider who is most famous for their middle-of-the-night eliminations and let them be close to the door.

We put the children against the walls and Todd and I in the middle. We began our nights with Sierra and I on one side, with Todd and Bryce, in his somewhat wild, pre-sleep state, on the other. There was peace until Bryce scrambled over Todd's body and got to Sierra and they began wrestling. It went on until they either bumped heads or Bryce bit his tongue. Then he'd cry and we'd move him over to his own side, where he went to sleep without any difficulty. That cry must drain him of his little bit of remaining energy.

Now we settle in with Bryce on my side, for he often needs tending in the middle of the night (and Todd does not sleep alertly enough to hear any child in the night), plus he usually wants his mom at night. Sierra usually does not need any tending to, so she sleeps on comatose Todd's side. That leaves Todd and I in the middle together. We can at least throw an arm over the other, even if that's all the "intimacy" we get. This set-up allows for some late-night talks too.

My favorite part is that the whole family sleeps together in the tent. I love the closeness, the holding and kissing and cuddling, and the before-bed wrestling. I imagine it's what having a "family bed" is all about. No wonder small children love it so: they have their parents all to themselves, all through the night.

Breaking Camp

It takes forever to break camp with babies and young children. There are more bodies to dress (and babies can squirm and kick and arch their backs in resistance); there are more mouths to feed; there is more food to cut up, bedding to put away, etc. The worst part with a fretful baby is early morning wake-ups—say, at 5:00 A.M.

After a bad night of frequent interruptions, Todd and I were not ready to face the day when our infant daughter woke us up. And she wasn't interested in facing it for long, but would need to be put back to sleep within the hour. She controlled us during those early days in the wilds. We were so concerned with meeting her needs—and rightfully so, for we felt if we didn't, we could jeopardize her well-being. We were young, and new parents. Not only were we learning to be parents in general, but we were learning to care for a baby in the backcountry, and we did not want to screw up.

Now that our children are a little older, the challenges are different. When Sierra's eyelids push open, she immediately wants to chat. She gets louder and louder, until she succeeds in waking up her brother. She needs something quiet to do, like play with paper dolls or read books, until he wakes. Have some quiet toys in the tent with you. It's as important as the bag of clean diapers.

Children are often cranky in camp in the morning. You are certain to be busy doing chores and often with haste. The children don't like this too much, even if you are doing something for them. They are often a little chilly too. When they're young, they don't know (or don't believe you when you tell them) that moving around gets them warm. They don't like staying in the warm tent either, but want to come out and see the day. Get something hot into them. Give them a snack to munch on until breakfast is ready.

Young children often want to help, and that can make the whole process take even longer. But you can't say no to them; that would be discouraging them from helping with chores, and it won't be long until their help is truly appreciated. Give them a task to engage their attention—kitchen chores, food preparation, morning rituals, etc. Sierra loves to help press air out of the mattress with her knees. Trouble is, she doesn't weigh enough to expel it and I have to not only wait for her to try to do it, but then do it myself anyway.

Older kids can have assigned responsibilities, including taking care of their own gear. They need something to occupy them. The ideal is for them to promote your progress of breaking camp, not hinder it.

It can all be discouraging if you dwell on what you used to be able to do. Those days will come again. Try to relax, forget about schedules, and learn to put more value on what is happening now, however slowly, instead of what you'd like to get accomplished.

Hints and Tips

- No matter what the outdoor sport, young children enjoy the camping part more than your method of arriving there. Allow ample time for their most favorite activity.

- Start small, with less remote destinations and shorter visits, until you know your family's interests and capabilities. Increase the wild element and length of stay in relation to your skills.

- Include the children in camp chores at as early an age as they are able. They'll not only have more of a part but, before long, they will become an asset.

- In public campgrounds, always be alert to and aware of your children's activities and whether they might be disturbing other campers. If you seek more freedom, learn to camp in more remote areas.

CHAPTER 7

Day Hiking

▲ ▲ ▲ ▲ ▲ ▲ ▲ ▲ ▲

*O*ne of the nicest things about day hiking is you have your car with you at the end of the day and can adjust gear, replenish supplies, and better care for your family's needs. For a spouse or family members who are not too keen on roughing it or participating in very rugged physical activity, day hiking from comfortable lodgings is a very good way to ease them into the sport because you are not taking away their creature comforts. And because there are so many options and you are not locked into a schedule, it gives them an out if the weather is not cooperating, if their muscles become sore, or if they simply want to take a break from hiking. Plus the rest of the family does not have to abandon their hiking plans.

Equipment

Day Packs

The youngest children find great delight in using a day pack. They can put their stuffed animal in there, a snack, their cup, etc. A hand lens, child's binoculars, etc., are other good gear ideas. Make sure their pack is not too big (very small ones can be found) and that they do not load it down with too much weight. Try to select packs that are designed like those for older hikers—adjustable, padded shoulder straps; webbing to tie as a belt to prevent the pack from shifting; etc. Small, child-size fanny packs are also nice for them to wear—in front or behind. It makes them feel like they are really participating in the sport.

Child Carriers

It is very important, right from the start, to have your babies enjoy being in their child carrier. After all, you might want to be using it a lot in the future.

Your child carrier should have a good amount of storage space in it. You can often buy additional side pockets (one-liter bottle size) and large zippered bags for under the seat. There is so much gear a baby needs to have along for even the shortest hike, never mind your own personal needs. You can "extend" your child carrier's load capacity by strapping gear on the outside—a sippee cup with a handle, vinyl pants, extra clothing, etc. Attach well with alligator clips purchased at a hardware store. Just make sure your child's clothing is very secure so that you do not lose it. If you're hiking with other adults, they can help carry some of your gear in their pack. Don't be afraid to ask.

If a young child sometimes leaves the carrier to walk, have a large stuff sack of gear available from another adult's pack, so you can relieve him or her of some weight. We keep our bag of rain gear and pack covers handy and shove it into the space where the child sat.

Hip carriers are not the best for trail walking, because they position most of your baby's weight on the side of your hip. You can use your arm to support baby's head and it is very comfortable for both you and baby as long as you are only walking gently. Choose another style for actual hiking.

Ask to borrow friends' carriers and try them out on yourself and your baby before purchasing one. All babies have their own personality and some cannot get used to a certain style no matter how often you put them in it.

It is possible to wear two, too. Some friends hiked with their infant on the front and their toddler on the back. You do what you have to do.

Front Packs

Many babies love being carried in a front soft pack which omits the frame and is made solely of fabric. It provides support for the baby's back, neck, and head. It may take a little practice getting into and out of a front pack, and it may need to be adjusted for the size of the adult wearing it or it will not fit comfortably. Front packs usually have features which allow them to expand to allow for some growth of the baby.

Some completely enclose the child inside the sack, making them very warm—an asset in colder weather, a deterrent in the summer months. They also hold them tightly against you (to give the wearer more support). Some babies love this snugly feeling, others feel claustrophobic and bored if they are alert, active babies who do not enjoy staring at your blouse for much of your hike. A mother can easily nurse while wearing one and even manage to do it while hiking, with some practice.

Other types of front carriers have a stiff backing with straps that allow you to carry your baby back away from your chest so it can look up and out. Alert babies may prefer this kind, because it provides an option.

Some front carriers also face your baby out away from you. They are enjoyable for your baby if he or she is active and likes to see where you are going. This type of carrier doesn't seem to be the most conducive for sleep, however, and does seem the most dangerous if you should trip and fall while carrying your baby.

As your baby grows and increases in weight, you can support him or her under the buttocks with your clasped arms to relieve some weight and pressure, but it won't be long before your baby feels too heavy to be carried in the front and you'll want to switch to your back. Some of the soft packs allow you to carry your baby both ways. But if you are genuinely committed to taking your baby on hikes, it is worth investing in a real child-carrier backpack.

Backpacks

Purchase the heftiest, largest, best-made child carrier there is. Price seems no object when it comes to both your comfort and your baby's. No other piece of gear contributes so much to your and your child's enjoyment and your success with the sport. Start out right.

Babies must be able to hold their head upright or must be supported with padding. The one that we used for Sierra at four months had a very narrow frame and dug into our shoulder blades when the load was heavy or we had to climb steeply and bend over.

Sierra did not always like being put in her carrier at four months, so we sang a jive juvenile jingle to her to occupy her mind while she slid in. Once she realized where she was, we were already moving and and she was enjoying herself. When she was fussy, we put her in it and went for a walk and it always quieted her. We put her in it to mow the lawn, can tomatoes, prune trees, etc. We couldn't have gotten along without it. We used it every day.

Bob Klein, who had two baby daughters with colic, would be up for hours walking the streets of his small town with the baby in his backpack, trying to get her to sleep and give his wife a break. Most children will enjoy their time spent in a carrier because they love to be

close to their parent and because they love the movement. Once it stops, however, they can wake up and become fussy. For this reason, you might want to keep hiking until they wake up on their own.

Stirrups are great for young children whose longer legs and feet can dangle annoyingly. The children seem to especially enjoy them when they nap in the pack because it gives their supple bodies a little more support.

It is wise to use the restraining strap inside the pack, as the manufacturer suggests, so your child does not fly out if you should trip and fall on your face. It's easy to become ultra-cautious with a baby on your back, so falling is a rarity.

We always used the restraining strap until we went on the Colorado Trail with one-and-a-half-year-old Bryce. We wanted him to be able to stand on the metal frame and relieve the pressure off his rear end. We were concerned that he would grow very tired of sitting during the two long months on the trail if he could not move around a little. He sometimes got out of hand—turning completely around, getting the wrong legs in the wrong leg hole, bending way down to one side and way back to the other. We did enjoy him standing up to put his arms around our head to hug us. But he was a monkey and moved around far too much for our comfort. He was sometimes so difficult to carry that I would rather have had sixty pounds of dead weight than his twenty-five pounds of live weight.

A sun awning does some good, especially if the sun is directly overhead. If it comes in from the side or if you are going to be in it for awhile and it is strong, you'll need other protection. A cotton bandanna can be tied and used as a shade on the side where the sun is coming in. This works fine as long as you aren't on a switchbacking trail and are continually changing direction

We tied rattles and gumming toys to the pack with nylon cord so the babies could pick them up to entertain themselves at will. However, do be aware of what their hands can grab while they're back there. Todd was carrying Sierra while he pruned one spring and didn't know she had reached out and grabbed a leaf and begun eating it until she started to choke.

Once Sierra was six months old, we graduated to our present child carrier. It is constructed like an adult's backpack, with a hefty suspension system and a wide range of adjustments. It allows us to carry up to sixty pounds, and we could not have carried our children the 1,500 miles that we did without it.

Hints and Tips

■ Purchase the heftiest, largest, best-made child carrier on the market. You'll get more years of use out of it and will enjoy the most comfort.

Boots

Children's high-top sneakers can be worn for day hikes and overnighters, but they do not offer the support that a genuine hiking boot does. Children also wear sneakers too sloppily for safe hiking. They are often priced higher than hiking boots, will not outlast them, and are less comfortable. Besides sneakers' inadequate tread on slippery ground, they lack the steel shank of hiking boots, which extends about half to two-thirds the length of the sole. Plus your children can wear their hiking boots to school.

Many companies make really wonderful boots for children. Some sizes will fit a one-year-old. They are usually lightweight hiking boots made of suede/leather and fabric. The tread and ankle support on these boots is super. Don't buy the most expensive hiking boots unless you are heavily into the sport, plan to backpack, and truly need the added features. The higher-priced boots have more support and prevent ankles from rocking. They have thicker, more shock-absorbing soles—important features if children will be carrying a load.

Children outgrow boots quickly, so buy according to your needs and not anything more. Steer clear of more expensive, waterproof leather boots, which are not feasible when children's feet are growing so quickly.

When fitting boots to your child, go to a reputable store and have a knowledgeable clerk fit your child, because this is probably the most important piece of equipment that you will buy. Your child should wear a liner sock and a thick sock, either a wool/synthetic blend or all synthetic. No cotton socks should be worn to try on boots, and should be used on the trail only for short day hikes if nothing else is available. There should be at least a thumb's width between the back of their foot and the heel of the boot once the boot is laced up. Or have your child put the boot on and kick down at the toe; there should be one to two fingers' width at the back.

Trail Safety

Have children hike at a respectable distance behind one another. Teach them at an early age not to walk on another hiker's heels, to take turns leading, and not try to run past the others. Teach your children that they need to hold aside branches or brush that could twang back and hurt the next hiker. We take these things for granted, but they do need to be taught to our children.

Everyone should have a stainless steel whistle, either around their necks on a cord, on a coiled bracelet, or in their front fanny pack, and they should know how and when to use it—not for fun, but only in actual emergencies or difficulties. Dress your young children in bright colors (as opposed to drab, dark, or earth tones), because they will be much easier to spot if you need to find them. See Keeping Them From Getting Lost, chapter 4, Health and Safety.

Young Children

Teach your young children basic wilderness skills as early as they can grasp them—how to build a fire, where to find water, how to look for shelter, etc. Check with a reputable outdoor guide book (see appendix C, Suggested Reading) for full coverage of this information. Help them learn to be aware of their senses—the smell of damp, musty earth when they are low in a sheltered ravine, the smell of dry, sun-baked rocks and earth on an open, exposed ridge. It will help them remember the land that they traveled over and help them develop a good sense of direction.

Don't let your young children run very far ahead. Keep them in sight and yell to them to slow down if need be. It is a special treat for them to lead the party and they love it, but stay very close. If the footing is treacherous and your young hiker is not confident with his or her footing, extend a hiking stick from one adult to the next and allow the child to walk in between, using it as a guard rail or railing.

Always carry enough toilet paper or facial tissues on even the shortest hikes. You might not be able to get back to the trailhead facilities in time, and no child should be encouraged to hold it.

Older Children

An adult should lead the group and one should sweep the rear. If there are more adults, they should be scattered at regular intervals throughout the group.

Once they grow older and want to lead and follow their own pace more closely, teach them how to follow a blazed trail, how to look for turn blazes at intersections, how to look backwards for a blaze if one hasn't been seen for awhile in the direction you are going. Help them learn and practice while you are with them by telling them to lead with you closely behind. This is great practice if you are hiking in an area with a lot of cross trails or intersecting woods roads. You will notice how well they are observing if they miss turns (with you right behind), which will help you determine when they are alert and skilled enough to go on ahead on their own.

For areas where intersections aren't blazed but are signed, verse them on these trails ahead of time, so they know to look for them. With older children, every individual should have a copy of the map (even a photocopy is fine) and the guide book to the area you are hiking in. At breaks, encourage the kids to pull them out and locate your position on the trail. This is great practice in map reading. Have them also read the data on the trail ahead and study how the trail crosses the land and the topo lines on the map. As they actually hike it then, the two-dimensional information will begin to make sense.

Older children who are able to lead should be well versed in your family's or group's trail rules. For example, decide ahead of time how you will handle intersections—whether everyone must wait and regroup at any turn so everyone is sure to make it; how often the hikers up front should break and allow the rest to catch up; whether this is done at predetermined spots along the trail or at predetermined times (watches must be worn for this).

Choosing a Trail

Determining the appropriate type of trail, length, and elevation gain or loss for your particular children is a very individual thing and follows no set formula. Consider the needs of your youngest member to even begin to determine this. But remember that what one five-year-old can accomplish on a trail (for example, one hiked the entire 2,100-mile Appalachian Trail in one stretch and was never carried), your adolescent could find impossible to do. You'll need to honestly study your family's capabilities to discover the kind of hike your family can handle. Your goal should be easy and fun and set up for success. You can only begin to learn this by going out on very short hikes at first to get them used to it—their bodies *and* their minds.

Naturally, if the youngest child is a baby and is carried all of the time, you will need to go to the next youngest child to determine the length or difficulty of the trail you want to hike. And while your three-year-old bounds down the mile-long trail to the lake showing no sign of fatigue, the mile back may be impossible for him or her. The age when a child turns into a real hiker varies from child to child, even within the same family. Just learn their capabilities and plan accordingly.

Take regular walks to parks and friends' homes early on to determine your children's abilities. Gradually increase the distance so their stamina will increase in proportion. Walking will become a natural activity for them and their bodies will not rebel so quickly once you hit the trail for more serious hiking.

Some things to consider: western mountainous terrain above 5,000 feet is very kind to youngsters. This elevation cannot support snakes or scorpions. Summer weather is mild, as in the Sierra Nevadas. You may want to stay close to treeline if the mountains are susceptible to frequent thunderstorms (as in the Rockies), with accompanying lightning.

Be educated on things such as when the summer snow runoff swells the streams to dangerous heights. This can last into July in the mountains, but every year is different (depending on the snowfall that year). Don't subject your children to any adverse condition if there is a choice, and always inquire about any trail condition before making too many plans.

Plan a one- or two-mile hike at first, just to get an idea of how everyone handles it and enjoys it. The youngest walkers can handle this distance, and they can be carried if necessary. What you're trying to do in these beginning hikes is to show, through your example, that walking is fun. Keeping your early hikes on fairly level ground and relatively short will help your children acquire the necessary strength and stamina that their bodies need to tackle greater distances and more difficult trails later.

Goals

Children live in the present. What they see along the way is more important than the destination, and parents must be willing to give up goal-oriented hikes for awhile in exchange for their children's company.

Climbing a mountain for the sake of getting to the top is often not enough for young children. They like to be entertained along the way. Creekside trails are wonderful for this—watching the water tumble over rocks, dropping sticks and leaves and watching them meander down, etc. They are more interested in what is close at hand—moss on rocks, lichens, wildflowers, hopping toads—than views. Views are nice, but eye-level wonders seem more within their comprehension.

They like to be active as they walk—looking for colored leaves in the fall, birds and butterflies, berries to eat. (Remember that children should only eat berries under parental supervision, and parents should know what kids are putting into their mouths.) On winter walks, they can look for animal tracks and try to guess what made them, where they were going, and what was happening, etc.

Since kids of all ages love all kinds of water, you can never lose if this physical feature is part of your hike. Hikes along streams are ideal with pools to throw rocks into, soak their feet in, etc. Lakes, waterfalls, and fire towers are all great examples of destination hikes. They act as a carrot in front of their noses, egging them on.

If lakes or rivers are the destination of a hike, then bringing along an ultra-light spinning or fly rod with a few appropriate lures or flies will provide unlimited enjoyment for youngsters. Children seem to have a natural affinity for tossing things out onto waters; whether they catch anything is irrelevant. Be sure to know the regulations for any area you or your child may be fishing in.

Be aware of swiftly flowing streams and rivers, especially during spring runoff, and make sure young children stay a very safe distance behind and under your supervision at all times.

Nature trails in parks and recreation areas are favorites of small children. The stations and different points along the way explain and identify the natural world to them. It's fun for them to look ahead and anticipate the next marker post. We've gone on exercise trails and, with our help, our children enjoy walking through the fitness courses. You can often find these kinds of trails in recreation areas, natural habitats, or refuges, and often close to home. Seek out these close areas to hike as alternatives to long drives into the mountains, especially when the kids are young and you're just learning what you can and cannot do and what you like and dislike in a hike.

If a trail is blazed, children enjoy looking ahead for the next blaze. This is also good practice to learn how to follow a trail, to be aware of turns, and to make them aware of where they are going. When we hiked in Vermont, Sierra liked to watch ahead for bog bridges and had fun walking on them.

Pacing

Young Children

Young walkers have the most enthusiasm during the early part of the day or the beginning of a hike. If they then rest for while, they are often good for at least another long stretch, often toward the end. Whenever the terrain is gentle and easy, children can come out of the child carriers. It gives parents a break too.

When Sierra walks, she is out in front, setting the pace. We don't tailgate her to try to get her to move, but keep a respectable distance behind her. When she needs a break, she sits down on a boulder or a log and takes one. She usually tries to get us to join her, but we often remain standing for the short breaks so they don't turn into long ones.

Sometimes she sees something really intriguing off the trail, such as a huge boulder with an easy way to climb up it. Todd and I try to allow her to deviate like this as often as she wants to, so she doesn't lose her sense of wonder and just begin plodding along, sticking to the trail. But sometimes we have to say no, just so we can get somewhere.

Todd wasn't always excited about the timing of when Sierra wanted to rest. It may have looked like rain, or we may have wanted to get to camp. I always felt like it was very important to let her walk when she wanted to. Our "schedule" would have no meaning when the trip was over, just the memories and the changes it made in all of us. Not allowing her to hike when she wanted to would have defeated our purpose for being there.

Older Children

Older children sometimes have a tendency to blast off and hike fast in the early part of the day. They too need to learn about pacing if

they haven't grown up hiking. It doesn't usually take too many days of hiking to learn this, however, and their fatigue will teach them more than your well-meaning words of wisdom.

If an adult is up ahead leading them, then they cannot get carried away with their pace and must hold back (as long as the adult doesn't have this same problem). Tell them a good rule of thumb is to be able to engage in a conversation while hiking without experiencing shortness of breath. You don't want them charging off away from the rest of the group anyway, so there are more important safety reasons to keep a wild pace in check.

Fatigue

Parents need to look for signs of fatigue, hunger, thirst, etc., because kids don't always know what is making them feel bad. They begin to find excuses to stop when they become fatigued. Sierra would become fascinated with every rock that poked through the soil and feel the need to touch every patch of moss and smell every flower. When they begin to trip and stumble a lot, you know they're getting fatigued. Some children may grow quiet, become argumentive or whiny, or begin to cry a lot. Tune into your children and learn to read their signals so you can properly care for their needs.

We hiked with our friends Frank and Lila Strauss and their grandson Solomon, who is close to Sierra in age. Solomon and Sierra silently encouraged each other to continue on, even after they were truly fatigued. We knew she had had enough when she had a difficult time remaining upright. Todd carried her for awhile to give her a rest. A parent needs to look out for these signs if a child is not telling you about his or her need to rest. This is when an injury can occur.

Young children might complain about fatigue when it doesn't seem like they ought to be tired if they slept poorly the night before or consecutive nights before. If children are not getting their proper rest, they simply cannot and will not perform.

If you can tell the difference between real fatigue and boredom, you can sometimes divert their attention away from themselves. Talk about something interesting, look for something, sing a song, play a game. I've grasped Sierra's hand on a gentle woods road and said, "Let's run!" and was amazed at the kind of ground she could cover when she was just "dying" seconds before.

Carrying Your Kids

Your pace and the amount of miles you can cover in a day will drop radically from what you were used to before parenthood. Whenever a child is on your back, you should proceed with greater caution, at least until you feel confident.

Babies

Following an obscure trail is much harder with a baby on your back. You don't know when branches will swat your child. Our first hike with four-month-old Sierra involved climbing up ladders to get over rock cliffs on Pennsylvania's Loyalsock Trail. It made me extremely cautious and slow moving. Rock hopping across streams made me nervous, too, with the thought of us both going under if I fell. I always used two sticks for support and would sometimes opt for the safer, though more inconvenient, way of crossing in the water.

When Sierra was between four and nine months old, she was happy in the pack for about sixty to ninety minutes at a time—long enough for us to hike two or three miles. When she was fussy in the pack, I clasped her feet and legs so I could make body contact with her and pretended she was riding a horse. When the trail was wide, Todd and I walked side by side and she loved to see her daddy's animated face.

We liked to get her out before her "desires" became strong "needs" and she had to cry to get her point across. When she needed to get out, it was also time to either change her, feed her, give her a drink, or merely let her stretch. We thought it was important for her to associate her pack with pleasure instead of discomfort and unhappiness, or we'd soon draw a fast close to our beloved sport. Sometimes we needed to stop for a break five minutes after the last one so we could change her diaper. In many ways, your baby is in charge of the day's agenda.

Half the time she napped in the child carrier, the other half she looked around. Sometimes we kept hiking if she slept unusually long, whether we were tired or not, just to cover some distance. Other times, we eased the pack off with her sleeping inside and let her continue. Someone must stay right with the child carrier, though, because as soon as they wake up and shift, they can easily knock themselves over.

Toddlers

The change from baby to toddler, from being carried all of the time to walking some of the time, can be a very radical, seemingly backwards step to your progress as a hiking family. If you found your young baby did not really hold you back from covering your normal distance in a day, it can be very frustrating now if your toddler is setting the quarter-mile-an-hour pace. You will need to redefine your limits and rediscover what your family's capabilities are.

Be of light heart. There are new joys to discover in this interim period. The most important thing is to take your children on trails where they can walk and learn to love the sport. You must resist the temptation to wish your children older and more capable, and relax into watching them discover the outdoors at their own pace.

Learning this was a very sobering experience for Todd and me. When Bryce was ten months old and Sierra was two and a half, our goal was a nine-mile loop over 5,100-foot Franconia Ridge, with a

couple thousand feet of elevation gain and loss. By the time we finished loading the two child carriers, a good chunk of time was already
gone from the morning. At the trailhead, the wind blew cold and stiff.
I was thinking that it might not even be smart to go. We couldn't get a
weather report, so we decided to try for it. We could always turn
around. It's a real possibility when children are involved.

Once we got into the forest, the wind died down. The trail climbed
very gradually along a stream at first, exciting Sierra into walking. She
needed a lot of help and had to go slowly, because there were rocks
and numerous stream crossings, but she had a great time. Once the
trail began to climb steeply, we put her into her child carrier. We hiked
most of the day and by 3:00 P.M. still hadn't reached treeline. Snow was
on the ground at this elevation and the temperature was in the high
twenties. We would never make it if we continued, and could place
ourselves in jeopardy if we tried. We had to turn around. Hauling children on our backs made us creep along. We simply could not do what
we had done before.

The next day we hiked along the Pemigewasset River on an old
railroad grade. It was an easy, gentle walk, full of sights, sounds, and
stimulation. Sierra skipped along and collected colored leaves. This
was the type of hike we were bound to for the next few years.

Very young children sometimes have a problem watching older
siblings hike while they remain confined in a child carrier. If mileage
and time is not an issue, by all means let them hike every time they
want to. You want them to come to love the trail and the whole
thought of moving down it under their own steam. Whenever the trail
is easy, we encourage walking. It makes them feel like a "big kid" and
look forward to the day they can hike all day by themselves.

Special-Needs Children

The O'Connor family's son Mahlon was born with cerebral palsy,
which impairs muscular power and coordination, resulting from brain
damage. He does not have control over his legs and is restricted to a
wheelchair. But that didn't stop his parents, Kate and Patrick, who
have a deep love of the outdoors. They were determined right from
the start to make things happen for Mahlon.

They purchased a "Bike Buddy" from Bike Caboose, which designed
this bike trailer to accommodate a large child and his wheelchair.
Besides using it as it was intended, they also use it as a rickshaw, which
Pat pulls as he hikes. Pat used a wide army belt with eyelet holes
already in it, and attached it to his waist to a leather apron that he
made. He padded it, because the trailer's arm has a tendency to swing

into you as you walk. This trailer is pulled from its center, unlike some whose arm is off to the side. On narrow hiking trails, they tied a stabilizing rope on the rear of it so Kate could control it on the downhills.

With this set-up, Pat was able to take Mahlon anywhere his wheelchair or Pat's bicycle could not go. As they hiked in the Ventana Wilderness between Carmel Valley and Big Sur in California, his parents brought things over to the trailer to show him. They gauged their hike lengths on Mahlon's needs, but they usually didn't need to stop any sooner than normal. A folding beach chair that sits low to the ground was always thrown into the trailer, so Mahlon could be lifted out of the trailer to stretch his legs on a break.

Mahlon enjoyed the trailer from ages three to ten, and could have continued its use longer if he had been able to straighten his legs out better. Even more so than hiking on trails, Pat and Mahlon particularly loved their runs on the beach together. They would play games of tag with the waves as Pat pulled Mahlon and the trailer right into the surf and then out again.

His parents want Mahlon to see the world. They want to give him a wealth of experiences while they are still in control of his life. It might take a bit longer and include more equipment and work, but it was so worthwhile. Mahlon wants to be a writer and these experiences will help him. His very special parents believed that their very special child should not be limited in his life, whether it's in the wilds or anywhere in this wide world.

Hiking with Your Kids

At those borderline ages—older toddlers and very young children—your children may sometimes need to be carried. They may ask to ride before they truly need to, because the empty pack is there, but it's much safer to bring it if you have it. You could have trouble getting back to the trailhead before dark if you estimate wrong and go their pace.

At three, Sierra could hike three miles without much problem, but not all at once and not without breaks. She hiked only when she wanted to or when we could encourage her to. We never forced her to hike, but then we never had to, either, because we had a child carrier for her. But at some point your child becomes too big to be carried for long, and you must choose hikes that your young child can hike nearly all the way.

Sierra is four now and weighs forty pounds and it is a real chore to carry her for any length of time. This year, our goal is to limit our hikes to three or four miles, allow ample time for her to cover it, and leave the pack at home. In an emergency, she can be carried for short distances on Todd's shoulders.

Young Children

To get young children enthused about hiking, you sometimes have to rig them up in their own hiking outfit—fanny pack (worn in front) containing sunglasses, a snack, a bandanna, and a few small "buddies";

and a day pack with a favorite stuffed animal in it. All these "props" make them feel like they are doing the "real thing" like the grown-ups. This is very important to a young child and should be allowed and encouraged. A stuffed animal friend will often dispel the difference between a boring time for the child and one he or she can enjoy.

Thomas Ricci has a life-sized stuffed raccoon hand puppet that either rides on the pack watching ahead or is on his arm, ready to greet unsuspecting hikers passing on the trail with a friendly wave of his paw. Thomas became very adept at imitating the behavior of a "real" raccoon, resting on his arm with an anthropomorphic twist of humor, a crowd stopper at times. While in Jacksons National Park in California, a naive ranger spotted Thomas with "Rascal" in his arms and informed him, very sternly, that visitors were not to pick up any wild animals in the park. At this juncture, "Rascal" proceeded to greet the ranger with a friendly wave and she had to turn away in a wave of embarrassment that made Thomas's day.

When your young children do well on a hike, praise them and tell them they are good hikers, and they will want to be good hikers. On the first day of our Vermont hike, three-and-a-half-year-old Sierra did really well with hiking. The next day she said she wanted to hike the entire day (which was about eight miles) by herself. We knew she wouldn't be able to, but didn't discourage her.

There are hiking techniques we adults take for granted, but if we try to see the world for the first time, as they are, it will open our eyes to their needs. When the treadway grew rocky on our Vermont hike, Sierra grew fatigued because she wasn't experienced enough to know where and how to place her feet for the greatest energy conservation. She enjoyed walking on rocks, and stepped up onto every one that was close by, even if it wasn't necessary. I took the opportunity to show her how to look at the ground quickly and select a spot to place each footstep, and to walk on the flat spots of earth between the rocks whenever possible, so it did not tire her out as much. After awhile, it will become second nature.

Older children's presence and performance sometimes influences younger children beyond their ability. It is your responsibility to watch young children and make decisions for them when necessary. On a hike with the Harris family in Vermont, our goal was Stowe Pinnacle—a 1,500-foot climb in one and a half miles—pretty steep for young children. The kids found a creeklet that was running from the same direction we were traveling—from farther up the mountainside, except that our trail switchbacked. We let them follow it and kept an eye on them, and they covered ground like no parents' encouragement could have yielded. Toward the end of the climb, the footing got very steep and rocky, and Sierra was having trouble. She didn't ask to ride in the pack because the Harris children, who were older, continued walking. But we encouraged her to ride in her pack at this point because I was afraid she would hurt herself in her fatigue.

When you reach your destination or if the weather changes, you must put warm clothes and wind protection on your child immediately. It does not matter if they say they are not cold yet. Once you stop moving for awhile, they will be cold very soon. You must put on warm clothes too.

On a descent, take the opportunity to teach your children how to side step down and get their center of gravity low. Whatever it takes for them to feel confident. The route down Stowe Pinnacle was very steep, muddy, and slippery, and Sierra fell onto her hiney a few times. She then decided it was easier to go down the mountain on her rump as soon as she came to those steep spots. As she did this, her raspberry wind suit turned dark brown with mud; my friend asked me if I wanted her to do this. But outerwear is supposed to handle abuse like that. Her clothes underneath got wet too.

You have to let them have some fun, even if they sometimes make a mess, as long as they aren't endangering themselves. Part of the joy of childhood is making a mess and playing in it. They won't want to go along with our plans if we don't let them have some choice and spontaneity when it comes to their play. At the bottom of Stowe Pinnacle, the kids had a tremendous time splashing and stomping and charging right through the middle of the flooded trail. We were done hiking for the day, our car lay a few hundred yards beyond, and the warm, dry inn where we were staying was only a short drive away. At the car, we took off her boots and her soaked socks, put on dry ones and pulled slippers on.

On that same trip in Vermont, we had a day of solid rain but still wanted to get out of the car for a short hike. We put Sierra's rain suit on her and gave her a fold-up umbrella to carry. It was light enough that she could hold it securely, and it kept her head dry. She enjoyed walking in the rain because, with the umbrella, it was fun and something different.

To determine how far your child can hike, many things must be taken into consideration—trail conditions, weather, individual kids, etc. Two miles for a four-year-old is pretty reasonable. If a child is physically fit and is used to hiking, it should be safe to try to go two miles less than their age. For example, an eight-year-old should be able to hike six miles if he or she is allowed as much time as needed to cover it. I would stop at eight miles no matter how old, even teenagers, until they have demonstrated that they can and want to hike more miles per day. But if your child is used to hiking, you should already have a good idea of his or her individual limits.

Starting around age five, begin to have your children carry a day pack with a few pounds in it. This will help them feel like they're doing their part, it will increase their stamina, and it will set them up for backpacking if your family hopes to enjoy this sport.

Older Kids and Adolescents

Once kids are older and able to walk well on their own, you can tackle more interesting and rigorous trails. Challenging trails alleviate boredom, and when they're interested in what they're doing, the less they complain of being tired. Long stretches of seemingly monotonous, easy trail is when kids complain of being tired (or, really, bored) the most. At home, get them more involved in the planning—where to go, what to eat, what to carry, etc.

Older children still need to break for rests and nourishment, but not as much as for diversions such as slopping in creeks. They still need praise for their accomplishments, and they still may need help to get their minds off the occasional discomfort of hiking in order to enjoy themselves fully. This is a time of growing independence and responsibility, so use their desire for learning to motivate them down the trail and keep them happy with the family. Teach them map and compass skills and have them lead the group. Get them binoculars and a bird guide, or any of the wonderful identification guides available—flowers, trees, ferns, etc. There is even a series for younger people (see appendix C, Suggested Reading). The idea is to keep their interest high in the sport, because this is the time when they may begin to think that time spent with their family isn't too cool.

It can be interesting to learn that children have their own leadership dynamics. In the Lewiston family of eight, the children turned to the older ones, naturally, but each person has their own individual skills and the children know them and use them to work together.

Hints and Tips

- Remember that young children live in the present. They are not as interested in the goal as an adult. Plan your outing with their needs in mind.
- Teach your children basic wilderness skills, such as how to build a fire, where to look for water, etc., as early as they can grasp them.
- Be sensitive to your older children's desire and need to follow their own pace. Devise a plan for covering the miles that enables them to do this, yet remain in a group and be safe.

- Learn to tell the difference between real fatigue and boredom. They are handled and remedied differently.

- Everything changes when a baby is on your back. Be more cautious of footing, when boulder hopping streams, in ducking branches, etc. Never forget you're carrying your baby.

- Adjust your pace, mileage, breaks, hiking style, trail activities, etc., to suit your youngest children's needs. Strive to make them happy hikers or you won't be a happy hiker.

- Encourage walking at as early an age and as often as they show the interest. It may be inconvenient and incredibly slow, but the idea is to eventually get them off your back (literally) and in love with hiking themselves.

- Have everyone know the group's rules for the trail—what to do at intersections, when to wait for each other and re-group, what to do if you become lost, etc.—and enforce them.

- Don't hesitate to give your kids pointers on how to do things, such as how to rest on a climb by pausing a second on the extended leg, or how to side step down a steep grade, etc. Make it easy on them by sharing your knowledge.

CHAPTER

Backpacking

▲ ▲ ▲ ▲ ▲ ▲ ▲ ▲ ▲

Equipment

Children's and Youth Backpacks

Children's muscles have often never carried weight before and their bodies may not be strong enough to carry it on their shoulders, when it's supposed to be on their backs. Never try to make your child wear your old army backpack or an old model that doesn't have a padded hip belt, a webbed belt/strap, or any belt at all. Don't try to rig up a dress belt to it, either. It will feel terrible.

One poor child hiked with a pack that was really a piece of luggage. He slid his arms through the long handles as if they were straps. His parents thought they could get better mileage out of this "combo" pack. The child was miserable the entire week of his backpacking trip.

Put yourself in your child's place. Would you want to deal with that piece of gear yourself? How can you ask your child to? And what kind of chance is there to have your child learn to love the wilds and the outdoors with such inferior, and even unsafe, equipment?

Go to a backpacking/outdoor store and get fitted by a clerk who knows gear and how to fit it. Parents often want to buy a backpack that is too big for their child in hopes of getting more years of use out of it. But if it doesn't fit comfortably, your child cannot possibly enjoy the sport.

Children come in all shapes and sizes. Some are all legs. Children can have the same torso length but have a one-foot difference in height, and the same backpack would fit them. What you need to focus on when fitting is their torso length—the distance between their shoulders and their hips. You want the weight of the backpack resting squarely on their hip bones. Children should have very few clothes on while trying on backpacks, if they are going to be hiking in the summer.

Backpacks come with many adjustments—spacers, cam locks, or pullout cotter pins to move bars. The shoulder straps shouldn't be so close together that they are cutting into the child's neck (not usually the case) or falling off of the shoulders. Move the straps in until they rest inside the shoulder. They do not not have features like load lifter straps and sternum straps. Most children's and youth backpacks fall short on padding and comfort compared to adult backpacks, but because their capacity is not very great, they won't weigh as much when loaded. Most kids are not going to be backpacking for long stretches or needing to carry heavy loads.

Don't allow your child to walk into a store and say, "I want a red pack," unless the one that fits best and suits your child's needs best happens to come in his or her favorite color. Ask to try on discontinued models; they are often discounted but perfectly good. Often someone in marketing decides that it is time to change colors and all stock must be cleared out.

External-Frame Backpacks

There are basically two sizes of external-frame backpacks that are available for children. "Children's" backpacks have a small frame— about twenty-four inches long. "Youth" frames are about twenty-eight inches long and fit kids of heights from four and a half feet to five and a half feet. Most children need to be about ten to twelve years old before they are large enough to wear an adult backpack.

You might think buying a youth backpack is not economical but if you have other children it can be passed down, or if your child is involved in scouts or youth groups that go out backpacking, you can easily resell it. Even if your children don't belong to these groups, you can advertise to them and sell to them.

If a child is going to be going on an extended trip, you can buy him or her a woman's backpack. A woman's backpack frame is the same size as a youth frame (twenty-eight inches), but the support and the suspension system are far superior. They are more costly, but your child will be much more comfortable with it. It can be resold if it is outgrown, and there are many colors available that do not look feminine to a male child.

Choose a welded backpack frame, as opposed to a sectional frame, if your child is rough or hard on gear. The more curved and anatomically correct the frame, the more comfortable it will feel. Plastic frames are thought by some to be more comfortable than metal frames, because they flex with your body.

Internal-Frame Backpacks

Another alternative is to fit your child into an internal-frame backpack. Not as many companies make them as external-frame backpacks, but your child may find them more comfortable to wear. They get a little uncomfortable when they are really loaded down, but that shouldn't happen to your youngster.

Boots

If your child is really into hiking and backpacking, and if you plan to get into more rugged, extended family excursions into the backcountry, genuine hiking boots should be considered. Their traction and support cannot be rivaled by any sneaker (see Boots, chapter 7, Day Hiking).

Overnighters

Before you consider backpacking with your children, think about your own personal desire to be out in the wilds. To have it seem worthwhile, your desire needs to be passionately high in order to deal with all the work bringing your children will create.

Some parents want to wait until their children can carry their own loads, are strong non-carrying walkers, are out of diapers, or sleep through the night. If you wait until your child is what you consider an ideal age before venturing out, you all may miss out on a lot of joy during those younger years. And your next child could come along and throw your good planning out the window.

Look at your personality and your child's. An easy-going child who adapts quickly and smoothly to new situations will do much better than a difficult child who falls apart with change. A parent who has a vast amount of patience, enjoys hard work, has cultivated a sense of humor, and loves to be with his or her children should be able to sail over any complexity or difficulty on the trail.

The smartest thing you can do as a parent who takes a young child into the backcountry is to take care of yourself. You are not much of a caregiver if you are keeling over from dehydration, hypothermia, or hyperthermia. Keep yourself safe and healthy so that you are in good shape to care for your children should they run into trouble.

Babies

The best time to backpack with your small children is definitely when they are young and when you only have one. The months before your baby can even crawl are some of the easiest. At this age, they are easily entertained by singing, looking around, chewing toys, or napping. The movement of walking and being close to their parent's body is very comforting to them. In camp you merely prop baby up with a stuff sack of clothes or sleeping bag and you can both go about doing your camp chores.

When backpacking with a baby, one adult basically carries the baby in the child carrier and not too much else. The older and heavier your child becomes, the less additional weight that adult can carry. This means more weight must be dumped onto the adult who is not carrying the child.

Because Sierra was small and light, I carried a lot of heavy items—about thirty-five to forty pounds—in the child carrier's storage pockets—water bottles, heavy food, etc.—in order to diminish Todd's load. But the child carrier's capacity was not huge and so Todd ended up carrying about sixty to seventy pounds. We hiked slowly and stopped frequently.

When we carried baby Sierra, we found that our daily distance limit was about ten miles, and sometimes less. This allowed for enough break time during the day to keep her happy. If we continued past 5:00 or 6:00 P.M., she would fall apart. There may have been more hours of daylight that remained and we may have had enough energy to continue hiking into the evening, but she had reached her limit and she was in charge.

We usually hiked an hour or two and then took a long break—at least a half hour to often an hour. In the eight hours we spent on the trail, about five of them we spent hiking. At a two-miles-per-hour pace, we could still easily get ten miles in per day.

After they can crawl, things begin to get interesting. One parent must always be on child duty and be ready to rescue the discovering babe. But as long as there is only one child, you can backpack until you cannot carry the weight happily anymore, or until another child arrives.

An older baby's desire to move can make life in the child carrier a little less agreeable for him or her. Sleep may not come as readily and the resulting crankiness can produce more tears. But if you started your child in a child carrier from birth, it is possible to sail through this stage with little more than noticing your load is heavier.

When Sierra was eight months old, we were able to go on an enormous number of trails and overnight backpacks with a minimum of driving in the Four Corners region of the Southwest. We went in September and early October because the desert sun was not as strong. We inquired at ranger stations for the best trails that allowed for backcountry camping and only went one or two miles in. We brought supper and breakfast and experienced this land when it looked its very best—evening and morning.

On such an overnighter into the backcountry of Capitol Reef National Park, we had to climb in the heat (although it was early evening), and Todd had twenty pounds of water weight alone on his back, shooting his total pack weight up to about seventy-five or eighty pounds. We never made it the two and a half miles to our destination. We simply could not haul the weight up and we weren't having any fun trying. We found an emergency camp spot on a narrow cliff, the only somewhat level spot around. We were depressed. We wanted to have another child soon and knew if they were close in age, both of us would be carrying a child when we hiked and we'd no longer be able to even go on overnighters. The next morning, conversation revolved around alternatives such as bicycling trips.

But on another overnighter in the Southwest, in Canyonlands National Park, we managed to hike the two and a half miles to the rim above the Colorado River to camp. We witnessed a light show in the canyon as lightning struck, brilliant rays of sunlight broke through the clouds, a double rainbow appeared, bighorn sheep with full curls drank water from a slickrock rain puddle ten feet away, a sunset blazed, the night was illuminated by a full moon, and a gorgeous sunrise greeted us in the morning. Not too shabby for only two or so miles from the road.

With a succession of nights like these in the backcountry, you begin to stop feeling sorry for yourself for having your dear baby to drag along and begin to accept that umbilical cord that ties you to your vehicle. Your style just changes a bit when you go out with little ones. It doesn't mean it has to be any less dramatic or magical, just a little more work.

Our most memorable overnighter on our Southwest trip was in the Grand Canyon. At first, we hoped to get a campsite at the very bottom. We didn't think there were any other options. But we discovered that the protected no-camping zone only extends one mile on either side of the trail. About halfway down the canyon is the Tonto Plateau. A trail leads along it for seventy-plus miles, connecting trails that lead from the rim to the floor. We took our loaded packs down to the plateau, hiked a mile off the trail, and stashed them. We then came back to the descending trail that leads down to the Colorado River at the bottom of the Grand Canyon and followed it to the floor to get fresh water at the campground and to experience the canyon's bottom.

It was on the canyon bottom that we realized what a wonderful decision we had made to camp halfway down. It was hot down there and the air felt heavy. We could see nothing of the rim 5,000 feet above us, and the sun "set" very early in the day. We didn't have far to climb to get back to our packs.

Most hikers were really beat as they climbed out of the canyon, but we noticed they hiked at a very fast pace and then collapsed on a switchback, panting and swabbing their brows and making up excuses why they needed to rest. We just took our time and paced ourselves, climbing slowly and methodically. When we stopped for short moments to rest our legs, we remained standing and turned our legs the opposite direction, downhill, to give them a break. When we reached our cached packs, we had a spectacular night and glorious sunrise in the canyon's wilderness—in utter solitude.

You may have to be a little creative to find overnight opportunities like this. All rangers don't offer them up. We didn't need any special skills to do what we did, just basic backcountry knowledge of low-impact, no-trace camping. We did have to do a little topo map reading to see if there was truly a suitable flat spot in the area. You don't have to go very far into the backcountry to experience the magic and the spirit of a place. If we couldn't stay out for extended periods of time as we preferred, experiences like our night in the Grand Canyon were a pretty good second choice.

Toddlers

The toddler years, from one to three, are when it's a sheer delight to share the wonders of the natural world with your children. Their minds are growing at an amazing rate and they are interested in everything. If your toddlers love being out in the wilds, it is worth struggling through this uncomfortable stage until they can walk well on their own.

But this age can be the most difficult to deal with. When your children are too young—around three to four years old—to walk very far and too heavy—around thirty to forty pounds—to carry for very long, backpacking is uncomfortable, especially if there is more than one child at that age. And the more children you have, the longer this period lasts. Your children may want to hike but can't for very far, or may lose interest rapidly. Their weight feels like twice as much on your back as compared to dead weight, and they move around in the carrier and can throw you off balance. They are in and out of the carrier a lot. Even after they all can walk, the distances you are able to cover will be small.

Try to go on hikes that combine easy stretches where they can walk without much difficulty. Think about their interests and abilities when deciding on a place to go. A slow meander along a creek to a lake to camp by, for instance.

There are a few ways to get your toddler into the backcountry. Because the parent who will occasionally carry this child will not be able to carry any more weight when the child is riding, all the gear necessary to camp must be shouldered by the other adult. If that person is capable of carrying enormous weight and still remaining happy, you're fortunate. You can also ask other adult friends to come along and help with the load carrying.

Another approach is to carry part of the load in—enough gear to set up camp—and then go back out for another load. You can't go too far into the backcountry by using this method, but you can go on a series of day hikes once your base camp is set up.

This uncomfortable stage does not last long, as frustrating as some parents find it. This endearing age is very short-lived, so try to adjust your thinking and expectations and appreciate the magical memories that are occurring in your family, despite the few miles that you cover.

Young Children

Once you simply cannot deal with carrying your child anymore, it is time to put the child carrier away so that the temptation to use it is removed. Then all hikes will be based upon your young child's ability to hike.

It could be tricky to convince your young children that it is fun to carry weight on their back unless they grow up carrying a tiny backpack at an early age. A stuffed animal, a few snacks—nothing to weigh them down—is how to start. Have them carry it on short errands with you. Let them play with their soft packs and pretend they are going on an expedition. This way, the whole idea of the backpacking experience will seem normal, comfortable, and fun for them.

As a child grows and strengthens and is capable of carrying more weight, add items such as a sweater, a small water bottle, more snacks, personal things your child will feel good about carrying. Sometimes if you ask your child to carry an item that the entire group shares, this makes him or her feel special and important and part of the group.

You might need to use some strategy to ease your young children into an overnight backpacking trip if all they are used to is day hikes and car camping. They will have to experience the dark without night lights, without their bed pillows and covers, without some of their bedtime rituals, perhaps. If the whole family does not go (say, mom stays home), separation anxiety may be a problem.

Bob Klein waltzed through this step with his daughter Adrienne. Adrienne had day hiked since she was four. Seeing his daughter's love of the outdoors grow and blossom encouraged her father to slow down his pace and experience the joys of the trail with his daughter. When Adrienne turned six years old, he decided it was time to take her on her first overnight backpack trip.

Her break-in period began by hiking a quarter mile from the road to a three-sided log shelter at Hawk Mountain Sanctuary, Pennsylvania. Adrienne was both nervous and excited about spending her first night in the woods, but she said she felt confident because her dad had so much experience. Before turning in that night, they hiked up to South Lookout by flashlight to watch the stars and lights come on in the scattered homes in the valley below. That first night she said, "Out of all those millions of people out there, only you and I are enjoying this wonderful peacefulness."

It wasn't a big production to go on this overnight hike. They scooted out after Bob finished work on Friday and were home the next day to catch the rest of the family at breakfast. Adrienne wasn't away from home and everything she was used to for very long. But it instilled confidence in Adrienne and a desire for a larger taste of what she had just sampled.

The only thing that spooked Adrienne on her first overnighter was the utter and complete darkness that the overcast sky provided. As with most children, she grew up with night lights illuminating the night. The nighttime sounds were different too. If there had been a real problem, it would have been very easy for Bob to get her out and home, because the car was only a quarter mile away.

Bob and Adrienne repeated this type of overnight hike eight times that year, but changed their evening stroll to a very early morning hike. By setting their alarm for 5:00 A.M., they got to see the stars fade, the lights turn off, and the sun rise from the lookout while they lounged on the rocks in their sleeping bags and cooked breakfast.

The next year, when Adrienne was seven, Bob took her on her first longer overnight backpacking trip. They were out for two days and one night and covered three and a half miles each day. She was not prepared for the wildness that she found—climbing up Angel Falls and seeing nothing but rolling ridges of forest and hollows with no sign of humans at all. The first time she experienced this, she grew a little uneasy, realizing how remote they were and how difficult it could be for someone to find them if they needed help. On successive trips, this fear turned into a feeling of contentment as she came to feel more comfortable.

The eroded trail that climbed up the steep side of Angel Falls frightened Adrienne a bit, and their return down it the next day remained on her mind until she traversed it. She was scared of falling—just because she knew that she could. She was also aware of the fact that two people had died there—one hiker who camped at the top of the falls and walked too close to the edge while taking a "late-night leak" and another who slipped on the ice. These were two situations she was not going to encounter. This was a very good learning experience for a seven-year-old because she overcame her fears, did something different, and was successful at it. A very important lesson to learn so early in life.

Bob took Adrienne on a total of seven overnight backpacking trips that year. On them, she experienced how incredibly bright a full moon in the forest can be, she imagined she was Diane Fossey as she watched the fog and mist dissipate in a canyon from a perch on the ridge, she listened to the night woods ring with sweet music when they shared a campsite with some guitar-playing hikers, she cuddled in the cozy tent in her sleeping bag as she and her dad took turns reading *The Hobbit* out loud by candlelight—such wonderful firsts in her young life.

Longer Hikes

Babies

Setting up the tent and sleeping out in the yard before venturing out on even an overnighter in the wilds is the best way to introduce your baby to backpacking. However, four months after Sierra was born, it had been a couple of years since we had backpacked for any length of time and we missed it; we decided to go cold turkey. We planned to hike for six days on the Loyalsock Trail in upstate Pennsylvania. Todd and I felt pretty confident taking our baby out with all the experience we had.

Still, we were embarking on new territory. We discussed options: packing into a spot a short distance from the trailhead and then going out to the car for another trip or two for more gear, caching extra supplies somewhere along the trail, etc.

We located a road crossing at about the halfway point and, before we began our hike, we drove to the road crossing to bury three five-gallon buckets with snaptight lids, which we loaded with clean diapers, diaper covers, wash rags, some clean clothes/sleepers for Sierra, and some food. Todd carried them a good distance from the dirt road, which saw very little traffic, and hid them well under leaves and branches. When we arrived on foot, we replaced the clean items with soiled items and the food with trash and items from our pack that we found we had no use for. After we reached the car at the end of our hike, we drove back to our cache and recovered our packed-out refuse. This strategy allowed us to enjoy a longer backpack trip with our infant.

Geoff Ricci carried his infant son, Thomas, into the backcountry in a different manner. Because his wife, Judy, is not a strong backpacker, Geoff carried much of the family's load in his backpack, as well as their son in a front-pack child carrier. Geoff could handle the load for most of the day with the usual packer's breaks when Thomas was quite young—up to two years of age and approximately twenty to twenty-five pounds. With this arrangement, Thomas tended to get pretty hot and sweaty, but when he was younger, Geoff would merely lift him away from his body by holding the bottom of the carrier in both arms, to help with air circulation and cooling. They went on backpacking trips of between two and four days, and covered distances of seven to twelve miles per day.

Young Children

For children under one to one and a half years old, there isn't much of a problem. A second hiker is a sufficient asset in loading and unloading the child, although an innovative solo hiker could manage to use a front carrier, if strong enough. Be sure to cross the shoulder straps across your back. It also helps tremendously if the child is aware of the difficulty of the added weight for the bearer and appreciates the break from his or her own "hard work" of walking, so that they avoid squirming and complaining too much and don't make any sudden moves at the wrong time to disturb balance.

When Thomas Ricci became older and heavier, Geoff just went slower and lived with it, although it did help to carry the load by using both arms under the child's bottom. When Thomas was three years old, weighing in at thirty-three-plus pounds, Geoff could handle about a half hour on an uphill grade (an hour was pushing it) before a break was required and Thomas would have to walk, with longer times on flattish or moderate downhill grades. Early in his outdoor experience, Thomas made the astute observation that traveling up a grade was not as much fun as moving in the opposite direction. While walking along the trail, he got to saying, "Downhill funny; uphill, no funny." This was an initial signal that carrying time was at hand.

When Thomas was in the front carrier, a disciplined, slower pace was naturally required, so Geoff didn't really have much of a problem with leg mobility for uphill walking if the carrier was adjusted properly. When Thomas felt rested enough or was getting too hot, he would usually ask to be let down, but would also do so if Geoff said that he needed a break as well. Mutual acceptance and cooperation were understood and they would chat or point out things along the trail to pass the time, or Thomas would even doze off for a while.

Because Geoff had much of the family's weight, his backpack's load ended up being heavier than normal—fifty-five to sixty pounds for these trips. His frame pack did feel fairly well balanced even when Thomas reached the thirty-pound level and had no overdue forward strain.

Thomas's third summer was the last one Geoff used this arrangement for. The ninety-plus total load was about all he could reasonably handle for an extended period. The following season, when Thomas was nearing four years old, he was expected to haul himself along for the most part. He even had a little pack to carry and only now and then, for the sake of morale, would his father pick him up and carry him in his arms for a short stint. Usually he would just stop and rest more frequently if it seemed he needed it.

Older Children

Never fill your child's backpack with a load greater than one-fourth of their body weight, and it's preferable closer to one-fifth. If your child is new to the sport or new to carrying weight, go even lighter. Bear in mind that your weight-carrying child will probably only be able to hike about half the distance he or she could hike burden-free. We all feel stronger and more energetic in the beginning of the day, so be prepared to unload some of the kids' weight as the day winds down.

After Thomas Ricci was older and had hiked a substantial amount, his parents tried to build up his sense of pride in his wilderness accomplishments and hiking prowess. When he reached 200 miles of trail hiking on his own at age eight, they had a gold trophy cup engraved with "Mountain Hiker Award—200 miles—Thomas Dean Ricci, Age 8, October 1986" and presented it to him at a special dinner celebration with his friends. He was very pleased and still keeps it on a prominent place on his dresser to this day. It seems to give tangibility and focus to all those good times spent in the wild—and compensation for the drudgery as well!

Bob and Adrienne Klein have now been backpacking together for five years. At the age of eight, she went on her first three-day backpacking trip, and at ten years old, she can cover ten miles in a good day. Bob found that the mileage she could comfortably cover was exactly the same number as her age.

Adrienne has some dreams for the future. She would like to hike a month on the Appalachian Trail every summer so that, by the time she graduates from high school, she'll have the entire 2,100 miles under her belt! Funny thing is, her pop has the same dream!

Age to Mileage Ratio

- Four- to five-year-olds: Could possibly walk two or three miles their first times out. They should not be required to carry anything on a day hike if it inhibits their movement and freedom to explore.
- Six- to eight-year-olds: They may be used to carrying little backpacks with school books during the school year, so they do better, but keep the weight and bulk down so that their bodies feel free on the trail.
- Nine- to ten-year-olds: They can start carrying weight, but keep it to ten pounds or under. A ten-year-old's body may not be proportioned or long enough to carry big, bulky items such as sleeping bags, so pack accordingly.

Adolescents

Once your children reach the adolescent years, you can begin to think of them in more adult terms when it comes to backpacking. If they are interested, they should be encouraged to read general books on back-packing and hiking to add to their knowledge of the sport (see appendix C, Suggested Reading). All things do not need to be learned through experience, trial and error, or their parents' teachings. They are now old enough to select gear, pack, plan menus, chart the route, plan itineraries, and follow the trail with your gentle, sideline guidance. They should be included in and taught all aspects of the trip, if they are interested—and if they are still happily going with you at this age, they are truly interested.

You should be thrilled that your adolescents still find joy in your family's presence, so work as hard as you can to plan the trip to meet their desires (as long as it's within the capabilities of every member of the family). They might be interested in exploring a certain area, or combining backpacking with another sport or skill such as orienteering by doing a little map and compass work. They might want to back-pack up to a mountain lake and do some fishing or climb a peak. At this age, your child is really stretching out and discovering and wants to challenge him or herself, so help guide your child in attaining the knowledge he or she now needs and the experience he or she desires.

It won't be long, however, before adolescents will want to go out with their own peers. Depending on the child, fifteen is not too young. I've shared an Appalachian Trail shelter and breakfast with very responsible fifteen-year-olds who evidently had a long history of feeling comfortable in the woods; these kids really impressed me with their knowledge and sensitivity for the natural world.

Fifteen-year-olds can be as strong as dad. If there are competing teenagers in the family or if friends are along, they may play macho games and try to out-carry each other. Teenagers are physically strong but weak in other ways. It's a hard age. There is a lot of peer pressure. There are often hormones flowing. They can get overstressed, so a parent needs to look out for them.

Naturally, a family's pace is set by the slowest member. Older, stronger hikers can be allowed to go at their own pace, but should always wait at intersections and should stop and rest and wait for the rest of the family at regularly timed intervals. All should be briefed in the morning on what the trail will be like that day. If they are aware that the trail remains on a ridge and they begin.to drop down, they would be alerted that they had gone astray, map or no map.

Once your child gets older and stronger and capable of carrying more weight and going faster and farther, you may have to juggle pack weights in order to keep everyone in the family hiking together. Dad may be overloaded and unable to move quickly, while the adolescent with his or her lightweight pack is itchy to zoom ahead. Throw some weight into your adolescent's backpack. You'll know when it's time.

The whole idea of not bathing for days disgusts some children at this age (not usually the boys), but they get over it quickly. The lack of bathroom facilities bothers some girls even more. I once hiked with a group of teenage girls who were simply refusing to go. They held it for days and were becoming very uncomfortable. I had had it one night and grabbed the flashlight and told them to follow me. I dug a hole, squatted with the flashlight over me and went about my business, put my toilet paper in the hole, covered it, tapped it down, and said, "There. Now you've actually seen it done. I don't want any more problems with it." They were mortified. But almost minutes after that scene, one by one they approached me for the community shovel and went off into the woods quietly and calmly; there was never a problem again.

One of the biggest problems with older adolescents is sometimes their attitude that they are "above" all those things like dehydration, hypothermia, etc. Some are still feeling naively invincible. They frequently don't eat, drink, or rest enough, or wear enough warm clothing. During a winter camping trip, one instructor told his students to eat some high-energy food before hitting the sack, to help keep them warm through the night. One young woman ate an entire box of chocolate bars and then washed her hair because she did not enjoy it feeling dirty. During the night, she became ill from the rich candy and vomited, and got hypothermia from her wet head and her inadequate "Winnie the Pooh" sleeping bag, and had to be taken to a hospital.

Although you might advise kids in this age group to take their time, enjoy extended lunch breaks, and admire views, some try to do more miles and do it faster than their peers. Those individuals suck in others through peer pressure. After a trip, during their debriefing, they all talk about their experience. The ones who raced through listen to what the slower ones saw and come to see all they've missed. There is a remarkable difference between how the first backpacking trip is executed and the second. More intelligent choices are made in every aspect of the planning and throughout the trip. The fast ones slow down. Everyone feels more comfortable and enjoys themselves more.

Hints and Tips

- Start backpacking with your child as soon as you feel comfortable. Even the smallest babies benefit from watching the night fall and the morning begin in the wilds.
- Don't think you have to hike far from the road to have a memorable outdoor experience. Even a mile or two down the trail will show you a world of wonder beyond the asphalt.
- Start your children on shorter backpacks close to home and increase in duration as they become comfortable in the wilds and with being away from home.
- The toddler/in-between years can be the most difficult to deal with when backpacking—too young to hike far alone, too heavy to carry. Keep your backpacking trips very short.
- Once you can no longer carry your child, your young hiker's capabilities will dictate most of the logistics of your backpacking trips.
- Do a trial run in your yard and simulate a campout, so you can see what pitfalls you'd encounter on the trail.
- Your adolescent backpacker can be thought of in adult terms in many respects. Give an adolescent as much responsibility as you are both comfortable with and he or she is capable of.

Special-Needs Children

Barry and Sharon Newman had fallen in love with the outdoors. With their first son, Clint, they had hiked, paddled canoe, and camped in the wilderness. But their second child, Kurt, was diagnosed at four months with glycogen storage disease (Von Geirkes disease), wherein his liver stores blood sugar but does not release it. As a result, his body must be digesting food constantly in order to maintain his blood sugar level. He needed to be fed a soy formula round the clock. (Because his body cannot break down complex sugars, his diet must be lactose-, fructose-, and sucrose-free.)

Many parents are terrified to allow their special-needs child to do anything remotely risky. The Newmans decided if they were going to take Kurt into the wilds and perhaps risk his life, they were going to

do everything they could to counteract those risks. A life-threatening emergency for Kurt could be as simple as him contracting the flu. If he became ill and couldn't keep his formula down, he could go into a seizure and then expire. It could happen in less than twelve hours. When the Newmans go out, they carry all the IV bags and the dextrose drip solution that an emergency medical technician would use. They know how to insert the IV and have a margin of six hours to get him out, if an emergency arises. They have everything they need with them, short of a doctor or a nurse. "You cover all of the bases," Sharon says. "And then sometimes you hold your breath and say a prayer."

Because spending time in the outdoors was something the Newmans dearly loved and was second nature to them, they did not want Kurt to be deprived of the experience. They continued to car camp and hike with him in a child carrier and had to get up every two hours, three to four times a night, to feed him his special formula. Working in a tent by flashlight was sometimes a tricky thing, but fortunately Kurt ate his formula cold.

When Kurt turned one, he went on nightly tube feedings that required an electric-powered pump. The pump continuously fed him and his parents only had to check him one to two times a night to see that the tube wasn't leaking or that Kurt hadn't pulled it out. This procedure, however, limited them to day trips and camping in a pop-up camper so that they were near a power source.

They preferred to visit parks that only allowed primitive camping. They asked to camp near the pump house so they could use the electricity. The parks never had a request for this before, and some refused to make special accommodation of their needs. Others, like Canada's Algonquin Provincial Park, were very pleased to help them out. The Newmans made telephone arrangements beforehand.

When Kurt turned eight, a doctor from the National Institute of Health in Bethesda, Maryland, pioneered and perfected the use of cornstarch for longer-term feedings. Now Kurt could go five hours at a shot by mixing six tablespoons of cornstarch with his soy formula. He gets a big dose before he goes to sleep and only needs to get up one time to drink a second dose to get him through the night.

The Newmans have now sold their pop-up camper and have gone back to wilderness canoeing and camping. Kurt loves it. He feels he is normal, and as long as he follows the rules and eats as often as he should and what he should, he is. He can do anything any other child can do and probably has seen and experienced a lot more than the average child.

These outings have given Kurt a much broader base of experience. He has seen dolphins close up in the Gulf of Mexico, and moose and beaver in wild rivers. He loves it out in the wilds. It has built self-reliance and independence in him, which is so important for every child but especially important for a special-needs child whom the world tends to look at as handicapped. Because Barry and Sharon Newman looked upon Kurt's disease as something they would learn to work with and continue to live their lives as normal, Kurt too, now, at eleven years old, believes he can do anything he wants in his life. That's a wonderful gift.

Leading a Group of Children

If you are an experienced hiker, you may someday find yourself leading a group of children into the wilds. They may be your child's scout troop, a 4H club, a church group, etc. Every child, group, situation, and trip is different; there are all types of groups out there, even if it is just your children's friends. Taking them into the wilds can make you feel like you'd like to tear out your hair and their's, but the experience is worthwhile because it is so rich and full for them. You can make a difference. If you can get them to love the earth and feel comfortable with nature, it's worth a try.

Figuring mileage can be somewhat challenging for a group of children. They can have a vast range of physical fitness levels and experience. If you try to cover too many miles, they will feel driven, have little fun, and fail. Covering too few miles causes boredom and encourages misbehavior. For eleven- to twelve-year-olds, you can probably cover about seven or eight miles a day without any problem (although there's always one child who is having a hard time—poor gear, overweight, etc.). Choose a trail with fairly easy terrain without a lot of elevation change, and go when the summer days give a lot of daylight hours.

Children can test you a lot too, and they may not know if you are being honest or feeding them a line of bull. You may be the exact age of their parents, but they cannot imagine you as their parents' age. Although you may be strict when it comes to safety, you are on a recreational outing, so they will probably like you and trust you. Plus, you all will have a good time together. If it is a first experience in the outdoors, encourage them to keep a journal every day and share it at the end of the trip. We had talent shows around our campfires and, as a result, the kids relaxed enough to talk about their homes, their families, and their lives with one another around the campfire.

Because backpacking made a lifelong impression on Ben Day and he wanted to give others the chance to experience it, he volunteered for the past five years with the Boy Scouts, taking kids ages nine to fourteen into the wilderness of California's Sierra Nevada. Kids are not the easiest to deal with and when Ben begins to get discouraged, he thinks about what his life would be like if he had not been introduced to the sport so many years ago. Plus, he gets to learn about dealing with kids, which will come in handy because he plans to become a parent someday.

The places Ben and other scout leaders take their kids are usually not accessible by trail, which means getting there is relatively harder. Being in a remote area also means that if one kid gets sick, everyone goes back, so they are very careful to have all the necessary first-aid equipment and that the kids have as low a chance as possible of hurting themselves. The remoteness of the area prevents the kids from getting into trouble with other people.

In preparation for a Boy Scout trip, the scoutmaster and Ben usually hold two meetings: one to discuss the logistics (trip route, gear, food) and the second one to actually do the packing. During the second meeting, they not only inspect the kids' backpacks but also ask the kids to help pack the meals. Each meal is packed in a plastic bag which is then marked with a two-character code designating what meal it is. For example, B-2 means breakfast for the second day, L-3 means lunch for the third day, and D-4 means dinner for the fourth day. They distribute the meal bags amongst themselves and weigh their packs for the record.

During the hike, either the scoutmaster or Ben is always last for two reasons. One, it's easier to catch stragglers, especially going cross-country, and two, some kids who get to camp last carry the stigma that they're slow. By having a leader last, they do a clean sweep and avoid the problem of a kid feeling down because he or she is last. And of course, one adult is always up front.

Once they completely establish their base camp, the teaching and the learning begin. They go on day hikes, fish, play games, practice making a campfire with one match, break illegal camps, collect trash, and learn other wilderness skills. On day hikes, they always bring, at the minimum: matches, a first-aid kit, and an emergency shelter. Although they most likely will not use them, one does not know when an emergency situation might occur.

Gear

Before departing, go through all of the children's backpacks, item by item. If there are items that are not on their gear list (given at the end of this section), ask them, "What's this for?" This may seem like an infringement of privacy, even into the lives of an adolescent, but the consequences that could arise from carrying too much stuff directly affect the entire group. If a child is succumbing to a heavy pack and cannot go on, comrades must either divvy up the extra weight or they must all bail out of the trip prematurely.

Watch their clothing, too. On a five-day backpack, kids sometimes take five or six outfits (with matching socks), and some boys can be as clothes-conscious as girls. One complete change of hiking clothes and one outfit for warmth is enough. Weed out the nonessentials.

You may also want to check for items that might be forbidden to your particular group of kids: cigarettes, huge bags of candy and gum, portable cassette players/radios, etc. There are new sights and sounds to discover, new thoughts to think, and new emotions to feel. Listening to head-phone music separates kids from the outdoors.

Good rain gear is essential. One young lady did not like the looks of her rain coat, even though it was pouring, and hung back toward the end of the day and changed into her heavy cotton hooded sweatshirt (which was not even advised for warmth) when we were out of sight. At the next break, Todd and I were alarmed to see this sopping wet shirt on this perfectly wretched girl and had to send her home, because she had nothing dry or warm left to put on.

Gear List

If the group cooks together, everyone is responsible for their own cup, bowl, and spoon, as well as clothes and sleeping bag. Food is divided among the group, as are the cooking gear, first-aid kit, tents, water purification system, shovel, etc. Below is a list of necessary gear each child should carry.

- matches
- rope/parachute cord
- flashlight
- toilet paper
- two one-liter water bottles
- cup, bowl, and spoon
- toothpaste and brush
- personal medication
- sleeping bag
- sleeping pad
- two bandannas
- sunglasses
- rain gear

optional: pocket knife (a scout group with proper training on knife handling might be allowed to bring this item)

Clothing List

Depending on the worst possible weather you might encounter on a particular trip, the following is a basic list for each child; note that no cotton clothing should be relied on for warmth.

- underwear: one pair per day, or one pair for every two days on long trips
- socks: two pairs liners, three pairs heavy socks
- T-shirts: two at the most
- something warm for the upper body: either a pile jacket or wool sweater/shirt
- something warm for the lower body: one pair of tights or synthetic long underwear bottoms; thin cotton leggings for bugs, not warmth, in the summer
- shorts or hiking pants

Optional Items List

- camera
- small comb
- insect repellent

Learning the Basics

Preadolescent and adolescent boys are usually tremendously good sports, for the most part. They don't seem to even notice the rain and continue to chatter on, goof with each other, and laugh the miles away. They do not care what they look like and seem impervious to the cold and wet.

Girls, on the other hand, are often miserable under these conditions. They do not care for looking like drowned rats, do not like feeling uncomfortable, and are still working hard at dressing "right," even in the rain.

Some of the solutions to their problems are so simple, or so the leaders think. The kids are cold: "change out of your wet clothes." Simple. Not until they begin to shiver do they seem to learn anything and take action. You can usually leave these older kids alone to learn their lessons for themselves. But when the situation changes a degree, as when real shivering begins, it is a different ball game, and you must step in to avoid a case of hypothermia.

The same thing occurs with sunburn. "I don't burn," they say. Try to catch them on their first break when their skin just begins to flush. They usually have the excuse that their suntan lotion is in the bottom of their backpacks, so offer your handy tube.

The most common ailment when dealing with groups of kids is dehydration. It is very difficult to get them to drink water, especially teenagers, who are not always crazy about "going to the bathroom" in the woods. Sometimes you must force kids to drink water. One girl refused liquids for two days (to hold her urine), until she was forced to drink hot soup.

Everyone is responsible for administering their own drugs. If they have a headache (which is usually from dehydration), they take their own aspirin, etc. The group's first-aid kit is a shared item, and the leaders should supervise the use of it.

Kids sometimes have problems giving each other the proper amount of space between them as they hike. They often hike crowded together as if at drill camp. Periodically make them stop and have each one count to twenty-five out loud before the next person can go. It spreads them out enough for awhile that they can begin to learn their own pace. Children at this age need to be encouraged to be independent and to listen to their own minds and bodies (as with finding their pace), and to not always follow like sheep; it seems as though there is always a dominant leader in a group like this, and you must help the less dominant kids experience some independence.

The kids should not be allowed to bring their backpacks into tents (only plastic bags containing their gear and clothing), because, for some reason, when they do they trash the tents. They are also extremely hard on tent zippers. The zippers get snagged and the kids pull and yank on them until they tear. When taking a group of kids out, remember these problem areas and try to take steps to avoid having this happen.

Teach them the importance of hanging all of their food at night. When night marauders arrive, they spend most of the night trying to get the food that is hung out of reach and snoop around backpacks. Some kids may be scared out of their skins, especially if they sleep under tarps as opposed to tents.

Your most difficult time may be at night. There is so much chatter going on deep into the night that it can wear you out from the lack of sleep. They are excited and it is all so new. As the nights and days pass on during longer trips, they quickly learn how important it is to get proper rest if they are to function the next day.

Mitch Tuchman has been taking groups of Explorer Scouts out canoeing ever since he was old enough to be a leader, for over twenty years now. He has never had any trouble with the kids staying up too late at night because he firmly believes in "exhaustion." He keeps the kids very busy and fills their day, and they cannot stay awake if they wanted to. Only the first night out poses any problems. He tells them they can stay awake as long as they like, but at 6:00 A.M., everyone is expected to be up. The adults also go to bed at the same time and do not sit around drinking beer, to set a good example. On winter camping trips, there are threats of putting snowballs in sleeping bags to get them roused, and the threats are carried through. Mitch's kids know he means business, they respect him for it, and their trips are enjoyable and successful as a result.

Drill the kids on how to dispose of their garbage. Everything goes into the garbage bag—eggshells, orange peels, etc. You may find things like partially eaten peanut butter sandwiches shoved halfway under rocks at lookouts when you take breaks, tons of wrappers, etc. Establish a rule that everyone has to pick up all trash whenever they see it, but, if the person in front missed it or stepped over it on purpose, the one who picks it up gets to put it in the other kid's backpack. So if they are alert and caring, they minimize carrying garbage themselves. It makes it worth their while to pick it up when they see it.

You have to be aware of what the kids are doing all the time. And some children need to be reminded over and over about good back-country ethics and behavior. It's important to make children believe that you are in charge and that they must listen, or an outing will not be a successful one.

It's important that they help out with all chores no matter what their home life is like. All children are equal out in the wilds and you must remind them that you are not their servant. Taking turns washing dishes in the backcountry can be a real eye opener for kids, as well as an opportunity to teach them about proper disposal of waste water, etc.

On one of our group hikes, it was a hot, dry summer day and the natural springs by the shelter were flowing very slowly. In order to get any drinking water, we had to dip very slowly and gently into the small puddle that formed where the water came out of the ground. A small group of boys went down to the springs and proceeded to soak their feet in it. A hot and thirsty long-distance hiker going from Georgia to Maine came into camp after a twenty-plus-mile day and turned livid when he saw where the boys' feet were. He came to me asking, "Who's in charge of these kids? Who is responsible?" I became even angrier because the children were drilled in good water-handling procedures.

Discipline

You probably do not need to inflict many rules on older adolescents, but the rules that are stated should be strictly enforced: no alcohol, drugs, tobacco, head sets, or radios. At orientation, start with a big discussion on when and why you'd send a child home for misbehaving. Do not tolerate repeated bad behavior, because you are not out there to be a disciplinarian but a guide and care-giver.

One group leader was questioned only once or twice on his tobacco rule. An individual smoked all of the time and thought the rule ridiculous. The instructor explained how one spark could set the highly flammable nylon tents on fire, that it was not good for his health, and he was polluting the air for non-smokers around him. They usually end up learning something about themselves that they've never known before.

On one of my trips, one young man worked very hard at getting the other children's attention—things like rolling boulders down the mountainside where there was a road below, when I had repeatedly asked him not to do it. Finally, all I said was, "I'm thinking of sending you home at the next road crossing. I'm thinking about calling your parents and asking them to pick you up." Terror swept over his face. An immediate and radical change took place in his behavior and I never needed to speak to him about it again.

Much of the conversation of preadolescent/adolescent boys revolves around their genitals. Nearly anything that is said, if it rhymes or sounds remotely like any word that has to do with sex, causes them to roll with laughter. They joke about things although they have no idea what they are talking about. Keep your sense of humor. Don't allow them to be offensive, but allow them to be young boys in the onslaught of puberty.

As their leader, you need to be conscious of any ill feelings or ostracizing going on toward another child. He or she may not fit into the group, for whatever reason, and so the group may act like they do not want this person. The group can be outright unkind or simply ignore the child. It is all painful to the child. You can find ways to include the unfortunate one by assigning him or her chores or responsibilities that make the child feel important and special. Pair such a child up with children who are kinder and more empathetic so a friendship may develop. You can help an outcast child be liked by liking him or her yourself and by making him or her feel as though he or she belongs. If the children respect you, they will mimic you and begin to treat that child in the same manner.

Accenting the Positive

Sometimes you need to allow the kids to do things that are a little adventurous and exciting. For instance, if it's hot and humid and you happen to pass a pond, even if no one brought a bathing suit, consider stripping to your underwear for an impromptu swim. The kids may be shocked at swimming in underpants, but they might have a great time. Some groups of kids may not be appropriate for this type of behavior— church outings, etc. And if this type of thing alarms you . . . beware of potential liability for adults in charge of kids. If there are some children in the group who cannot swim well, they can go in the water but should just stay by the edge and in shallow water. Sometimes it doesn't hurt for you to be a little lenient and flexible. It makes them trust you and listen to you when you do draw the line and say, "No, that is unsafe."

On Ben Day's scout trips, he and the scoutmaster teach the kids how to fish. They teach them the basic use of a rod and reel, the use of a lure and bait, and the not-so-popular cleaning of the fish. The kids get very excited, or in some cases, very emotional, when they catch one. Once a kid hooks a fish, the two leaders try not to assist the kid in bringing it in. The reeling in of a fish is probably the most exciting part of fishing. It is only when the kid lands the fish that they give him or her a hand. If the child does not want to keep the fish, they usually let it go as long as it is not badly hurt. If the child decides to keep it, they have a rule that whoever catches the fish must clean it. For first timers, they show them how to clean it.

Children at this age are very impressed with their accomplishments and need to feel good about what they have done. If there is a vantage point or lookout on the trail, they can clearly see how far they've come, and they can see where the hike will conclude. Their mood and tone changes, they mature, become proud, and feel bonded to their comrades (even those that do not get along). They begin to realize that they are accomplishing something that is not only difficult but that, through it, they are finding a sense of freedom and independence they've never before experienced—good lessons for an adolescent to learn. It teaches them to reach for other goals—to have larger and more complex dreams in their lives and to not be afraid of trying something that may be difficult.

Teaching Advanced Skills

With groups of older adolescents, you can begin teaching them more advanced wilderness skills. Make sure that everyone knows all the basics, including hands-on skills such as lighting stoves and setting up tents. When you've selected a destination, say to the group, "Here's the trailhead on the map. Here's where the vehicles will be parked. You will have three days to do the hike. Plan your trip."

The kids can then break up into groups and plan their mileage, campsites, and menus amongst themselves. They can either pitch in for food and cook as a group, or plan meals as pairs or individuals. Tell them the usual high and low temperatures in the area they are going to visit so they can decide what gear and clothing to bring. Do not go through their backpacks to see if they are carrying adequate gear. If they make the wrong decision, they learn. Step in only if it is a life or death situation.

Teach proper campsite selection (well-drained or sandy sites, away from fragile meadows, 200 feet from any water source, etc.), but let them choose their campsites, even if they make mistakes. "If they screw up," one group leader says, "they won't do it a second time." They are learning by experience, and although it's the hardest way sometimes, these are choices the kids are making for themselves.

To teach kids the use of map and compass, have them lead on some parts of a hike. But be aware that giving kids this kind of responsibility can have serious consequences—and sometimes that's part of the learning experience too. The type of organization you're leading for will determine the extent to which you can allow the children to learn by their mistakes. Be sure you consider your personal liability as well as the kids' safety and well-being.

On one of Ben Day's scout trips, during a fifteen-mile loop day hike the kids were leading they got off track about halfway through. It took four hours to do the first half. With about six hours of daylight left, they took a vote and decided to continue around. When they encountered a wide stream, they lost about an hour's worth of time looking for a suitable place to cross, thereby eating up more of their precious daylight. It began to get dark. On some parts of the hike, they were on a foot of snow. They were cold and tired. They had numb feet because they had not taken a break since lunch. By 10:30 P.M., they were too tired to continue or even eat, so they spent the night where they were.

They needed rest, but they also needed to keep warm. The most anyone had along was a flannel shirt. Fortunately, the area they stopped in had plenty of dried wood. The two leaders built two campfires and had the kids sleep close to them. They placed emergency blankets on top of them to protect them from wind while they slept. They kept the two campfires alive all night by taking turns gathering and feeding the fire. Although the two leaders did not sleep too much, they managed to keep warm. By morning, everyone was feeling a lot better and after a few mouthfuls of food, they hiked another two hours before reaching their base camp.

This experience clearly shows what could happen in cross-country day hikes. You just never know and you need to be prepared to spend the night out. For all involved, however, surviving the hike only boosted their self-esteem, and for the children, especially, this is very important.

To teach kids how to pick the right type of wood for a campfire and to pile it properly in the fire ring, when making a campfire use a method called "round robin campfire." Each kid is only allowed one match, to make sure the kids really think about what they are doing. If the first child does not get the fire lit, then the next kid gives it a try. The cycle continues until they have a campfire. It is very important that you keep track of which child had the first try for the last round robin campfire, so that another child can have the first try next time.

It is also very important to teach children the proper use of handling backpacking stoves. Have each older child take a turn filling and lighting the stove under adult supervision, so he or she is not afraid of it. Pouring fuel into the stove needs to be done slowly and carefully and away from food and cooking utensils. Priming can be touchy if a pump is used to establish pressure. This can take a sensitive, practiced touch, so tasks like this may require assistance on several tries. Teach them to keep their faces away from their stove when they are lighting it, to keep their fuel bottle far away from their lit stove, and to keep a safe distance around it while it is in use—no rough-housing is allowed and it should be treated with respect. Also teach them what to do if the stove malfunctions and blows up, sprouts a fuel leak, splits a seam, etc.: smother it in dirt.

In addition to teaching advanced skills such as building campfires, using a stove, traveling cross-country, etc., always emphasize to kids that whenever they are in the wilderness, they must always do at least one good deed before the end of the trip. The deed could be collecting trash, breaking up an illegal campground (a fire ring in a no-fire or no-camping zone, too many fire rings in an area, etc.), clearing a trail, or anything that keeps the wilderness as wild as possible. Explain to the kids that the wilderness belongs to everyone, and that if we do not take care of it, no one else will.

Hints and Tips

- Your group's capabilities may be extremely varied from individual to individual. Gauge your planning for/to the youngest, smallest, least fit, etc., child.
- Be strict when it comes to safety, childlike when it comes to good-natured fun, and patient when it comes to stressful times; never lose your sense of humor.
- Make certain they have the right gear (for example, proper rain suits) and are not bringing too much of some items. Do not let them have control of this unless they are older and strong, and you are positive they can handle carrying the weight of their own "mistakes."
- The older kids become, the more invincible they think they are. Step in when you see them not taking care of their needs.
- Always be aware of where your kids are and what they are supposed to be doing. In the end, it is your ultimate responsibility.
- Make backcountry ethics and low-impact camping techniques a part of their lives out in the wilds. You're training future stewards of our earth.
- Be sensitive to children who are being left out and find ways to nonchalantly include them. Strive to promote harmony and acceptance amongst your group.

Stock Animal Packing

▲ ▲ ▲ ▲ ▲ ▲ ▲ ▲ ▲

Llama Packing

It all began at a party. We were listening to some people talk about Colorado, how it was their home and how they loved the mountains. Todd mentioned that we longed to hike the 470-mile Colorado Trail, but the children came along and our long hike had been put off until they could walk under their own steam. Wally and Katy Blanca, llama breeders from Durango, Colorado, who have taken their two daughters hiking all over the Rockies with llamas, said that with llamas we could get back onto the trail *right now!* There was a flutter of excitement inside of us. Premature, to be sure, but a magic was creeping into our dreams with the possibility that something wonderful might happen.

Although packing with llamas may be a novelty to us, they have been used for over 5,000 years in South America to transport goods. In some remote villages of Peru, these "trucks of the Andes" are still the only means some families have of carrying their potatoes and other goods many miles to town to sell.

Contrary to what many people think, llamas are not "exotics" in the true sense of the word, but are really native to the western hemisphere. The camel family first originated and evolved on the plains of North America (flourishing as recently as 10,000 to 12,000 years ago). They are just now returning to the home of their ancestors as llama breeding and packing is widely spreading.

In this country, llamas are now being used by the U.S. Forest Service and National Park Service for a variety of tasks in managing their lands. Because of the llama's calm disposition, relatively inexperienced trail maintenance and work crews can safely and efficiently use them to transport tools and supplies. Llama trains are also used for packing trash and human waste from wilderness areas, in search and rescue, and for transporting the fragile equipment of scientists who are going into the backcountry to collect data.

One option for a llama-packing hike is llama rental for privately led hikes. Any private group who wishes to lease a llama for their own personal trip must attend orientation sessions to better acquaint them with llama handling and care. You must also possess the necessary backcountry skills to safely care for yourself and the other members of your party. This is a wonderful way to get your family into the backcountry and still be in charge of the trip, if this is the style you are used to and desire.

If you are seeking a guided experience, there are commercial pack llama outfitters throughout much of the country who lead scheduled trips. Many will also create custom trips for your family or group. An annual list of outfitters can be obtained from the Rocky Mountain Llama Association (see appendix B, Organizations).

An experienced pack llama is capable of carrying 60 to 100 pounds and covering eight to fifteen miles a day. Llamas carrying a full pack will follow you anywhere you can walk or climb without the use of your hands. Because of their unintimidating size (averaging six feet tall and weighing 300 to 400 pounds), they meet you at eye level and become genuine trail companions.

We'd seen llamas on the Pacific Crest Trail, carrying gourmet picnics for clients. We had no desire to hike with them while we were fit and strong, but llamas are our ticket back into the wilderness with our young children. They make it possible to carry the twenty pounds of dry diapers (forty pounds when wet!), the diaper rinsing bucket, rubber rain boots, golf umbrellas, bibs, balloons, dolls, trucks, tons of clothing for accidents in the night and slopping in creeks, plus all the other normal gear needed to survive with kids in the backcountry for days on end. We couldn't do without them, so we were determined to like them.

We like animals but we are not intense lovers of them. The "boys" we would be taking on the trail were looked upon as workers, laborers. Llamas do not require a lot of attention, but we thought we should become as well acquainted with them as possible. We went on a short day hike with Wally and Katy and their llamas, and immediately grew fond of their companionship. Sierra felt comfortable riding, which was a great relief because, at forty pounds, she was too heavy to carry for an extended period of time. She had to enjoy riding or there would be no trip.

We depended on llamas to carry our three-year-old safely over those high Rocky Mountain passes. A uniquely designed wooden saddle called the Mount Sopris, which resembles a cross-buck pack saddle for horses, was chosen. We filled the two panniers with sleeping bags and rolled-foam sleeping pads which were lashed to the tops of the bags. They supported Sierra's sides so she could not easily fall off should her llama spook or leap. Across the back, we rolled another pad that was placed on top of the two side pads, perpendicular to them. This prevented Sierra from flying backwards because it rested right in the middle of her back. Riding up there, she looked like a cross between an Indian princess riding on an elephant and the Blessed Mother riding her donkey into Bethlehem.

The only inconvenience in using llamas is the considerable amount of time needed to saddle, load, and unload their panniers. Their panniers must be of equal weight, so with the help of a hand scale daily adjustments of their contents must be made. It initially took us three hours in the morning for four llamas, but with practice,

we got it down to one and a half. A small inconvenience when we considered that they are our ticket back to the trails as a family and they enabled our children to experience the wilderness at a far younger age. The llamas helped make our Colorado Trail adventure a wonderful experience for the whole family. Our children came to love the wilderness, they bonded as siblings, we became strengthened as a family, and we really had the time of our lives.

Llama packing is a wonderful way for families with young children to get out onto the trails. Senior hikers who can no longer carry the weight, injured hikers (with bad knees or backs), and handicapped children all have an opportunity to experience the backcountry because of llamas.

Low Impact

Llamas are well adapted to fragile trails and alpine areas because of their two-toed padded feet, which not only make the llama sure-footed in the most rugged terrain but also have a very low impact in comparison to the hooves of other traditional pack animals.

All the world is a salad bar to llamas and they usually can subsist on native vegetation due to their ability to browse on a wide variety of vegetable matter, meeting all their nutritional needs from what grows alongside the trail, bark and dried pine needles included. A small amount of grain can be offered at day's end, a job children enjoy. Since they are cousins of the camel, they do not require a lot of water (usually a gallon a day, including what moisture they get from their food).

Good With Kids

The greatest thing about llamas and kids may be llamas' keen ability to sense a child's vulnerability. No one really understands why, but their high intelligence may help them tolerate the abuse doled out by small children. Llamas rarely spit at humans. They only try to move away, never kicking or spitting. Children are constantly entertained by their presence and curious behavior, which helps tremendously to combat boredom on a hike of any length.

Sierra's llama, Berrick, was incredibly cautious as he crossed plank bridges and gently stepped over rocks on steep descents. He knew there was precious cargo on his back and she let him know when she got upset. They became the best of friends. As they hiked, she pointed out flowers, animals, waterfalls, and views. At the end of a long day, she consoled him and told him to look ahead for a campsite.

There were occasional problems. Sierra became frightened when we crossed high passes in the Rockies. Her llama would sometimes jump up a steep slope when he went off trail to avoid a snowbank. The suddenness of it caught her off guard and startled her. Going steeply down rock-strewn trails frightened her, too, as her llama held back and she was forced to hold her body upright and balanced. But Sierra became a natural at riding and handling the llamas after a week on the trail. She stopped holding onto the wooden saddle horn right away.

Sierra hiked and led Berrick about two or three miles every day, often in the morning or at day's end, but mostly when the trail was gentle and smooth. At first, she spent as much time looking back at him as she did watching where she was going. "He's running too fast, Mom!" she'd wail. I told her, "He will only go as fast as you. You slow down and so will he." Before she caught on, she tripped a few times from not looking ahead, but Berrick never walked on her. She became quite a hiker, and even rock hops across creeklets didn't deter her as she confidently placed her feet and led her llama to the other side.

Special-Needs Children

Steve Jackson was born with spina bifida, a defect of the spinal column which results in paralysis of the legs. Up until Steve was five years old and weighed forty pounds, his father, Bill, carried him into the wilderness on his back in a child carrier. Then Bill began taking Steve into the La Plata Mountains in Colorado via the back of a trusty llama.

For the next five years, Steve's llama took him over 400 miles of trail every summer on four- and five-day trips into the backcountry. Steve has to hang on tighter than most children, because he is top-heavy and his body behaves more like dead weight. He cannot hug the animal with his legs as a normal rider does. He uses the unique Mount Sopris Saddle to ride on. Bill told me that Steve's llama senses his child's uniqueness and compensates for it.

In five years of riding, Steve only fell off his llama a few times and only once his father wasn't able to catch him. Steve would call out to his father, "Dad, I'm going to fall," and Bill would reach for him. There is no string of other llamas that is ever attached to a riding llama, so his father was always close at hand.

Ever since the age of five, though, Steve has enjoyed walking part of every day's hike. He uses Canadian-style crutches with metal arm bands and can move along at a rate of about three miles in four hours. His brother, Peter, rode a llama only a few times when he was four and chose to walk from then on. Steve enjoys hiking with his brother now.

Goat Packing

Trained pack goats are strong, intelligent, hard-working, loyal, disciplined, and friendly. This is important for families with children because they are a safe and fun way to get everyone into the backcountry. The adults can carry the young children on their backs and the goats can carry all their gear and supplies on their backs—between fifty and sixty pounds. Pack goats are extremely gentle animals once broken to pack and it is very unlikely that they cause accidental injuries to people. A goat's size is smaller than other stock animals, making them easier to saddle and handle and less intimidating for children.

Perhaps their greatest advantage in the backcountry is their unique ability to negotiate steep, slippery escarpments, cliff edges, boulder fields, and even glaciers. However, you can't take any goat and turn it into a good pack goat, because, as with children, it's the initial months of their lives and how they were handled and trained that determines their success as a packer. For further information on goat pack trips and leasing or buying goats and equipment, see appendix B, Organizations.

Low Impact

Goats have an extremely low impact on the environment, less than any other stock animal, because they prefer to walk on the high points of the trail and dislike the feeling of mud under their cloven hoofs. In wet conditions, they will step from rock to rock or walk along trailside logs whenever possible. Their droppings and tracks blend with those of antelope, deer, or Bighorn sheep and, because their appearance resembles that of Bighorn sheep, they blend well aesthetically in the wilderness environment. Goats nibble small amounts of plants and move from one to the next, leaving little noticeable damage.

Good With Children

A calm, well-trained goat is just as important a requirement as a mature, responsible child, but with the right goat, children can ride all day long. With training, a small child in the proper weight range can ride a goat with a little padding on the saddle. The saddle must be kept cinched tightly and the trail should be smooth in case of a fall.

Because they are companionable animals, goats will go where you go and easily follow a child, either on or off a lead rope. They enjoy affection and will allow you to sleep with them (an advantage on a cold night), or let you use their body as a pillow on a trail break.

Horse Packing

Traveling by horseback is as American as you can get, but environmental times have changed and horsepack parties need to keep up with the new backcountry ethics.

Before you decide to take your own horses out onto the trails for a backcountry trip, your animals should be familiar with packs and walking on trails. Bring along a first-aid kit for you and your companions, and have the animals wormed, vaccinated, and properly shod.

Contact local land managers for details on regulations concerning party size, grazing, trail closures, weed-seed-free feed, etc.

Horsepacking is magic for children—and we adults! It is the closest thing you can get to cowboys and the Old West in the 1990s. It's sitting around campfires and riding through some awesome country.

Minimize Impact

On the trail, check regularly that their packs are balanced and fitting comfortably so their loads ride better. This will help to reduce wear and tear on the trail. Stock should travel single file to avoid creating multiple parallel trails and should be led through puddles, mud, etc., to prevent trail-widening.

In camp, stay at least 200 feet from trails, water sources, and meadows. Tie stock away from the immediate campsite and use tree-saver straps for short breaks. Stock should be fed weed-seed-free feed to prevent the spread of noxious weeds. Supplemental feeds such as alfalfa pellets and processed grain help reduce the amount of grazing. See appendix B, Organizations, for a great free book on stock packing put out by the U.S. Forest Service.

Use Carefully With Kids

Horses are the most skittish of all trail stock, making them the most dangerous around children. But in horsepacking, most of the emphasis must be on the adult's experience with horses and packing, and all decisions pertaining to the children must hinge on this. Adults should be very familiar with trail riding before they take children out with them, and children should not be afraid of the animals, but have a healthy respect.

Equipment

It's important for even the smallest riders to have a place to put their feet and hold themselves on the horse. The youngest children ride in the saddle with an adult and simply lean up against them for support and balance. There is a wide variety of children's saddles available, and an outfitter that caters to young children will have a saddle whose stirrups will fit a four-year-old. As the child moves into adolescent years, small adult saddles are available to accommodate their junior size.

Rain is never much fun for anyone, and kids can tend to get unhappy when their hands get wet. Carry riding gloves for occasions like this. Ponchos are not the best choice for rain gear while horseback riding, because the loose corners tend to blow around, create noise, and make the horses edgy and a little nervous. Rain pants and jacket or oilskin slickers in children's sizes are preferable. Try to anticipate the weather and put rain gear on before a storm hits.

High winds are not always enjoyed by children, but the biggest problem seems to be keeping their cowboy hats on. A hat is important for keeping the sun off children's sensitive heads, and any good sun-hat will do, but for the children (as well as the adults), wearing a cowboy hat is a big part of the fun.

Family Horsepacking

What better way for a child to live out his or her fantasy than to go west for a horsepack trip? Ranches that offer horsepack trips can be found throughout the country, but the West is peppered with them. Many take children, and some even take very young children. The trails should be gentle and friendly and the wranglers should be spread throughout the line so that if anyone has trouble, they can get to them quickly.

Young Children

Young children may be able to ride and be led, or ride alone (about age five), if they are big and mature enough. Of course, it takes a certain kind of horse for such a young child to feel safe on its back. Docile, dog-gentle horses are the "kid-carriers." A child who is not used to riding may sit up stiffly instead of relaxing his or her body and sitting into the saddle and moving with the motion of the horse. For the most part, though, children are pretty fearless and tend to relax more than an inexperienced adult and perhaps learn more quickly because of it.

Kids, for the most part, won't slow you down as you ride. You'll just have to make some adjustments with your pace and not ride as hard. They can go all day, covering eight to twelve miles, with a lot of breaks to go fish and look at things. Getting up onto and down off of the horse helps the children a lot.

One outfitter has never had any kids "sore-up" on them. If there is a tendency to rub, it is where their legs hit the saddle, because they have a tendency to wear their jeans looser. Children never seem to complain about their bones and muscles aching either, unlike the adults, whose knees, ankles, and butts tend to feel badly on those initial days. The children get to camp and run around like wild because they are so resilient.

Jim and Deb Elliott's children have grown up on horses. Riding is as natural as walking to them. They took their two sons in the saddle with them as early as one year old, when they were able to sit up themselves. Deb held onto her child by putting her arm around him and resting her other hand, holding the reins, on the saddle horn. Her body supported his. Their rides lasted two and a half hours at this young age.

Before going on their horsepack trip, Garret and Clay Gamble were a bit apprehensive, even though they both had ponies at home and had been riding for a year or two already. The horses on the pack trip were much larger and five-year-old Garret was on the biggest horse in the string, because it was the most well-behaved. But the boys had learned the basics beforehand, which can also be taught during the first day.

Garret and Clay grew in confidence on their horsepack trip, for even though the trail horses were well-behaved, some incidents occurred where the rider had to let the horse know who was in charge. Some of the horses that they rode were "lead" horses at one time, and wanted to lead again. The adults instructed the kids to take the reins and pull back on them and make the horse do what they wanted it to do. It may sound like a little thing, but for a five- and a seven-year-old, this is a big deal. After the long ride into base camp, everything else that occurred on the trip was taken in stride.

Children seem to handle frightening experiences better than we adults do sometimes. Perhaps it is because of their innocence. On the very first day of his horsepack trip, five-year-old Garret's horse's saddle got loose and rolled under to its belly. As it slid, Garret moved over the front of the saddle up onto the horse's neck, and hung on to its mane for dear life. While the horse was slowing down, the wrangler moved quickly to his side and plucked him off his horse and put him onto her's. After he composed himself, he felt very good and was tickled with his performance and said, "We almost had a wreck, but I stayed on!" There were a few steep descents on the trail ride that caused even some adults to become uncomfortable. But Garret's parents, Greg and Carey, decided not to say anything to Garret and his seven-year-old brother, Clay, beforehand. They just wanted to see how they did, and they breezed right down them.

Older Children

I asked the Whitaker children what the biggest thrill or memory of their horsepack trip was. For twelve-year-old Josh, it was a local cowboy who they met up in the hills, riding the range and looking for strays. He rolled his own cigarettes and said to Josh, "The only bad coffee is no coffee." Right out of the movies.

Eight-year-old Jonah remembers with extreme clarity the time his horse slipped on some loose shale and laid down. He was not scared but "tentative," and he realized that this is real life stuff. Good for a kid.

They all remember the fishing and this is not a family of avid fishermen. The guide or camp boy would take the kids down to the stream, teach them how and where to cast, showed them where the fish were hiding, and if they did not catch beautiful native trout, something was wrong. There is just something magical about catching a fish in a wilderness stream and taking it back to camp to fry up for supper.

Hints and Tips

- Using pack stock can give you back some freedom of mobility that you lost when your children arrived on the scene. With their convenience, however, comes additional work. Determine if it's worth the exchange.

- Choose a method of stock travel or assistance that you feel most comfortable with. You need to trust and like the animals that you will be using on the trail.

- Adding stock animals can increase the odds of having an injury or accident occur to your child. Be very knowledgeable about handling the animals to diminish this risk considerably.

CHAPTER 10

Cycling

▲ ▲ ▲ ▲ ▲ ▲ ▲ ▲ ▲

When your children are too young to hike any distance on their own and too big to carry for very long, consider the alternative of bicycle touring. Families with small children can consider the vast network of rail trails that our country has established, adding up to over 500 trails. There are state chapters and a national organization (see appendix B, Organizations). Rail trails take you away from the hazards of traveling on the same roads with motorized vehicles. They are usually well graded and you can often pick the gradual downhill-sloping direction to travel. This can be a life-saver for parents who are pulling a loaded trailer or for young riders who cannot physically handle pulling hills.

A cycling adventure like this does not take you to pure wilderness; it can't beat hiking beautiful trails with glaciers and wildflowers—but it is a very safe way to have an outdoor family adventure, especially if it includes very young children. For families with older children who can handle their own mountain bike, off-road mountain bike touring is another real possibility.

Equipment

Bikes

Put some thought into what type of cycling experience you and your family are interested in before purchasing your bikes. Do you plan to use your bike for rough mountain travel without your young kids or with your older children, aside from slower, more tame family adventures? It is all a matter of taste and needs. But keep in mind that even the flattest rail trail can have quite rough sections. Visit your local bike shop and talk it over and try a few kinds out.

If you want a road bike for touring or carrying over twenty to twenty-five pounds of gear, a loaded touring bike is for you. It is constructed with a longer wheelbase for a smoother, more comfortable ride; it is outfitted with cantilever breaks for greater stopping power, extra-low gears for climbing hills and pulling loads, etc. Mud guards or fenders may be standard equipment on these bikes, but if not can easily be added. They prevent the rider (and those in the trailer behind you) from getting wet and muddy from spray thrown up by the wheels.

Mountain or all-terrain bikes are fat-tired, off-road bikes with flat or upswept handlebars that will take you over dirt trails, gravel roads, or any paved road where a road bike can go. The upright seating and low-pressure tires will make your ride slower than on a road bike.

A hybrid bike is a cross between a mountain and a road bike. Its frame is closer to a road bike, giving you a faster ride than a mountain bike, but it can still handle packed dirt, gravel roads, and modest climbs. Unless you want to jump logs and boulders in a single bound or do some serious mountain cycling, a hybrid may be the bike for you.

Most mountain and hybrid bikes come with twenty-one speeds. You may wonder why so many, especially if much of the terrain you plan to travel over is relatively easy. But you can easily top out a trailer's weight at 100 to 150 pounds, forcing you into a very low gear when traveling through loose gravel, etc. And why work harder than is necessary? Anything that makes your life as an outdoor adventuring parent easier, take advantage of it.

If your children are big enough to ride a ten-speed bicycle, they can go touring and carry full gear for themselves. It is important that children's bikes are the right size. A bike bought too big for a kid so that it can be grown into is a serious liability and drastically increases the chances of spilling. The smallest multi-speed bicycle made for a child (sixteen-inch frame) will fit the average nine-year-old. Because this wheel diameter (twenty-four inches) is not common, it is a good idea to carry a spare tube and tire on extended trips. Between the ages of twelve and fourteen, the average child will fit an adult-sized bike. Seat adjustment ought to be somewhat lower than on an adult's bike, to provide extra security and stability; for an eight-year-old, the seat should be at about hip level.

Another option for kids old enough to cycle is a tandem, with a parent riding in front and the child riding in back. This arrangement requires less responsibility of a child than riding on his or her own.

Consult your local bike shop for available tandems; every major manufacturer makes a model.

No high-quality tandem is going to be inexpensive, but this sort of bike bridges the gap between kids riding in a trailer or child seat to cycling under their own steam on their own bikes. They learn techniques of riding on a tandem, how to handle traffic, the rules of the road, etc., by doing it right alongside their parent.

Most standard tandems are manufactured for a height variable between riders, usually the rider in back being smaller than the rider in front. Even so, you may need to get your tandem custom built to accommodate your youngster, who must be able to pedal when you pedal. A Junior Pedaling Attachment or "Kiddy-crank" kit will transform your tandem, but it is not something do-it-yourselfers or even every bike shop mechanic can do. Hunt around for one who has this experience.

Trailers

Bike trailers fill that gap between babies who can fit into a child seat (up to forty pounds) and children who can ride their own bike (about six years old and on up). They are not inexpensive, but they can be used as a cargo carrier on a long tour after your children have outgrown them, or you can resell them to a younger family. They are a very safe way to transport your children. Your children can move in the trailer and not disturb the rider like they do if they're in a child seat. Many trailers are extremely difficult to tip over.

There are probably over a dozen different companies making bicycle trailers. They range from the lightest models that hold only children and no gear, to heavy-duty models that can carry 150 pounds or a handicapped child and a wheelchair. No matter what brand and model trailer you have, they all seem tight for two children sitting in them side by side for great lengths of time, and some are miserably tight. The trailers that close up entirely can be quite warm and comfortable for your child in even the wettest weather—the plastic windows even get steamed up. There are also solo trailers for carrying one child, which are lighter and narrower versions of the full-scale trailers. Children can face either forward or backward in either one-person or multi-person trailers.

The trailer can attach in different ways to your bike. Some trailers attach to the bike seat and are directly behind the bike, with equal parts sticking out on both sides. This width is an important image to keep in your mind as you pull it. The other type is attached to the bike frame, down on the left side by the rear wheel, so the trailer sits

considerably off center. This type of trailer interferes with some designs of rear panniers and doesn't allow you to use them. However, any gear that you'd put in your rear panniers could easily fit in the storage compartment of the trailer. Look for trailers which have a low center of gravity and a stable, wide wheel base.

Trailers are much safer than child seats because they are more stable: their center of gravity is lower to the ground. If there is an accident, a child will not fall as far. It is important that your trailer be equipped with a flag so it is very visible.

We use two differently designed bike trailers. For day trips we use a very lightweight, collapsible model that fits two young children rather tightly. For overnight trips when we had one child, we used a larger, heavier trailer that could fit three children or a handicapped adolescent and wheelchair. After we had our second child, we needed both trailers on an extended trip. The children were in their own separate trailers ninety-nine percent of the time. We thought they might have wanted to be together more for company, but they ended up enjoying their own private space.

Child Seats

When choosing a child seat, look for safety features such as wheel guards/leg shields to protect small feet and legs from encountering spinning spokes. Make sure the child seat doesn't rub your brakes or tires. Padded head rests are nice for naps. Keep in mind that most seats can hold children up to forty pounds. A child seat that is protected with some sort of fabric, rather than being just bare plastic, will not heat up from the sun and burn your little one's skin. Bring your bike to the dealer when you buy your child seat to make sure it can be fitted properly.

Don't ever leave your child in the child seat unattended or leaning against something without someone there to hold the bike. Children can easily wiggle and topple the bike. And practice with something other than your precious cargo when you first get your child seat. Strap a stuff sack of heavy gear onto the child seat to get you accustomed to your new center of gravity. Practice banking some turns and braking.

You will probably notice a big difference between a young child—say, two and a half years old—riding in a bike seat compared to a toddler of, say, one and a half. The older child's legs can get in your way and jab your back. The increased instability caused by the child's weight on your bike will probably make the arrangement undesirable for long periods of time

Bring along your child's bike seat in addition to the trailer; you can use it when your child is fussy in the trailer. The change of perspective is what keeps them going—having a parent close by, and being able to see better because they're sitting up higher. You can take advantage of the extra space in the trailer by strapping a large stuff sack of supplies in the bike seat when your child rides in the trailer, and then switching it when your child moves to the child seat.

Bike-Carrying Racks

If you do not have a bike-carrying rack and have to put your bikes inside your vehicle, all the rest of the gear has to be put in afterwards, piled on top of the bikes. It all has to be unloaded in order to pull the bikes out, and then whatever you're not taking with you has to be put back in before you can leave for a ride. The whole process has to be repeated again when your ride is over. It is fatiguing and time-consuming. Invest in a bike-carrying rack before taking even a series of day trips.

Racks that hold two bikes can be attached to the front or back of the car. Consider access to the trunk when placing this type of carrying rack. If you are a family with more than two bikes, you will need a carrier that goes on your roof. You'll need to check your car's gutters, width, etc., for models that fit. If you have a cap on your truck, you may have to custom fit the roof rack and drill holes down through the cap to fasten it.

Panniers and Racks

When you are touring, you'll probably be carrying all your gear on your bike, usually on a front rack, a rear rack, and the handlebars. Avoid racks that are bolted together rather than welded, because welded racks can withstand much more abuse. Choose a front rack that rides low and places the bags over the axle. This enables you to have more control over your steering.

Don't decide to be economical and choose huge rear panniers that have the volume to carry all your gear. It's much easier on your bike if your load is distributed between your handlebar bag (5 percent), your front panniers (35 percent), and your rear panniers (60 percent).

The new bicycle bags are designed to be used for both road bikes and mountain bike touring. Off-road riding demands much more from your gear, so panniers for this type of riding must be made of heavy fabric that can withstand abrasion and have a more secure system of fastening the bags to the bike rack to withstand all the bumping around. Some of these panniers may convert to backpacks or fanny packs—a nice feature if you're traveling.

For a child who is touring on his or her own bike, the style of panniers designed for the front wheel can be used on the rear wheel; they are smaller and will not throw a young rider off balance as much as full-size rear panniers. However, they also hold less gear. If your child uses a handlebar bag, be careful that you do not overload it, because its added weight can throw balance way off and making steering difficult. Twenty pounds of gear on each child's bike should be your limit.

Helmets

Both adults and parents should wear a bicycle helmet at all times and on all kinds of trails or roads. A child could easily hit a rock or other natural obstacle and be thrown from the bike. Helmets should have an ANSI or Snell seal of approval on them.

Helmets for babies can weigh as little as eight ounces, which is a good thing to look for, because babies' necks are not very strong. When a young child rides in a child seat, the high back sometimes pushes the head forward into an uncomfortable position. By distributing the helmet mass, some companies have successfully designed a child's helmet so this doesn't happen and the child has a more enjoyable ride. Many companies' helmets have kid-appealing graphics on them and come with decorative stickers, to help excite children about wearing them.

Of course, the best thing to do is to make sure you always wear your helmet and set a good example. Some helmets come with visors, because wearing sunglasses with a helmet can be uncomfortable for small children. Lots of vents to keep heads cool is another feature to look for.

Bike Accessories

Toe clips or straps, or one of the new strapless pedal-binding systems, are important for any rider, because they enable you to pedal more efficiently. Without them, you can only pedal down and away, not up, as you can with clips, which makes your cadence much smoother and brisker.

All bikes should be equipped with a bell or horn to give a warning sound. Every bike should also be equipped with a water bottle. You should also consider a bike pump and tire-patching kit for every bike; a family tool kit can either be carried by one person or divided among the riders. Be sure to bring spare parts on extended trips, or even on shorter trips if the parts are hard to come by.

Make sure your child's equipment—saddle, gear ratio, helmet, etc.—is just as user-friendly and dependable as your own.

Rain Gear

Ponchos are much too flappy and dangerous for use as cycling rain gear; their ends can catch in the chain ring, spokes, etc. Your regular outdoor rain pants and jacket serve well, as long as your pants cuffs can be tightened closely around your ankles to prevent them from catching on the moving chain. Velcroed straps can be purchased or easily made, or wide rubber bands carried in the jacket pocket work well too—as long as there is no danger of them cutting off circulation.

A baseball-type hat or a visor with a brim is a good thing to wear to keep the rain off your or your child's face and hold any type of hood away from the forehead.

If the rain looks like it's going to be short-term or light, you can get by with just keeping your kids in the trailer without their rain gear on. Some trailers are not absolutely weathertight and, depending on how hard the wind is blowing and how hard the rain is falling, children riding in them can become wet. If there is that chance, stop and dress them in their rain gear. At the very least, put warmer clothes on them, because rain and a front moving through invariably makes the temperatures drop.

An umbrella provides you with very nice shelter when you're stopped en route. Golf umbrellas are an invaluable piece of gear. If the rain comes down too heavy to ride in, it is much more comfortable to sit out a bad storm under an umbrella than exposed in the open. You may decide to just keep your child in the safety and comfort of the trailer while you wait it out, but with the umbrella, you at least have a choice if your child wants to be close to you.

Even a very short summer shower can leave an unpaved bike trail muddy. Even if it's only a tad muddy, it can be enough to cover your child's face, clothes, hair, and trailer with mud as your rear wheel slings it back. A rear fender is a good thing to have if you are pulling a child in a trailer. You can also pull down the plastic shield on the trailer and enclose your child, or put him or her in the bike seat during a rainy spell.

Clothing

All members of the family should steer clear of jeans or cotton pants that do not stretch and give, have thick seams that cause rubbing, and soak up water like a sponge. Tights are readily available at all department and clothing stores for every member of the family. Wear long tights in cold/wet weather and spandex shorts when it's warm.

Nylon/spandex jerseys aren't necessary, although they will keep you cool and dry. If you wear a cotton shirt, you may soak it with sweat and become wet and chilled. If the temperature lowers, slip your basic polypro thin long underwear top on instead and strip off that wet cotton. A long tail is nice too for keeping your back warm in chilly weather.

When your children are old enough to pedal along with you, it's important that your children have as much "real" bicycle clothing as possible—padded bike shorts, tights whose legs will not get caught in the chain ring, reflective jackets, etc. Because reflective jackets are expensive and quickly outgrown, you can instead buy a roll of reflective tape and put it on their jackets.

Your children's comfort and performance is very important to the success and enjoyment of your trip. Parents need to determine how much of this specialized gear they want to invest in. Keep it to a minimum at first—good rain gear, helmet, gloves—and build on this as your family really gets into the sport. Some major outdoor catalog companies carry bike gear for children.

When your child is being pulled in a trailer, you must remember that you are exercising and your child is not only stationary but catching a breeze as well. Children must wear more clothes than you do, and wind-protection gear is especially important (see chapter 1, Clothing and Equipment). Keep a hat handy and whenever you stop, check their body temperature by feeling their hands and noses.

Also be aware that your children need much more insulation compared to an adult, even if they are working like you. Their bodies just don't contain the same amount of body fat and muscle mass. If you are comfortable in just a sweater, your child might need a winter coat.

Children's Gear

- two pairs of shorts: at least one of them should be lycra/nylon/spandex; cotton with wide legs
- one pair of tights for riding
- one pair long pants for in camp/off-road
- two short-sleeve shirts: T-shirts or nylon bike jerseys
- two long-sleeved shirts: at least one should be polypro long underwear
- one warm wool sweater/pile jacket
- one rain jacket and pants
- four pairs of socks
- underwear
- hat
- balaclava
- gloves

Conditioning

A family cycling adventure may sound ideal to some, but a lot of building-up work must go into it if everyone is going to hold up reasonably well. It is important to know your limits before you even attempt an adventure. This will be determined by many factors and variables, taking into consideration the ages and capabilities of the members of your family, the terrain, weather, etc. Even if your family does a lot of riding at home, do a substantial amount of training before your trip.

At between six and seven years old, children's ability to concentrate and focus on a task, such as moving a bicycle through space at a steady pace, increases. Their motor skills have also improved to the point where they are now able to ride on a substantial tour. But because of this, conditioning becomes important because they can have a muscular injury just like an adult.

To build up strength for a trip, you and your older child should ride at least two to three times a week, or every other day preferably. Condition aerobically to develop endurance. Ride at a steady pace with a brisk cadence, but don't ride so hard that you wear yourself out quickly. Increase to twenty-five-mile rides, then thirty-mile, then thirty-five-mile, as the weeks pass. Never increase more than ten percent from one week to the next.

If you have normally active children, you shouldn't have to worry a lot about conditioning before going on a trip. If your children are sports-minded and accustomed to using their bodies, they should be able to slip into a cycling adventure with no problem. Your puberty-aged children may easily last longer than their parents, and can handle anything you can. *You* may need to condition more than they.

More book-minded, sedentary children need to be helped along a little with their conditioning. Go out on short trips often to help them build up stamina and strength. Ride to lakes, to playgrounds, to restaurants for breakfast—a ride with a destination and a purpose in mind. On these destination rides, everyone's muscles strengthen, their tolerance levels increase, and they become more and more excited over their coming cycling adventure. If you don't ride regularly like this, do so before a trip.

Mental conditioning may be the most important for the young riders. You can get your young children psyched ahead of time by all wearing your helmets around the house, playing in the bike trailer, etc. On the road, you will need to have control over them. They must listen and know they cannot "play on the road" and do their own thing. You don't get a second chance on the road.

Have a good idea of what your family can do by using shorter day trips as a gauge. Always be conservative and build in down time for poor weather, diversionary activities, etc. Even if the bike route you choose is a flat, even downhill grade that is a piece of cake to roll over, remember that you'll be pedaling a bike that is fully loaded. A strong nine-year-old who is used to riding may be able to carry about fifteen to twenty pounds of gear and cover about twenty-five miles a day, but even some adults would find this impossible. Keep the heaviest things in the rear panniers and only put the lightest things in the handlebar bag so it doesn't interfere with steering.

As soon as you add that loaded trailer, you lose a lot of freedom and mobility in where you can place your tires. A solo cyclist can weave back and forth and aim for the smoothest, firmest sections of trail, needing only a tire's width to be concerned. When towing a trailer, you search for a two-foot-wide smooth area to run its wheels on, and it can be difficult to accommodate all your tires. You pick and choose and usually one wheel drags. And so you need to be a fairly strong rider to be able to pull a trailer on an uneven surface such as an unpaved rail trail and not become extremely fatigued. Just don't underestimate the degree of difficulty and work that may accompany a bike trip like this. Its surface is far different than paved asphalt.

Choosing a Route

Of course, you should aim for the most scenic, gentle, least hilly route for your children. If you are pulling a trailer, or if your children are young riders, the more gentle and flatter the better. Rail trails are great choices for this age group (see appendix B, Organizations, for information on rail trails). They are usually unpaved gravel or dirt, which may be easier to execute on mountain or hybrid bikes. But because of mud, it's advisable to avoid an unpaved bike trail for two days after a good rain. Hills are hard on kids who are riding (and nearly impossible if you're pulling a loaded trailer), although they love the downhills. Stay away from heavy traffic, no matter how old they are, and if they are very young, try to avoid it altogether by sticking to the rail trails or other bike paths.

If your children are older, the relatively unchanging terrain of the rail trails may not be stimulating enough for them. Try touring on back roads, then, on a hybrid or road-touring bike. Plan to ride where the countryside is interesting and varied; for example, a ride through Amish lands to see draft horses plowing the fields. If you want to tour off-road or wild areas on your mountain bikes, your children will need to be older and quite strong riders to handle it. Many publishing companies have wonderful cycling guides to every area imaginable, domestic and foreign (see appendix C, Suggested Reading). There are also bicycle trail maps that cover large areas, through trails such as the Washington to Maine, Maine to Florida, etc. (see appendix B, Organizations).

Day Trips

You will most likely spend most of your cycling hours on day trips. Find the best part of the day for you to get out and make cycling a regular part of your life. You may decide to ride to and from work, at lunch, or in the evenings. When summer and the warmer months come, you may want to start the day with an early morning ride. If your day is more open, aim for the most comfortable weather of the day (not midday in the heat of summer) and when the least amount of traffic is on the road.

Bicycle Camping

If you plan to stay at inns and bed-and-breakfasts on your tour, your loads will be lighter because you won't have to carry your sleeping gear, but you will be more limited as to where you can stay (no campgrounds), and your costs will rise considerably. You have the most flexibility and freedom when you are able to use both types of accommodations: inns and campgrounds. Children love to camp, and spending the evenings and mornings outdoors in a place adds an element to the experience that one could never get if within four walls all the time. A sense of the place becomes more firmly imbedded in your soul.

When we first got our bikes and trailer, we tried them out on a mountaintop dirt road we remembered as being gentle with very little elevation loss or gain. However, on a bike while pulling a child in a trailer, the rises were extremely laborious and sometimes impossible to pull. We got off and walked. We weren't hauling any gear except for a diaper change and a bottle of water. We learned something there. Hills were out of the question. We could only bike on flat and extremely gentle terrain.

We dove into cycling with our child cold turkey. We went for a few short rides and then began making plans to ride the entire 185-mile Chesapeake & Ohio (C&O) Canal trail from Cumberland, Maryland, to Washington, D.C. With campsites and water every five miles and level to downhill terrain, this route made our initiation into the sport easy. The riding was much easier than we expected. There were some ruts where the ground turned muddy during a rain and then hardened.

On some rail trails, there are lots of historical things to keep the trip interesting. These are excellent places for a family adventure. For variety, you can pedal into nearby towns for treats. Parks are often located in these areas; one of you can stay behind with youngsters and gear while the other goes in search of treats like ice cream and pizza (for the salt!). The C&O Canal trail had boat locks, lock houses, stone aqueducts, replicas of barge boats, etc. The trail was easy enough for a child of young bike-riding age to cover the distance needed for an extended trip.

In some areas, the bike trails consist of lots of black-topped roads that are being reclaimed by the forest. When the asphalt peters out and turns into sand, you will immediately feel the difference of the weight of a child. A child in the bike seat makes your rear wheel drag in the sand, and a bike trailer is like pulling a ball and chain behind you. Your steering is affected too, so you may have to reroute. Toting children on sand does not work. Even getting off and pushing them for any length of time is laborious. This is one thing to be cautious of when riding in coastal areas, which is a very attractive place to ride.

Biking around campground parks, where the services and the facilities are spread out, is very convenient. You can bike to a nature trail, and the kids will delight in stretching their legs and doing a new activity. When you are through hiking, your child won't be the least bit reluctant to get back into the trailer. You can also ride over to a playground, because children are always ready for a swing and a slide. This combining of activities is really very enjoyable for the kids, and keeps them much happier longer.

In some parts of the country, there are many many miles of packed-dirt roads which may not see traffic for days and, hence, will not make you uncomfortable taking your children on them. Coastal states are good places to look for biking opportunities, as are lakeshores, and, of course, converted rail trails. One thing you have to be cautious about in areas like this is the wind, which children never enjoy.

The most wonderful part of many rail trails is the fabulous swimming. If the water is clean and shallow, it will be tepid in many places, enabling you to sit out on flat rocks and let the kids play by the sides—throwing stones, finding snails, digging in the riverbank sand, etc. It's a good idea to have some sort of water shoe or sports sandal for your kids so they can walk around the river and stream bottoms without danger or care. Playing in streams and rivers is really living to a kid. And this is one of the most wonderful assets of rail trails: they are often along flowing bodies of water.

A good time of year to cycle with your kids if they are not yet of school age is September when the parks and campgrounds are very empty. The cooler temperatures make it easier on everyone too.

Touring Inn to Inn

A family cycling vacation, an adventure where you can do something memorable in someplace exquisitely beautiful, requires a safe place that is friendly and ideal for cycling and contains enough wonder to keep your kids entertained. Other countries and cultures are very open to families traveling with children. They enjoy the young ones and seem more tolerant of children's behavior. Your children will find playmates everywhere that they go, regardless of the language.

The relatively untraveled, untouched area of western Ireland with its misty mountains, thatched cottages, and fairytale castles fit the bill for Joe Parker and his family. They planned to be on the road for seventeen days and cover 450 miles, while averaging 35 miles per day. Joe's wife, Maria, pulled their four-year-old-daughter, Claire, in a trailer, and Joe captained eight-year-old Paul on a tandem bike, which was equipped with a "child-stoker kit" to raise the rear pedals so he could help power the bike. A support van transported their luggage and eased their burden.

The Parkers did not carry full gear on their bikes and in their trailer. They did not do any camping and carried only essentials. Joe feels traveling with children is enough work in itself. To ride all day in the rain, as they did in Ireland, and then have to set up camp would have buried them. Staying at bed-and-breakfasts took away one large hardship, provided one less thing to worry about.

Each day's specific route was decided upon at breakfast, and some nights they just winged it without reservations for lodgings. Accommodations included bed-and-breakfasts, farms, and a castle. They tried to remain flexible to give themselves the freedom a traveling family needs. Stopping at local pubs was a very big part of the magic and success of their trip because they used them for diversion as well as for nourishment. The pubs also offered them a much-needed break from the unexpected frequent rains.

In Ireland, people are so very accepting of families and children. You are just as likely to find a child behind the family-run country pubs as an adult. If your children get loud and rambunctious, it is better tolerated than in the States. Because the children were in their separate spaces most of the day, very little bickering went on compared to at home. There was so much to do, so many new things to experience, every day was a new adventure.

For those who cannot consider a European cycle tour with their kids, there are options closer to home. Hostels date back to 1909 when German school teacher Richard Schirrman began the movement so that young people and adults could travel freely and inexpensively from country to country and stay in hostels everywhere. There are now over 100,000 worldwide and more than 200 in the United States. Members can find accommodations for as low as $8 a night in their traditional bunkrooms, including kitchen facilities, but many hostels now have private rooms for couples and families at a higher rate.

There are two ways you can plan a cycling adventure using hostels. One way is to use them as a base of operation and go on day trips departing from there. Many hostels are located in an area where there are a lot of varied rides to take. Many hostels do not allow you to hang around all day (although the large ones, as in Washington, D.C., have a day room), but you can store your things there and return after your day's ride.

The other way is to incorporate the hostels into your trip as you would a motel stop. It is difficult to stay in hostels 100 percent of the time, because there aren't enough of them in most places. (Although in the Pacific Northwest they are so plentiful, it would not be difficult to revolve your trip around them.) But you could camp some nights, and also motel or bed-and-breakfast it, in addition to using hostels for your accommodations. Decide on the mileage you can and want to do and plan your overnight stops around them.

Once you join a hosteling organization (family membership is $35 and renewal is $25), you will receive a book listing the hostels and all the pertinent information on them. Once you decide on the area you'd like to visit, call to see if those hostels are open and if you need reservations. In the summer, the hostels in the cities or in populated areas may be booked well in advance. You should not have that problem, however, with hostels that are located in rural or remote areas.

The American Youth Hostels Association also has Discovery Tours that are open to families with children over thirteen years of age. Your family will have very enriching experiences as they meet new people and are placed in new environments and cultures.

The Strauss family went on cycling trips that took them into towns where the kids could eat "normal" food and spent their nights in American Youth Hostels where they could socialize with other traveling children. For the kids, it was the best of both worlds.

Safety

Riding Safely

Make sure everyone knows the rules of the road and practices them. When traveling on paved roads with traffic, it is an especially good idea to put an adult in the lead and one in the rear. The adult's larger size will provide greater visibility for traffic.

Riding directly behind each other in order to have conversation is not a good idea on a rough-surfaced trail. It does not give you enough lead time to avoid rocks and roots and ruts that come up. The proper space that allows you to scope out the surface ahead of you is too far to hear conversation. Riding side by side is only possible if the trail is not crowded and you can see ahead.

If you are traveling on a trail that allows walkers, etc., remain in single file when sharing the trail, use your bell, and announce aloud "bikes on the left" as you pass around them.

Road Hazards

One day, we had to take a detour on black-topped roads because a flood had permanently destroyed part of the trail. There were hills on the detour route. Would Todd be able to physically pull that loaded trailer up the hills and would he be able to hold it back on the downhills? He had to ride with extreme caution because the roads were busy and narrow and vehicles couldn't swing out around us to pass. The experience was enough to make us realize that with such small children, roads with vehicles were not the way we wanted to go.

On another day, we had to cross a pedestrian trestle bridge over railroad tracks and had to ascend and descend a set of metal stairs to reach it. Todd needed help to carry the trailer and our bikes up the stairs. We felt very uncomfortable leaving gear behind down below, especially our baby, while I helped Todd, so my assistance was not an option. I had to stay with the cargo. I asked a group of people, "Would someone mind helping my husband carry our trailer up?" and one young, strong man flatly said, "No!" Another said he would "later," and didn't stop to explain what "later" meant. I kept asking until someone was kind enough to help. Whenever you're out on the open road, it's best to be as self-sufficient as possible, but sometimes you just need other people, and you need to be humble enough to ask.

Trailer Safety

You have to be very aware of different things when pulling a trailer. Be conscious of where those trailer tires will run, and steer so that tree roots or rocks are in between them. This often means that your bike tires will hit the object, but this is a lot safer. A very bumpy and rutty trail really disturbs your passengers, especially if they are tired. Ride very slowly over such terrain and try to avoid as many objects as possible to keep your child happy and comfortable. During the first day or so of pulling a trailer, use extra caution because you're not used to thinking about where the trailer's wheels are.

I wasn't keeping this in mind early in one trip, and got one wheel close to a twenty-foot drop-off above a river at times. Todd was riding behind me and would warn me. Some sections of the Greenbrier River Trail in West Virginia are built up very high above the river and if it were an automobile road, it would definitely have a guard rail on it.

Be careful not to flip the trailer. One time, Sierra was in the child seat and Todd was barreling along at a fast pace, not bothering to look for rocks and roots, and flipped the trailer, *boom,* just like that. We were happy that Sierra was not in it but felt confident that it probably would not have happened if she were, because Todd rides much more cautiously at those times. Still, it was a good experience to see what could make it happen and how it actually flips.

Because the rail trails are often constructed with a built-up bed, many picnic and campsites are located below you. The rail trails are often uneven surfaces and the ground can be hidden by high weeds and grass, leaving you unable to predict how the trailer will react. It is better to simply take your child out to go up and down these inclines, and it is easier on both of you. I dumped Bryce in the trailer once while going down such an incline off the side of a rail trail. Bryce's trailer rolled over on its side and I stopped and plopped the whole thing back up. He wasn't fazed. Bryce could have just as easily walked down himself in this instance.

We usually kept a waist belt on our two-year-old in the trailer—at least at first. For four-year-old Sierra, we did not bother. They both listened well and remained seated. One time, however, Bryce was not buckled in and began to get out of the trailer when we stopped for a break. We weren't aware of this and changed our minds about the area to rest in a few moments after we initially stopped. When we began to move again, Bryce had already begun to get out and fell to the ground once the trailer began to move—running over his body. He wasn't hurt badly. The cart wasn't that heavy with him out of it, and only one tire ran over him. If he had had his seat belt on, however, it would not have occurred.

Weather Conditions

During inclement weather, the children might be in the trailer longer than they'd prefer. You can try to ride for a greater period of time then, because resting in the rain is an uncomfortable experience. Breaks do not last as long either.

Heat

There is always a breeze blowing when you're riding. Even at 105 degrees Fahrenheit on the C&O Canal trail, we were all comfortable as long as we were moving. Our faces were slightly damp from perspiration but our constant movement kept us cool. We only noticed the heat when we stopped for a break, and then we headed for the water to soak our heads and shirts or to swim.

Wind

Wind and rain storms can be a very difficult thing to deal with, especially if you are pulling a load and if you have young children aboard. It can scare them and make them very uncomfortable. If children are exposed on a child seat, they can only put their heads down and try to shield their faces and tough it out. This is when a bike trailer that closes completely up is so wonderful.

Listening to the forecast is something you should always do, for safety reasons, especially when dealing with coastal weather. Experiencing storms is an education for all and it is the stuff that memories are made up of, but they can be very dangerous if you are unprepared. Adults can push themselves through a lot, but not children, and it's very unsettling for parents to make their children endure such hardship.

We were out on Chincoteague Island in Virginia when we got hit by fierce winds and blowing sand. Sierra moved to the trailer with her brother, which was designed for two. But it was so crowded and they were under such stress, they were miserable. There were no protected places to get out of the storm, so we just had to persevere and close our ears to the crying. The storm we were caught in was a hurricane that was teasing the shore. Had we listened to the forecast we could have made other plans.

Rain

Long, soaking, cold rain (late September) is weather you can't have your kids out in. There is no sense in staying. If the weather turns really bad and stays that way consistently, you have no choice but to abandon your plans. If you keep a watch on the weather and notice it deteriorating, it's a good idea to seek out shelter or keep your eyes open for it as you proceed.

When it is raining, choose your breaks according to what the weather is doing and let the kids out of the trailers when the rain ceases, or when you find some shelter, such as an overhanging ledge or a porch of a vacant summer home. You might toy with the idea of remaining under the shelter you've found and camping right there and foregoing riding in the rain, but it is much more difficult to entertain children who are stuck in one spot for a long period of time—be it a tent or a barn or a porch. To continue often ends up being the lesser of the two evils.

During stormy weather, of all times, sleep is very easily induced—your children are warm in their moving trailers, and they know they can't get out for awhile. It gives the parents an advantage to cover some distance, because they don't have to expend energy on dealing with the kids.

A bad electrical storm came up on us one day along the Greenbrier River Trail. We had just finished swimming when the sky darkened and the wind picked up considerably. We took cover in a hay barn whose roof was very high and all four sides were open. The rain fell so hard and the wind blew so violently that it came in horizontally and seemingly on all four sides. We sought shelter between the hay bales, ate high-energy snacks, and held the kids.

What we thought would be a rather quickly passing storm turned into many hours of rain. The sky did not brighten and clear but continued to rain softly. Because it was important for us to get to our destination for the day, we decided to ride in the rain. We wore our rain jackets and left our pants off, because the heat that we generated from riding warmed our legs. The children were snug and dry and warm in the bike trailers.

Family Cycling

Grasp every opportunity for fun and diversion, even if it takes time from cycling. As in any sport, children are not motivated by reaching goals but live entirely in the present. They will be happier and more content if you embrace this philosophy.

Although you might not always feel like you need a rest, stop frequently, especially where there's water. Kids and water just naturally go hand in hand. Many rail trails follow rivers, providing a great and frequent place to cool off on a break. Just be careful the river is not deep or swift, or polluted. We usually just put our feet in or sat in the shallows.

On our way through Virginia to the C&O Canal trail, we stopped at a picnic site with a stream by its side. Sierra and I held hands and happily walked up the streambed, sometimes stepping on top of the big, flat, exposed rocks, sometimes walking right in the water. Sierra loves to take her shoes off and splash in the water. We let her slop in a creek whenever she could. (We brought two pairs of shoes along—open sandals and sneakers for when her feet needed protection.) Todd and I learned shortly after we arrived there to strip them down as soon as they got close to water. Both kids fell into the shallow water and totally soaked their cotton clothes, making them colder than in their bare skin. It is too much of a nuisance for us to put their bathing suits on every time we get near water, so we just either keep their underpants on or take everything off. I believe that if a child cannot run around free and naked and swim in their youth in the wilds, they are missing out on a great joy of childhood. If we are in a remote area and are alone with our family, mom and dad may even join in.

Besides swimming, there were the turtles to enjoy, the butterflies, and the intoxicating sweet fragrance of the wild flame azaleas and the pinkster azaleas, the autumn olive, the honeysuckle, the multiflora rose, and the countless other flowers and flowering shrubs that filled the air with their perfume. And always that river, wide and rolling to our side, framed by the high Allegheny Mountains. And the chance to be together in this beauty with our children. The sore bottoms and the rain and the tight thigh muscles all fell to the background in this picture.

Babies

The earliest you should take a baby on a ride is when it can fit into a helmet and is strong enough to hold its head up—about six to eight months. At this age, your infant is not yet ready to ride in a child seat on your bike, but babies can ride in their car seat or other carrier placed inside a trailer. They will need to be well strapped into the carrier and the carrier must be well strapped into the trailer. They seem to enjoy the movement and the rolling along, looking at the leaves in the trees and the wind and the light. Their needs remain the same as in normal life—diaper changes, nourishment, etc. Sleep isn't usually ever a problem with this age and they sleep when they feel the urge. The important thing is to make sure they are warm and protected from the sun, if you are riding in open sunny areas.

Young Children

Averaging thirty to thirty-five miles a day isn't usually a problem. Your days will likely be filled up, though, with the frequent stops. They are necessary for your child as much as for you. Todd and I never got fully rested unless we laid down on our breaks. Our rear ends were beginning to ache so sitting to rest was out of the question and standing isn't too rejuvenating.

One of the most difficult things to plan is your schedule. To a great extent, your children are in charge. When they need to get out, their wishes should be respected. You can push them, but there is a definite limit. What you don't want to do is to make them dislike being there. At first, you can't be sure how long your child will allow you to ride in a day, so bring along extra provisions.

A youngster of a year and a half or so is comfortable in the trailer about an hour or so. In that amount of time, you could probably cover five miles. Then you might have to take an hour-long break with lots of walking, cuddling, snacking, and swimming. With a schedule like this, you might get in about six hours of riding (thirty-plus miles per day) and six hours of playing and resting a day.

Keeping small children entertained while you cycle can be a challenge. Point out things as you ride, such as airplanes flying overhead, crows cawing, turtles sunning themselves on rocks, etc., so your child learns to be observant and is better able to entertain him or herself when older. Point out baby duckies, snakes, and turtles on the path. There was a remarkable difference in what grasped and held the attention of our two children. Todd and I both pointed out many things of interest to each child, but four-year-old Sierra could focus and see what we were explaining far better than Bryce.

Pick wild flowers for them to hold, walnuts to play with in a cup, and long strips of sycamore bark to crack and break apart. Play peek-a-boo as you ride, dropping back behind your partner's trailer to hide behind the trailer roof. Give the kids a sippee cup of water, which you can tie to the trailer with a nylon cord, to splash with when days are hot or to feed to a doll. Just be sure the cord isn't so long that the toy can get tangled in spokes or run over.

A nice toy for in the trailer or child seat is a pinwheel. The child can hold it or mount it somehow to the trailer nearby so he or she can watch it and enjoy it as you ride. On breaks, young children may be more interested in gathering walnuts, pine cones, and small green wild apples and putting them in a cooking pot than with the toys that you bring along. Reserve them for tent play.

Bryce didn't need many toys to keep him happy. Besides the scenery going by, he enjoyed playing with his small metal cars and trucks in the trailer. The same went for our friends' grandson, Solomon, who enjoyed playing with his plastic movable figures that he brought along. He sang to himself a lot too, which he really enjoys. Many times, I'd look back at Bryce and he'd be examining where the trailer was attached to the bike, or was staring down at the ground as it moved quickly by. The close-up, nearby world held much more fascination for him at his age. Spatial relationships did not make entire sense to him yet.

Sierra had her teddy which she'd talk to and show things to. She is a talker and discussed things with me as she rode. This wasn't always the easiest thing for me to do, because riding on a gravel surface can be very noisy. Bryce, on the other hand, is happier entertaining himself. With both types of personalities, the children were usually happy in the trailer. We don't usually keep them in there long enough for them to become very bored and we usually stop often enough and long enough to keep them occupied.

Extreme and prolonged fussiness might mean that your child is tired and needs to nap. Your child might not look very active while riding in the trailer, but it is fatiguing none the less. Compare it with riding in a bumpy jeep. Your body grows fatigued from the motion as you try to keep your body centered and steady. Don't underestimate a child's need to nap on a trip, especially if the surface you are riding on is bumpy. The fresh air, the activity, and the jostling simply fatigues them.

It's important that you make the trailer as comfortable as possible for napping. It is difficult for your children to nap in a trailer that they are sharing with a sibling. A stuff sack of clothes pounded into a triangular shape fits in the corner of the trailer seat where your child can lean against this sloped surface while still in the seat belt, and lay his or her head down whenever he or she feels sleepy. If another child were there in the seat, there would be no place to rest their heads. One of our trailers has high fabric sides with clear plastic windows, making it easy and comfortable to lean their sleepy head right on it. The other trailer does not and so must have a stuff sack of soft items wedged in the corner to lean against.

The harness must be positioned just right. It can work up to your child's neck when he or she becomes fatigued and slouches down, choking your child slightly. Rework it so it just goes around the waist during naps and not over the head. When your child is very small, you can strap him or her in a car seat right in the trailer, without bothering to prop up his or her body.

When our children were four and two years old, we were anxious to go on another bike trip while they were still small and light enough to easily pull. The weight on this trip was evenly divided, with each of us pulling a trailer, gear, and a child. My trailer and its contents maxed out at 100 pounds and Todd's maxed out at 150.

We planned on three days to do the seventy-five-mile Greenbrier River Trail, and we didn't think this would be a problem at all. But things do not always turn out as planned. The shuttle took six hours on account of the incredibly winding, steep grades. Right from the beginning, it left us with a half day gone.

There had been severe flood damage done to the trail a few years back and reconstruction work was in full swing when we were on it. In many places, the surface was not packed down very well from continuous use, and it was difficult and slow at times to pull the trailers through the loose gravel. It felt like you were plowing through oatmeal. (In a few instances, the surface had been laid the week or the day before!)

As soon as we realized that a large chunk of our available riding time was eaten up by the shuttle, and the going would be slower and more difficult than we anticipated, we had to rethink our schedule and our pace. We realized that "pushing" would be required to reach our goal. We still rested every hour, rarely went beyond the five-mile mark before taking a break, and enjoyed at least one two-hour swim every afternoon. But we still had to do our miles when we may have felt like resting more. This re-evaluating is a common need on any trip because factors change and the unexpected crops up. You must always remain flexible and be ready to adjust. When children and other companions are involved, more needs and considerations often crop up and can complicate things.

Hints and Tips

- Choose areas to visit where you have the option to change plans en route.
- Adjust your itinerary, mileage, etc., according to the evolving needs of your group.
- Periodically examine your schedule/plan and make changes if necessary.
- Energy levels, lack of sleep, and inclement weather all contribute to schedules gone haywire. Build in bail-outs, alternatives, etc.

■ If an alternative is not available (or very attractive), try to cover the distance in the least painful way (i.e., move quickly, do not stop when kids are asleep, etc.).

Older Kids

Although the Parkers are avid cyclists, they waited until their children were older for their family's first cycling vacation, so they would be more aware of their surroundings, be more controllable, and be more involved in the whole adventure. They feel a child younger than four years old is too difficult to please and too difficult to reason with.

Although they were cursing the rain on their Ireland tour and some of the more difficult days got them down, the way their family bonded over those seventeen days was invaluable. There is a big difference between a typical family vacation, where you travel in a car and are insulated from nature and the world you are traveling in, and an adventure. There is no tour guide giving you an itinerary. You need to make many decisions daily. Some of it rubs off onto your children and provides them with a tremendous learning experience.

The Parkers' four-year-old daughter, Claire, was quite comfortable in her trailer and looked on it as her own little rolling room. She lined the inside with stuffed animals and books, and it lulled her to sleep (too often sometimes, giving her too much energy in the evenings when mom and dad were ready to rest). When the rains wouldn't let up, she rode in the van and gave mom a break from pulling the fifty-five-pound load.

Their eight-year-old son, Paul, did very well riding on the tandem, considering he had to continue pedaling. Even the rain did not dampen his spirits, for the most part.

Sometimes you have to push your children to their limits or slightly beyond because of unforeseen changes. No parent enjoys doing this to their child and no child enjoys experiencing this. But it is part of any adventure and it needs to be embraced and dealt with, along with the joy and ease. It teaches children good lessons too. The important thing is to know where to draw the line, never jeopardizing their health and safety. And often we can make it easier for them to get through it.

Paul Parker was pushed close to his limit only one time on their Ireland trip. The rain was falling hard and cold and every ten minutes he asked how much longer it would be until the ride was over. His father explained that they had no alternative but to keep going because the van was already at the bed-and-breakfast for the night. They had to get there under their own power. They refueled at a pub with a sandwich and Paul was much better able to continue.

It is hard to get Paul on the tandem at home, Joe admitted—not exciting enough. But on their Ireland trip, Paul was really into the cycling. Joe had very small-scale maps on which they highlighted that day's route every morning. It provided excellent incentive for Paul and gave him a real sense of accomplishment that helped him continue through the seventeen days.

Joe is not used to being with his family twenty-four hours a day, as many fathers are not, but he did truly enjoy it. Kids are only kids for a short time and the memories you create will last a lifetime. Now, Joe hopes there will be more of these cycling family adventures, and soon. His dream is to get two tandems and ride across the country with his family. He feels the ages of ten to fifteen are the best, for the children are perfectly capable of doing the miles physically, will learn a huge amount, and are still connected enough to their parents to enjoy their company.

Family Touring Tips

Joe Parker offers the following:
1. Do a few shake-down day trips before departing to give them a sense of spending time in the saddle. Outfit your bike exactly as it will be outfitted for the tour.
2. If you'll be pulling a trailer or cranking a fully loaded bike, then train that way.
3. Make them responsible for their own stuff (packing, carrying suitcases, etc.). You'll go crazy otherwise.
4. Bring any special medicine they might need (don't depend on doctors abroad) and carry a good first-aid kit.
5. Realize that children don't view cycling like you do. They're not interested in building fitness, losing weight, or improving performance. They have but one criteria for enjoyment: fun.
6. Involve the children in planning both before and during the trip. Let them make some route or accommodations decisions.
7. Scale back daily mileage to half or a third of what you normally do.
8. Stop for breaks often.
9. Encourage them to drink plenty of water and eat frequently. Small bodies deplete quickly.
10. Don't make them adhere to the same strict high-carbo diet you do. Kids need some fat.
11. Dress them a bit warmer than you do yourself. Kids generally have less body fat and chill quicker on a bike.
12. Encourage them to decorate their bikes and trailers with things they find. By the end of the Parkers' trip, the rear of

the tandem was adorned with feathers, twigs, pins, bells, buttons, and other treasures. Let them play.

13. Buy them an inexpensive single-use camera so they can take their own photographs.
14. Encourage them to keep a trip diary, complete with sketches and taped-in treasures.
15. Highlight your daily progress on a small-scale map to instill a sense of grand accomplishment.

Adolescents

At this age, they are moving closer toward being an equal, a contributor, and it's important for the parent to recognize this and allow and encourage it to happen. Parents need to be tuned into subtle changes in their child and move in the direction that their child is interested in.

Things changed for the Strauss family when their boys reached the ages of eleven and thirteen; being just with mom and dad and their younger sister in the wilderness wasn't enough anymore. Their own interests became stronger and they had a clearer idea of what they thought was fun.

The boys were into their bikes, learning how to fix them and care for them and propelling them down the road. Their new strong bodies needed to be tested and pushed. Their parents, Frank and Lila, were fond of backpacking, but believed they would have to do a little bending if they wanted their boys to happily vacation with the family in the outdoors. So they switched their backpacks for bikes.

The boys' love of the sport was enhanced by the fact that they knew how to repair and condition their bikes—more so than their parents—and this empowered them. Many kids love machines and there is nothing that can go faster and longer on a bike than a fourteen-year-old. Their parents knew that, at this age, it was important to their children to know they were contributing something worthwhile, playing an important role, and not just following mom and dad along and doing what they said. This led to their playing a larger role in planning and executing their cycling adventure too.

Hints and Tips

- Test out your sizable equipment before you invest in it, because this sport's good-quality gear is not inexpensive.
- Know your needs. Make sure the gear fits them.
- This is one sport where the rules (of the road) must be followed to a tee. Enforce them. Your child's life may depend on it.

- Remember that pulling a loaded trailer severely limits what kind of terrain you can comfortably and safely traverse. Stick to flat and very gently rolling country.
- Make the trailer as comfortable as possible for napping. A rested child isn't just a happy child, it's a happy parent too.

CHAPTER 11

Canoeing

▲ ▲ ▲ ▲ ▲ ▲ ▲ ▲ ▲ ▲

*T*ruly unforgettable experiences are shared by a family while canoeing along the banks of a lake, such as seeing carp spawning in the shallow waters. The children can reach down and touch them as the canoe quietly moves through the water. You might see beavers, mergansers, western grebes, and deer watching from the banks; you are truly at an advantage for seeing wildlife when you glide noiselessly through the water. This is the part of canoeing that all children love.

Equipment

Canoe, Paddles, and Related Gear

For your family outings, choose a canoe that is stable, is a good load carrier, and is easy to paddle. It should be at least sixteen to eighteen feet long, at least thirty-four inches wide, and thirteen inches deep in the center. This type of "tripping" canoe will accommodate a family of four, including two young children, and their gear for an extended trip. Once your children get older and are able to paddle well, a family of four will have to travel in two canoes.

Shoot for a lightweight paddle that is shoulder height and no higher than your chin. Carry an extra paddle in the stern. Junior paddles come in two lengths—thirty-six inches and forty-two inches. This is a very important piece of equipment for your child, although you might think he or she is not contributing much to moving you further along. Before long, with a little practice, your children will be able to contribute significantly. It makes them feel part of the adventure too. Adult paddles are too big and clumsy for them and their interest won't kindle nearly as quickly if there isn't an appropriately sized paddle for them to practice with.

Comfortable seats and back rests to lean against make life much more enjoyable for your canoeing children (and you!).

Racks and Canoe Carriers

Choose a canoe rack for your vehicle that can be used for more than one sport if possible (such as carrying your bicycles) if you are a family who enjoys the outdoors.

If you will be doing a trip which includes some portages, you'll

need to carry your canoe on your shoulders. Many canoes come with an optional built-in yoke for carrying. Pack plenty of padding for protecting your shoulders and an efficient method of carrying your gear (and babies too—a child carrier).

Personal Flotation Devices (PFDs)

Of course, personal flotation devices (PFDs) should be worn at all times and they should be U.S. Coast Guard approved. Adults need to keep theirs on too, no matter how strong a swimmer they are. At the very least, they need to set a good example. When kids are trying on PFDs, have them sit down to do it. They seldom will wear them standing up. Some shapes and designs of vests are cut differently and are more uncomfortable than others.

We did not try one-year-old Bryce's new life jacket on him before purchasing it because he was six pounds below the upper figure of recommended weight. When we first put it on him during a canoe trip, it pushed his head up high and enveloped his entire neck. I had to squeeze it together to get it to zip. The confinement was not to his liking. It is much better to have your child try the PFD before you are out on an excursion.

Marcia and John Barla also had trouble with their baby's PFD. Michael was also in the infant style that had a handle behind the head for lifting the baby out of the water should it go overboard. But it was too small for him, even though he too was well within the weight range. They too neglected to try on his PFD before leaving on their first outing of the year. Mike had outgrown it over the winter, and actually needed the next size up.

Clothing

Clothing for canoeing need not be anything special or different than your all-round outdoor gear: Polypro underwear, pile for insulation and warmth, etc. Your feet will get wetter in this sport, so it's important to have appropriate footgear. Sports sandals are excellent choices if the water and air are not too cold. They allow your feet to dry. Old sneakers (with or without holes) are another choice, but they can hold in water and chills. Rubber boots or boots with leather uppers and rubber bottoms are great if you are canoeing in cooler climates or anytime other than in the heat of summer. Children are not happy when they are cold and wet, and wet feet can make their whole body feel miserable, especially if they are not exerting.

Remember that the younger your children are, the wetter they can become. Have more than a change of clothing along for anything longer than a day trip. To keep the kids warm when canoeing in Canada, Mom Newman brought along their snowsuits.

John Moran began his two- and three-year-old girls canoeing by getting them initially psyched with their "canoe outfits." His wife sewed "Holly Hobbit" outfits of cool, comfortable cotton—long-sleeved blouses, pants, and matching bonnets to protect them from the sun. Plus, they looked like their heroines on *Little House on the Prairie.*

Rain Gear

Canoeing in the rain can be very unpleasant for anyone, but especially for children. Good rain gear is essential, because the young ones are not expending much energy. Ponchos do not work well in canoes because of the wind which often accompanies rain. Your basic, well-ventilated, seam-sealed rain suit that is versatile for any sport is recommended. Look for a hood that has a tightly drawn and protected neck enclosure. Bring along a hat with a brim for sun and rain. Wet suits may be necessary in cold weather; if you do not want to invest in them for growing children, canoe only during warm weather.

Watertight Packing Gear

Packing your gear is extremely important because you must keep your extra clothing dry. Package complete clothing outfits in individual resealable plastic bags so that all of your children's pants, or all of their shirts, etc., don't get wet. Some families put their clothing and other things that need to be kept dry into five-gallon plastic buckets with snap-tight lids.

Dry bags are the very best way to go, where the tops of vinyl or nylon bags are rolled down and fastened to prevent any water from seeping in. If you do not have dry bags, you can also keep your belongings dry by double bagging them in plastic bags and "goose necking" their openings. Gather the opening and twist it tightly. Then loop it around (like a "goose neck") and tie it off with a long, sturdy twist tie. Then, you must just watch out for punctures.

Choosing an Outing

Before you begin to plan a trip, be certain that you have mastered the basic skills of canoeing and that all children are Red Cross "water safe" or can swim. You'll need access to a boat if you don't have one.

If you plan your trip in the summer months to a popular area, you'll most likely have a lot of company. From late August, September, and October, there will be fewer bugs in the northern climates. Bugs and people are usually gone after Labor Day. You can also get on the water in early June before the bugs and crowds hit. But later in the year the water is much warmer—something to consider with young children who easily get wet and love to play in water.

In a family with small children, where the parents are the chief movers of the canoe and must do all the portaging, plan to cover between five and ten miles per day and no more than fifty miles in a seven-day week. Stick to a chain of small lakes for a young family's first trip, which are connected by very small portages of, say, a quarter mile long.

Once your skills move from basic to moderate, you'll be able to tackle rivers where the water volume and gradient increase to four to eight miles an hour. With this comes the danger of downed trees or "sweeps," low dams, etc. You will need to know how to read the river, spotting obstacles ahead and knowing how to safely maneuver around them.

In choosing an outing, start small and build up. Pick the safest, most gentle of locations to travel in: quiet, meandering streams, a small lakeshore, protected, quiet waters. Go on day trips and then a short weekend at first to familiarize your family to the sport and see how they handle the restrictions that the canoe and the water impose.

You'll want to first visit sheltered waterways or canals where there is some population (compared to wilder routes), in case you need assistance. As your skills, conditioning, and experience build up, you'll be able to tackle longer trips into more remote wilderness areas.

Once you decide to go on an extended trip (a week or longer) which encompasses overnight camping, decide on the area you'd like to visit. See if there is an outfitter in the area from whom you can rent equipment and get a detailed route and map for a trip. If you are planning your own extended canoe trip, allow for inclement weather and high winds by padding the schedule with off days. Every other day is free to hike, paddle up a side drainage, or just hole up in the tent, waiting out inclement weather. With these built-in down days, you *can* paddle every day if you have lost too much time, say, waiting out a storm.

One of the worst things is to start off too ambitiously. Start with an outing that is short and easy, something you can bail out of. Parents must be extremely conservative when it comes to submitting their children to certain paddling experiences. They must be very skilled themselves if they are going to increase the risk and danger factors. We are sometimes too careless with our children's lives. Drowning happens too easily. Young children should not be subjected to their parents' adventurous desires if they are frightened and not capable of understanding what to do if their lives become endangered.

Never go on a solo canoe trip when children are present; plan on a minimum of three canoes (if this is not possible, two are better than one). Because parents' first responsibility is to their children, they could be busy tending to their needs and more easily get into trouble—like losing a paddle and hitting a strainer—if they are not paying attention. If you are far from civilization, you are more at risk. Other canoeists in your group can be a tremendous help in these situations.

Canoeing in a group or with friends that include other adults is very beneficial because, unlike hiking, where you can aim for loop hikes and use only one car or just retrace your steps, in canoeing, you need to shuttle upriver to your pick-up point.

If your family chooses canoe outings without anyone but the immediate family, you will not be able to run rivers that do not enable you to paddle back upstream to your vehicle. You can get around this by canoeing on canals and on very gentle-moving waterways like tidal streams near a coast.

Canoe club outings may be a good place to gain experience as a family. It depends on the nature of the club and where its interest lies. Some clubs have members who are very strong and experienced and paddle hard and fast with their goal—the end of the run—held clear in their minds. This style isn't so good for families with young children who impose frequent interruptions. If the club is sensitive to families, you are very fortunate. Some clubs have programs designed for the kids—silly races and things that get the children used to canoeing and draw them closer to the other members.

Water Classifications

There are six classes of water conditions: Easy, Novice, Intermediate, Advanced, Expert, and Extreme.

Class I—Easy. Fast-moving water with riffles and small waves. Few obstructions, all obvious and easily missed with little training. Risk to swimmers is slight; self-rescue is easy.

Class II—Novice. Straightforward rapids with wide, clear channels which are evident without scouting. Occasional maneuvering may be required, but rocks and medium-sized waves are easily missed by trained paddlers. Swimmers are seldom injured and group assistance, while helpful, is seldom needed.

Class III—Intermediate (difficult). Long rapids requiring extensive maneuvering. Waves and ledges are up to three feet high and waves are often irregular. Course is not always recognizable. Rescue opportunities are spaced further apart.

Class IV—Advanced (very difficult). Extended sets of rapids where boulders and ledges block the course. There may be powerful crosscurrents, requiring abrupt and intricate turns. Scouting is often necessary and rescue is difficult.

Class V—Expert (exceedingly difficult). Long, heavy rapids with high, irregular waves and powerful crosscurrents, or steep, complex, boulder-clogged rapids with poor visibility. Turbulence and big drops are unavoidable and rescue is very difficult.

Class VI—Extreme (utmost difficulty). Class V characteristics only more extreme. Running this water poses an extreme risk to life.

Nothing greater than Class I should ever be attempted with any young child on board, no matter how skilled the adults are. Young children can demand your attention at a second's notice. In that second, you may need to maneuver around a stringer or a rock and you can't be doing two things at once.

Safety

Know Basic Skills

To safely navigate quiet sheltered water, know your basic canoeing strokes. They can be self-taught with a good manual or, better yet, through formal instruction. Take a canoe course before taking your children out. Inquire through the American Canoe Association (ACA) where the closest canoe club is. If they do not run courses or if they are too far away, find out where the closest member is and try to work out some sort of way to get the instruction from them. (See appendix B, Organizations.)

You'll need to learn and decide which side is your strongest and most natural for you to paddle on, and then stick to that side. One should not be changing sides at random. You will learn how your strokes complement your partner's and learn to work together, not against, toward moving your canoe in a straight line.

Your outside hand grasps the paddle halfway down, while the other hand covers the top of the handle. Your power should come from your top hand as the bottom one guides the paddle and keeps it away from the canoe. Don't just use your arms for power, but let your entire upper body contribute to the stroke.

The paddler in the bow position (front) is the person whose chief purpose is to power the boat through the water. The stern paddler's most important job is steering and keeping the canoe moving in a straight line. This is accomplished by using the J stroke—your wrist is twisted, and a hook away from your body and boat is added to the normal power stroke. In the stern pry, the blade is turned upward at the end of the power stroke and the paddle pulled, as though you were prying the water. All paddlers need to learn both bow and stern strokes. Once your children begin to paddle, your positions in the canoe may change.

A draw is used when you want to pull your end of the canoe over. You plant your paddle, wide end facing the canoe's length, into the water and pull toward you and the boat. If this stroke is done on the same side by both paddlers, the canoe will make a turn. This stroke is necessary for moving your boat into a shore or moving around on tight streams or rivers.

If the wind comes up and you are unable to make headway and need more stability, have the paddlers move down off their seats, especially the bowman.

Be competent in Class I water. Mitch Newman, canoe instructor for ACA for twenty-plus years, believes your child, as well as you, should take a River Course before attempting Class II.

Make sure you don't overload your canoe. You need to have a minimum of six inches of freeboard showing above the water after it is fully loaded.

One of the most important things young children in a canoe must be made to realize is that they absolutely must sit still or they can tip the canoe. Make sure your kids know the basics of water safety, and if they're old enough, make sure they know how to swim.

All children love to lean over the gunwales of a canoe and play in the water. John Moran continually reminded his two young girls to keep their hands in, because it put the canoe out of balance. They always stopped when he mentioned it, but the attraction was too great and they always had to be asked not to do it many times during a trip. That is, until they were in the Okefanokee Swamp. They noticed an eleven-foot alligator slip into the water from the bog, not three feet from the side of the canoe. Little girls' hands stayed as close to the center of the canoe as two hands can get after that.

When a situation gets a little hairy, Mike Barla and his dad have an understanding. His dad alerts him by saying, "Put your hands in the canoe and give me all the room that I need." There is never any need to ask twice.

It's a good idea to practice capsizing the canoe when it is warm out, so the children can experience it and erase their fear in case it happens by accident. Let the kids get underneath, yell and scream, and get comfortable with the canoe.

Hazardous Conditions

Weather contributes greatly to hazards while canoeing, especially on open water. The wind in particular can slow you down or make your direction of travel very difficult to follow. High winds also generate waves that can swamp or capsize your canoe.

Lake canoeing can be very dangerous, for winds can change at any given time and pick up with tremendous speed. Waves can crash over the boat, making capsizing a reality. Shorelines are safest with young children and certainly the most interesting. If you must cross large expanses of open water, be very careful to monitor the weather and, if possible, make the crossing at the calmest time of the day.

You could also get severe weather on a lake without a storm if it is positioned alongside a mountain. Winds shift up and down a mountain at different times of the day, which greatly affect the conditions of the lake. Be aware of this "turnaround" affect and plan accordingly.

A good rule of thumb for playing it safe on the water is to cut out of a situation before it gets serious. When storm clouds begin to appear or the wind picks up, get off the water and set up camp, even if it is early in the day. Never push it when children are involved.

Weather

Sun

When you're on the water, the sun's rays are reflected onto you constantly—there is no cover as there is in a forest. Even during overcast

weather, be relentlessly careful of sunburn on young children. Use strong sunscreens or adequate coverings of hats and clothing. The current increase in UV radiation levels makes the exposure of a child's sensitive skin even more serious. Be sure to use a minimum of 15 SPF for faces or even 25 SPF, and apply it every couple of hours on hot days. Check out your local health food store for lotions that leave out a lot of questionable additives.

The Tuchman boy did not enjoy wearing a hat. He simply refused to. Different hats were tried and all types of bribes were made, to no avail. Then a relative brought back a Donald Duck hat from Disneyland. Its brim was a hollow, yellow plastic bill that squeaked. His father told him that he needed to wear it at all times on the water, for you never knew when you'd come upon a duck and they needed to know he was a "duck friend." He also needed to say "hello" to them and so would happily squeak his hat's bill. He never took his hat off in case he'd meet one by surprise. As a parent, you have to do what you need to do in order to get the results that you want.

Cold

Exposure and hypothermia are other weather-related hazards. Check on what the recommended date is in your area for when it is safe to be on the water without a wet suit. The sum of water and air temperature should equal or exceed 100 degrees Fahrenheit. This does not include wind chill, however. If it is less than 100, the risk of hypothermia increases greatly should you get wet, and wet suits should be worn. Most parents do not want to invest in them for growing children and because of this they canoe in the warmer months of the year.

Family Canoe Trips

All children really love canoeing because around the water is where the wildlife can be found. All animals must go to water. A canoe slips along quietly compared to tramping through the woods in dry leaves and you can sneak up on animals—moose and deer, otter and egrets. Two-year-old Mike Barla was enraptured on the Snake River in Idaho with the enormous trout that he saw in the water and the buffalo lounging by the side.

Normally, you set your pace, as in hiking and cycling, by the slowest member. They must be in the lead because if they get behind, they can never catch up unless the ones up front stop, for there is no way for them to communicate. You should also have a designated "sweep" or last canoe to see that no one falls behind. Most families remained in the canoe for a maximum of three hours before taking a break, but generally one and a half to two hours was what they strived for.

Babies

A baby can ride in a canoe when big enough to sit up on its own and wear a life jacket. You could attach a tether from your child to a parent. In the event that you do capsize, your child will not be able to drift away. Of course, to be safest you will only be able to go on small lakes during mild weather when canoeing with a small baby.

Once babies reach one year old, they can understand when you tell them they must sit or lie in the little bed that you've made. They cannot lean, crawl, or stand up. They truly do love the changing scenery and motion. And as long as you shield the sun from their eyes, they are able to lie down and nap too. The Newmans gently rocked their canoe back and forth to get their babies asleep. You have to learn how far you can push your canoe (tipping it over once or twice on purpose in warm weather will teach you its limits.)

Some babies' personalities are not conducive to canoe travel and they will let you know if this is true, right from the start. Wait a few months and try again. Perhaps the added maturity will stretch their attention span and enable them to sit better.

Young Children

Canoeing is very confining, and very young children can become extremely frustrated with these limitations. Because of this, the Lewiston family never went on trips longer than four or five hours until the children were old enough to help portage. They began canoeing when their children were four to five years old. They were never bored when on the water.

Until your children are two or three years old, be prepared to work solo most of the time. At one year old, Bryce still couldn't be left unattended while we packed up and carried the canoe down to the water's edge. Only one of us could work. This is typical of this age.

Small children do not belong in the stern with the person who has the important job of steering the boat. They are too much of a distraction and if you are on a moving river or stream, sometimes quick decisions and movements need to be made.

We didn't know this valuable piece of information when we went on our trial run down the wild and scenic Little Schuykill River in Pennsylvania for Mother's Day. We waited until late in the afternoon to run our stretch, so the hot sun would be lower and the river would be in shade. Bryce sat with me in the stern, either on an inflatable pillow or standing between my knees. He fussed a lot and I was frantically trying to steer us away from hanging tree branches and rocks. I was supposed to be steering and handling a baby at the same time. Those two big jobs were too much for me. I had to raise my arms above my head to clear him in order to paddle, and still I bumped his head. Todd kept telling me to keep the boat straight. Todd tossed me back a pound of cheese to feed Bryce and he immediately threw it overboard. I would have been happy had the run lasted ten minutes.

A child as young as three can begin to learn skills such as reading a river. Teach them anything they show an interest in learning. When Todd and I read the river out loud to each other on that Mother's Day run, three-year-old Sierra wanted to know where and what we were talking about. I explained how the water looked different around the rock ahead. As we passed by it, she could see for herself how the water moved and crested.

She sat on a chair in the middle of the canoe and looked at everything wide-eyed. At this age, with her inquisitive and cooperative personality, we had no problems. But all children are different, with different attention spans, interests, etc.

A mink ran on the shore. Geese sat by the riverbank. Ducks took off in front of us. We showed her how to look ahead on the water for their dark bobbing heads. We had all settled down and relaxed. The lowering sun shone on the water and dazzled like diamonds. A warm, refreshing breeze blew over the water. Our canoe cut through the water as though it were butter. I looked over at Todd and he was smiling. "I like this," he said. It turned into a fine Mother's Day after all.

Children should never be taken down any Class II river unless they themselves have taken a river running course. Parents may feel confident themselves, but including young children really multiplies the risk.

Todd Hudson and his family had lake canoed a dozen times before he got the urge to tackle the Piedra River in Colorado. He ran it solo the day before and felt confident that his family could handle it. Snow melt was occurring and the water was swift and high.

The oldest child, Cody, age seven, loved it and had learned to ride rapids earlier, in the event that she'd fall overboard or capsize. Her parents taught her to keep her feet up and her arms crossed on her chest while holding her life jacket on. She knew that as soon as she reached a shallow or calm spot, she should get to the bank, because riding rapids is dangerous and her goal is to get to safety.

The two younger boys, West, age four, and Logan, age two, did not care for their father's idea of adventure. West was very nervous and Logan hated it. He remained in a scissors lock between his mother's legs in the bow for the entire six-mile run.

Their mother, Elizabeth, who has a strong maternal instinct and wisdom besides, felt that they would have been in trouble had they dumped the canoe. The boys will not run a river like that again until they are older and will practice going through rapids like their sister.

The Tuchman child was taught his strokes as soon as he began to use a paddle and could talk and communicate. By the time he was three, he knew the draw, the pry, and the forward and backward sweep. He invented some of his own names, like "the motorboat" for a brace stroke; when he spun his paddle, he called it "the tornado." To a child, this is play and entertainment, but he is also laying the foundation for good canoe skills.

Most of their canoeing was done in the Pine Barrens of New Jersey, where the rivers have current but they are not very wide or deep. The children could learn how to maneuver a canoe and hone their skills so that when they got older, they'd be ready to experience rapids.

Once children turn five, they want to paddle and they are able to paddle. They participate enough at this age to think that they are doing something. The Lewiston family had only flat-water canoed on slow-moving, narrow rivers. They did not go near a rapid until their children were teenagers and were strong enough to handle their own boat.

Games and Diversions

The Barlas always canoed in the summer months with their two-year-old son Michael and took advantage of the warmth and friendliness of the season. To keep Mike occupied on short trips, his dad filled the canoe with twenty-five pounds of stones that he could toss into the water. When his stash was depleted, they filled up on the next river bank on the next break.

They took along sand pails and shovels so he could dig and build jetties on shore when they took breaks. Whenever there was something interesting to see, they pulled over and tried to break up the day for him. When you see a nice stretch of beach or area that's a good spot to take a break, take advantage of it because you can't assume that in another half mile there will be another good place to stop. They looked for campsites with nice sand beaches, too, so Mike could entertain himself while his parents set up camp.

The Newman children were kept entertained in the canoe by being allowed to eat as much as they liked. When it was time to take a break out of the canoe, or portage, they were all fueled up and ran around, getting the exercise they needed. The Newmans also got the children little toy fishing rods that they could reel in and cast out. By the time they were four years old, they could cast a real rod and used worms on the hooks, which they put on themselves.

For diversion, the Tuchmans play a Canadian canoe game called "Rooster" when canoeing with a group. You must get your bow to tag the stern of another canoe and say, "Cock-a-doodle-doo." Then that canoe is "It" and goes off in search of another boat to tag. On hot day trips, you can break up the day by having water fights using empty bleach bottles that are cut into scoops for bailing.

Discipline

The Barlas never had a discipline problem with their young child. Instead, the movement of the canoe seemed to soothe and sedate him. If there was any problem, it was trying to keep him out of the canoe while his parents loaded it, for he was so excited to begin the trip.

There is never a discipline problem with the Newman children on canoe trips. Dad lays down the ground rules ahead of time and announces that it is not going to be like it is at home. He won't be telling them more than one time to do something because it may be a life and death situation. The Newman children wanted to solo paddle a canoe on a lake and could, by the time they were six years old.

Sleep

To get Mike to sleep in the canoe, his mother would just hold him in her arms and sometimes rock him gently. Sometimes she'd lay him down on a foam pad in the canoe or just continue holding him when he was very small. Fortunately, he had gotten used to sleeping in a brightly lit room before he began canoeing, so falling asleep in strong daylight was not a problem.

When a child is laid on the floor of a canoe to sleep, remember that the bottom is the same temperature as the water, which could be quite cold. Insulate it sufficiently. Water can get into the bottom from waves and rain, so they must be kept above it.

Older Children and Adolescents

At thirteen, the Newmans' eldest son began to pine over missing his girlfriend, the lack of TV, and the telephone when he was on a family canoe trip. Family trips did not challenge him anymore. He needed to go somewhere where he could push himself—test his skills and find his limits. He and his brother are five years apart and the differences in their needs revealed themselves when the eldest son hit thirteen. Dad Newman knows that this is the year he must take his son to run some Class II rapids.

While they are on family trips, this eldest son really enjoys paddling a solo canoe. He and his mother do not do very well as partners, because his younger, less strong brother, usually has to pair up with his father. This puts mom back in the boat with dad and young bro, so the eldest son can have the independence he so desperately needs at his age.

When your older children are in their own canoe, specific plans, directions, and rules must be made so that they do not become dangerously separated. Older children like to be up ahead and they exult in the power found within their bodies and want to test it.

The Lewiston family had an incident while canoeing in the Jersey Pine Barrens, when the children did not do as they were told, by accident. They missed the take-out point, going half as far again as they should have. The three children in the boat were fast paddlers and got much further ahead than they thought was possible. One friend in the canoe wanted to go off on the riverside trail and try to find a road. The Lewiston son had it drilled into his head to stay put if he ever got lost, and perhaps the trail only led deeper into the forest instead of out to a road. He talked his friend out of leaving and his dad did find them. They were never so happy to see an adult.

Mitch Tuchman has been taking groups of Explorer Scouts out canoeing ever since he was old enough to be a leader, for over twenty years now. Mitch forces the kids to switch positions in the boat so one child is not doing all of the work or learning only certain maneuvers and strokes. The kids do not volunteer to do this on their own.

Hints and Tips

- Make every effort to keep clothing, sleeping bags, etc., dry on a canoe trip.
- This is one sport where lack of experience and expertise can get you killed or in serious trouble. Be educated on handling the boat before you take your children on the water.
- Avoid any waterway listed as having water rated as Class II

on up until your children are old enough and knowledge-able enough to handle it.

- In a canoe on the water is not the place to be in severe weather. Get off the water before conditions get serious. Watch the weather and adjust your plans ahead of time.

- Unless you have wet suits, stay off the water if the air and water temperatures, added together, do not equal or exceed 100 degrees Fahrenheit (take wind chill into consideration).

- Because young children may find this sport more confining than most, with their mobility greatly limited, have a good repertoire of entertainment ideas up your sleeve—in advance.

- Canoeing safety rules are some of the most important, because water is a very dangerous element if not treated with respect. Your children should know and practice them fastidiously.

CHAPTER 12

Cross-Country Skiing

▲ ▲ ▲ ▲ ▲ ▲ ▲ ▲ ▲

C ross-country skiing is a very easy and enjoyable winter sport that the whole family can participate in. You have control over how gentle or wild the terrain you ski on. Introducing your children to this sport could give them a lifelong love, for participation in this sport can reach long into the golden years.

Make sure the area that you live in gets a considerable amount of snow and is consistent enough to warrant the purchase of equipment for your children. If not, and if you have to travel far to find reliable snow, consider renting until they're older.

It's a good idea to have your child take an introductory lesson from a professional at a ski resort/center. Your child will listen more attentively and learn much quicker and forego any frustration that may result from a parent playing the teacher role.

The most important factors that will contribute to them either loving the sport or deciding it's not worth the effort is if they can stay warm, if the terrain does not prove to be too difficult, and if their equipment works with them, not against.

Remember to try to have fun yourself. Don't set yourself up for a disaster; don't bite off too much. They pick up on your mood and attitude, so if you want them to be happy and join you again on an outing, make sure your message is that cross-country skiing is a great sport.

Equipment

Before you buy any cross-country gear for your children, look into ski rentals at outdoor equipment stores or ski centers. It is not very expensive to rent and it beats having to buy new skis every year. The people who rent you the skis will help out on what size to get (weight and height are taken into consideration). Some rental places sell their used skis at the end of the season at a fraction of their cost. And some places let you buy them and then trade in the skis for another size in the next season.

Skis

You should only purchase waxless skis for your child. Children do not need the speed that the correct wax gives a waxable ski. To size your child, go by his or her height from age five on down. After age six, they can successfully use longer skis, but don't go more than twenty centimeters beyond their height. If you must decide between longer and shorter skis, always go shorter, because your child will be more concerned with stability and balance at this age, than with glide.

Boots

Children under five years old can wear the same warm, waterproof snow boots that they wear for general winter wear, and attach them to their skis with a simple cable or strap binding. Don't buy boots that they will "grow into," but take advantage of the many trade-in offers at the stores.

Poles

Poles may be more of a hindrance than a help to children under five years old. They may have a hard time coordinating the arm/leg movement, they can get tangled up in them when they fall, and they actually do better, slushing along, propelling themselves with just the movement of arms and legs. Younger kids usually don't need the stability of poles because they stick to flat terrain, not hills. Once they reach five years of age, they may be ready for poles. Keep them shorter in proportion to their height.

Child Carriers

You can ski with your very small baby if you carry him or her in a child carrier and make sure baby is kept very warm. It is important that your carrier is the best type for the baby's size, age, personality, etc., because balance is much more important in this sport than when you are carrying them on the dry trail.

You don't want your child making any sudden weight shifts when you are trying to balance and maneuver on your skis. A child carrier with a nylon webbed belt—a poor excuse for a hip belt which takes no weight off your shoulders—is not recommended at all. If you do take a fall and your child is in one of these inferior packs, he or she will have a tendency to "bullet" out of them when you fall.

Our friends Todd and Cindy Harris of Vermont first skied with their daughter, Hannah, when she was six months old. One time when we were skiing with the Harrises, Hannah bulleted out in a fall while Todd was carrying her. Todd could not strap Hannah into the carrier, so she moved all around and threw him off balance and they took a spill. She wasn't hurt, but she wasn't happy either. It convinced her parents that they needed a much better child carrier.

A child carrier that can handle a heavy load has a much more substantial suspension system on it. It's important to have a sternum strap to tighten and pull the pack close to your body, and to have a good restraining strap system for keeping your child in place. Your baby has to be old enough to sit upright and hold its head up to be in a child carrier designed for your back.

With very small babies, some parents ski with them up front in a soft, fabric pack. One advantage of this set-up is you are able to cover them better and keep them warm by zipping them into a large coat or jacket with you. The greatest inherent danger is that if you fall forward, your child would go into the snow too. There is a tendency to put your arms out to catch yourself, but this is still the most dangerous way to ski with a child. If you use a front pack, only the most gentle trails should be attempted by the best skiers.

Sleds

When kids begin to exceed twenty pounds, skiing while carrying your child can be very difficult, because the child's weight doesn't balance as well as gear does. Another way to get onto the trails when your children are young is by pulling them behind you in a sled designed for carrying children or gear.

They look a little like the plastic sleds that the kids play with, but they are state-of-the-art. The hull is made out of a multilayered fiberglass or impact-resistant plastic, and it holds up to two children or cargo filling about 6,500 cubic inches. The pulling system is rigid, with aluminum and fiberglass rods that extend from the sled to a wide harness belt that the skier wears. This enables you to ski without bothersome jerking, and enables you to maneuver downhill turns. It stays directly behind and does not wander or go crosswise.

Sleds weigh in the neighborhood of seven to twelve pounds empty and are about four and a half feet long and two feet wide. The zippered nylon cover protects your children from snow and slush and helps to keep them warm. The children are enclosed in a sack that either zips or drawstrings closed to make a hood like a mummy sleeping bag if desired. You can first put your child in a down sleeping bag and place him or her on a sheepskin and be very assured that the child will stay warm. In this sack, body warmth is not being separated from extremities as it is in a baby sack with legs.

Some models have plexiglass windshields, because if there's one thing kids don't like, it's snow blowing in their faces. Some models have a "trunk" space behind the seat which is handy for holding extra clothes and food for your child. Some sleds convert to backpacks with the contoured hull doubling as a backpack frame and the zippered covering doubling as a pack bag. Once the children outgrow them and learn to ski themselves, the sled can be used to haul gear for the family's backcountry ski touring/camping adventures.

Disabled older children or adults can ski alpine and cross-country runs in a sled called Sit-n-Ski (see appendix A, Equipment Suppliers). The rider sits strapped into the seat of the sled which has aluminum rudderlike skis mounted to the sled, and uses short ski poles to lean on, drag behind, or propel them along. You can attach a tether line to a helper who is skiing behind to help control the sled's speed and direction. The zippered nylon cover protects the rider from snow and slush. There are even opportunities for competition using this sled, at the major ski areas.

Clothing

Whether your child is in a child carrier or a sled, the most important thing is to make sure he or she is kept warm. (This is more difficult in a child carrier.) Put lots of layers of insulation on and add and subtract as you need to.

Avoid all cotton and stick to wool or silk or synthetics such as polypropylene, capilene, polyester, etc. A windproof, waterproof, breathable outer layer is very important for skiing children. Young skiers fall down quite a bit, so it's important that they do not get wet. The one-piece suit prevents snow from getting into their backs too.

Snowsuits should only be worn if the child is riding in a pack or being pulled in a sled, when no activity is being done. If you think the temperature may fluctuate and warm up considerably during your run, avoid putting snowsuits on, because you cannot pull layers off and help ventilate when your child heats up.

Hats and mittens/gloves are very important. If the hat is made of wool, make sure it has an itch-proof lining such as a polyester pile; it's better if the hat is made entirely of polyester pile. Mittens are much warmer than gloves. If your child falls a lot and the snow is wet, the mittens should have a waterproof shell over them. If your child has a tendency to pull off mittens, pin them to cuffs with a large safety or diaper pin. A lost mitten can ruin an otherwise great ski.

Gaiters are great for preventing snow from going down your boots and socks, but you may not be able to find them to fit your small children. Invest in them as soon as your child is old enough to fit into them.

Bring along a foam pad to sit on and insulate yourself from the cold and wet.

Dress your baby in multiple layers of warm clothing, balaclavas, etc., and then put him or her in an insulated baby bag. These bags have two legs in them for use in car seats and in backpacks, and the top can be zipped and drawstringed closed around the upper body and head. Still, your child is being sedentary and cannot last more than a few hours without getting chilled. Babies may need to wear several hats, and socks make excellent layered mittens.

Choosing an Outing

Out of all the outdoor sports which involve your children, cross-country skiing has the greatest potential for hardship and danger, whether you're carrying them on your body as you ski or pulling them behind you on a sled. There are a few things to consider right from the start.

First, assess how good a skier you really are. You should have a fair amount of experience. No matter what your level of skill, bring your challenge level way down, not just for safety reasons, but to insure that you have a little fun. Anything that is going to cause you trouble, such as inconsistent snow conditions, lots of uphill slogging, breaking through a crust, deep snow, and unbroken trail, will be doubly difficult as you haul your child through it too.

Stick to fairly gentle trails without a lot of fast downhill through trees. The less competent a skier you are, the more tame your course should be. If you are fairly inexperienced, you might consider first going to a ski touring center with groomed trails that are rated for difficulty.

Days when the sun is bright and warm with little or no wind are the best kind of days. The wind chill is more important to consider than temperature.

Safety

Dehydration is a real danger during outdoor winter activities. Without the presence of perspiration to remind us that we need to drink, it often gets ignored. Freezing-cold drinks don't always sound appealing to anyone, especially chilled children, so carry a thermos of hot cocoa or hot cider for breaks. Carry your water bottle in an insulated case that you either buy or make by fitting, cutting, and gluing pieces of closed-cell foam pad together using contact cement. This prevents your water from freezing so you have something to drink and keeps the temperature lower to make "gulping" more appealing. You can even put warm water in before going out so the temperature doesn't have as much chance to drop very low.

Always carry plenty of wholesome snacks. Food with a higher fat content, such as cheese or bars with oil or butter in them, will not freeze as quickly and give you much-needed calories.

Always carry some "spare parts" such as another set of mittens, a hat, etc. It could make a big difference in a successful trip.

When you come to a bridge, don't be afraid to take off your skis and walk across, especially with a child on your back or in tow. Your poles could stick into the slats and wrench your arm or get broken.

Never take any chances crossing frozen water that is iffy or skiing in avalanche-prone areas. If your children are old enough to be in these more dangerous, wild areas, consult a good mountaineering guide to learn about avalanche awareness, etc. (see appendix C, Suggested Reading).

Weather Conditions

Be very careful of the sun. The brightness and glare could badly sunburn your children's sensitive skin and harm their eyes. Use a highly protective sunscreen and put sunglasses, ski goggles, or a wide-brimmed hat on your children.

Your children cannot adjust to altitude as readily as you, so refrain from skiing very high, especially if they are very young and cannot communicate. All children respond differently and it depends on what elevation you live at, what elevation you are staying at, etc.

Don't plan on staying out more than an hour or two at first. Later, you can prolong it to four or five hours if the weather is pleasant and that time frame is within everyone's capabilities.

Protect your children's skin from wind chill by applying glacier cream, which seals the pores to a degree. Pay attention to their face, especially their nose and ears, which protrude from their face. If the temperatures and wind chill are low enough to make frostbite a possibility, perhaps you should pick a warmer day to take your children out.

Bad weather could blow in at any time in the mountains. Always listen to the forecast before venturing out, watch the sky for impending storms, and turn back if conditions begin to deteriorate. Sometimes you may get caught and you need to just put your head down and get your family out. Make sure everyone's fuel is sufficiently high to tackle the pushing needed to quickly get out.

Plan your outings out of a lodge or an inn if at all possible. You have a better chance of having someone know you are out in case of an emergency, and the children will thoroughly enjoy ending their day in the comfort and warmth, with a roaring fire and something warm to eat.

Family Ski Outings

Babies

Your baby must be old enough to sit upright and hold its head up if you use a child carrier designed for your back. Alternatively, you can use a front pack. You will not be able to ski on anything but gentle, moderate trails while carrying a baby, no matter how competent a skier you are, because you could lose control and plunge into a tree.

You may not be able to stop or rest much when carrying a baby, because it may not like the motion to stop and may awaken from a nap in tears. This sport isn't like backpacking, where you can stop, take baby out of the pack, and let him or her freely move around for a break. Because of this, the skier may need exceptional stamina.

A big problem with this sport is diaper changing. Most parents change their baby's diaper right before going on a run, then put extra diapers or liners on and only stay out as long as it takes for that diaper to fill up. Changing them out-of-doors in the winter can be terribly uncomfortable for them, as well as dangerous.

Young Children

You may reach your limit of carrying ability earlier on skis in snow than hiking on a dry trail. You also get a break when hiking as your three-year-old can walk a bit, but this isn't the case on skis. You could combine carrying your children in a child carrier and alternating with a sled to give yourself a break.

Our friends in Montana skied with their daughter in her sled from six months on up to four years. She loved it in there and would listen to tapes of children's music while she rode. If the weather wasn't too cold, she'd sit with the sack open and look at books and even color. Because the child is kept so warm, the length of time you are able to ski increases considerably. Our friends typically skied into a Forest Service cabin that they rented for a three-day weekend and went on day trips while based out of it. The ski-in was six hours long, however, and still their daughter was happy. When they did get her out to care for her needs, she never wanted to remain out for long because it was cold, so there was never any coaxing to get her to go back in.

Sleds are good for carrying children up until four to six years old, when they will begin to get antsy and want to ski themselves. Then you can use your sled for simply carrying gear (as they do in Antarctica) or use it to give your larger child a break from skiing. One of the nicest things about these sleds is that your child's skis can fit on them, so when he or she tires from skiing and needs to rest, you can still continue moving.

The Harrises started Hannah on her own skis when she was about three years old. At that age, they are just generally testing and experimenting with how to get their skis to move. Tooling around in open meadows is just the thing to introduce them to the sport. Some touring centers offer lessons for children as young as three and four. It isn't really until they are five and six years old, however, that they usually begin to get the hang of it. They are bigger and stronger and more coordinated by then and can even handle downhills. The most important thing to remember is to keep their outings very short and fun.

Have no expectations. Don't think about your own skiing, but rather view it as an outing where you're going to take your child out skiing.

Older Children and Adolescents

Cross-country skiing enables older kids to connect with the quiet and beauty of nature. It also presents them with an opportunity to learn some new outdoor skills—critical winter ones—and test themselves physically on technique, slopes, etc. This is the age at which to take them to a place where they can learn to telemark. This is a very graceful turn for skiing downhill in powder. You need the heel-lifting freedom that you can only get with telemark cross-country gear. Investing in some telemark lessons at a lodge or resort could be just the thing to excite them into going on a ski outing with you. It also gets them onto steeper, more exciting slopes, which is just what this age group may need.

Hints and Tips

- Buy new ski equipment for your children only if your area gets considerable snow. Otherwise, rent.
- Waxless skis are the only type of ski a child should use.
- Protect your children from the sun by having them wear glasses/goggles, creams, and protective clothing.
- Plan short outings with plenty of snacks and stops to ensure a good time.
- Be sure you are a competent skier yourself before carrying your child on your back. Choose terrain and plan trip length, etc., according to your skill level.

Appendix A:

Equipment Suppliers

For the reader's convenience, manufacturers are listed under the heading that best reflects their specialty in terms of items for chidren, rather than their entire production.

Backpacking

General Equipment

Campmor, 810 Route 17 North, P.O. Box 997-D, Paramus, NJ 07653-0997; (201) 445-5000

Crazy Creek Chairs, P.O. Box 1050, Red Lodge, MT 59068; (800) 331-0304

Land's End, Inc., 1 Land's End Lane, Dodgeville, IL 53595; (800) 356-4444

L.L. Bean, Inc., Freeport, ME 04033; (800) 221-4221

Recreational Equipment, Inc., P.O. Box 88125, Seattle, WA 98138-2125; (800) 426-4840

Clothing & Outerwear

Cherry Tree, 166 Valley Street, Providence, RI 02909; (800) 869-7742

Chuck Roast, Odell Hill Road, Conway, NH 03818

Columbia Sportswear, 6600 North Baltimore Avenue, Portland, OR 97203; (800) 622-6953

Hanna Anderson, 1010 Northwest Flanders, Portland, OR 97209; (800) 222-0544

Helly-Hansen, P.O. Box 97031, Redmond WA 98073-9731; (206) 883-4313 (children's clothing)

Newport Kidsport, 10775 Northwest McDaniel, Portland, OR 97229; (503) 644-5064

Patagonia, 1609 West Babcock Street, Bozeman, MT 59715; (800) 638-6464

Wicker's, 340 Veteran's Memorial Highway, Commack, NY 11725; (800) 648-7024

Wilderness Experience, 20675 Nordhoff Street, Chatsworth, CA 91311 (clothing and packs)

Wyoming Woolens, P.O. Box 3127, Jackson Hole, WY 83001; (307) 733-2889

Diaper Liners

Family Playhouse, 6 Chiles Avenue, Ashfield, NC 28803

Boots

Coleman Co., 250 North St. Francis, Wichita, KS 67201; (316) 261-3485

Decker's Corp., P.O. Box 5022, Carpinteria, CA 93014; (805) 684-6694 (sport sandals)

Fabiano Shoe Co., Inc., 850 Summer Street, Boston, MA 02127

Hi-Tec Sports USA, Inc., 4801 Stoddard Road, Modesto, CA 95356; (800) 521-1698

Merrell Boots, P.O. Box 4249, Burlington, VT 05406; (800) 359-3050

NIKE Inc., 1 Bowerman Drive, Beaverton, OR 97005-6453; (800) 344-6453

Pacific Mountain Sports, 910 Foothill Boulevard, La Canada, CA 91011

Puddleduckers, Inc., 840 Summer Street, Boston, MA 02127; (617) 269-5556 (rubber boots)

Technica Boots, 19 Technology Drive, West Lebanon, NH 03784; (800) 258-3897

Vasque Boots, 314 Main Street, Red Wing, MN 55066; (612) 388-8211

Backpacks

Camp Trails, P.O. Box 966, Binghamton, NY 13902; (607) 779-2200

Jansport, Paine Field Industrial Park, Everett, WA 98204; (206) 353-0200

Kelty Pack, Inc., P.O. Box 7048-A, St. Louis, MO 63177; (800) 423-2320 (also child carriers and sleeping bags)

Tough Traveler, 1012 State Street, Schenectady, NY 12307; (800) GO-TOUGH (also child carriers and sleeping bags)

Children's Packs

Diamond Brand Canvas Products Co., Inc., P.O. Box 249, Naples, NC 28760; (800) 258-9811

Lafuma USA, P.O. Box 812, Farmington, GA 30638; (706) 769-6627

Mountain Masters, P.O. Box 1831, Grass Valley, CA 95945 (children's backpacks and child carriers)

Mountainsmith, Inc., 1100 Simms Street, Golden, CO 80401 (children's backpacks and child carriers)

Day Packs

Dolt of California, 10455 West Jefferson Boulevard, Culver City, CA 90230

Eastpak, 17 Locust Street, Haverhill, MA 01830

Child Carriers

Gerry Baby Products, Inc., 150 East 128th Avenue, Thorton, CO 80220; (800) 535-2472

Snugli, 12520 Grant Drive, Denver, CO 80233; (303) 457-0926

Sleeping Bags

Baby Bag, 138 Hartley Street, Portland, ME 04103

Caribou Mountaineering, P.O. Box 3696, Chico, CA 95927; (800) 824-4153

Cascade Designs, Inc., 4000 First Avenue South, Seattle, WA 98134; (800) 531-9531

Eastern Mountain Sports, One Vose Farm Road, Peterborough, NH 03458; (603) 924-6154 (sleeping bags and general gear)

Henderson Camp Products, 300 West Washington Street, Chicago, IL 60606

Jack Wolfskin, 920 Mendocino Avenue, Santa Rosa, CA 95401; (607) 779-2755

The North Face, 999 Harrison Street, Berkeley, CA 94710; (501) 527-9700
Sierra Designs, 2039 Fourth Street, Berkeley, CA 94710; (800) SIERRA-2
Wiggy's, 2482 Industrial Boulevard, P.O. Box 2124, Grand Junction, CO
   81502; (303) 241-6465

Food Dehydrators

American Harvest, P.O. Box 159, 4064 Peavey Road, Chaska, MN 55318;
   (612) 448-4400
Harvest Savor Dehydrator, Vita-Mix Corporation, 8615 Usher Road, Cleve-
   land, OH 44138; (216) 235-4840

Bicycling

Bailen Bike Helmets, 2680 Bridgeway, Sausalito, CA 94965
Bell Helmets, 15301 Shoemaker Avenue, Norwalk, CA 90650; (800) 456-2355
Bell Wether, San Francisco, CA; (415) 863-0436 (children's clothing)
Bike Burro, Inc., P.O. Box 2594, Carson City, NV 89702; (702) 885-7767
Bike Caboose International, P.O. Box 1088, Sandpoint, ID 83864; (208)
   236-8606
The Bike Farm, Route 1, Box 99, Cushing, WI 54006; (715) 648-5519
Blue Sky Cycle Carts, P.O. Box 704, Redmond, OR 97756; (503) 548-7753
Burley Design Cooperative, 4080 Stewart Road, Eugene, OR 97402; (800)
   423-8445 (tandems, child stoker kit, trailers, etc.)
Cannondale Corporation, 9 Brookside Place, Georgetown, CT 06829; (800)
   BIKE USA
Cycletote, 1828 East First Street, Loveland, CO 80537; (303) 669-4283
Cycle Trailer, 3330 North Webster, Tuscon, AZ 85715; (602) 296-6536
Equinox Industries Inc., 1142 Chestnut Street, Cottage Grove, OR 97424;
   (800) 942-7895
Expressline, (313) 426-1000 (gloves)
Giro Sport Design, 2880 Research Park Drive, Soquel, CA 95073-2000; (408)
   479-8020
Gita Sporting Goods, 12600 Steelecreek Road, Charlotte, NC 28273; (704)
   588-7555 (jerseys)
Kidde Kart, (612) 774-1312
L.L. Bean, Inc., Freeport, ME 04033; (800) 221-4221
Mel Pinto Imports, P.O. Box 2198, Falls Church, VA 22042; (703) 237-4686
Patagonia, P.O. Box 150, Ventura, CA 93002; (800) 638-6464 (reflective jack-
   ets, etc.)
Pearl Izumi, 2300 Central Avenue, Boulder, CO 80301; (800) 328-8488
Performance, One Performance Way, P.O. Box 2741, Chapel Hill, NC 27514;
   (800) PBS-BIKE
Rhode Gear, 765 Allens Avenue, Providence, RI 02905; (800) 456-2800
Santana Cycles, Inc., Box 1205, Claremont, CA 91711; (909) 596-7570 (child
   conversion kits)
Tandems East, RR 8, Box 319 East Gwynwood Drive, Bridgeton, NJ 08302
Tandems Ltd., Route 19, Box 248, Birmingham, AL 35244

Troxel, 1333 30th Street, San Diego, CA 92514; (800) 288-4280

Winchester Originals, Kool Stop International, Inc., P.O. Box 3480, Lahabra, CA 90632; (714) 738-4973

Canoeing

Coleman, 250 North St. Francis, Wichita, KS 67202

Easy Rider Canoe 7 Kayak Co., Box 88108, Tukwila Branch C9, Seattle, WA 98138; (206) 228-3633

The Jersey Paddler, Route 88 West, Brick, NJ 08724; (201) 458-5777

Kayak Specialties, P.O. Box 152, Buchanan, MI 49107 (life jackets)

L.L. Bean, Freeport, ME 04033; (800) 221-4221

Mad River Canoe, Box 610, Waitsfield, VT 05673; (802) 496-3127

Old Town Canoe Co., 58 Middle Street, Old Town, ME 04468; (207) 827-5514

Cross-Country Skiing

Mountain Man, 720 Front Street, Bozeman, MT 59715; (406) 587-0310 ("Cross-country Touring Sled")

Ridge Runner Products, Inc., P.O. Box 270373, Fort Collins, CO 80527; (303) 282-8785 ("Snow Otter Sled")

Appendix B:

Organizations

Associations

American Bicycle Association
P.O. Box 714, Chandler, AZ 85244; (602) 961-1903
American Canoe Association
7217 Lockport Place, P.O. Box 248, Lorton, VA 22079
American Hiking Society
243 Church Street, Suite 300A, Vienna, VA 22180; (703) 255-9304
American Youth Hostels
733 15th Street Northwest, Suite 840, Washington, DC, 20005;
(202) 783-6161
Appalachian Trail Conference
P.O. Box 807, Harper's Ferry, WV 25425; (304) 535-6331
Bicycle Federation of America
1818 R Street Northwest, Washington, DC 20036 (runs bike education
programs for grades 4-6)
Family Cycling Club
FCC RR 8, Box 319E, Bridgeton, NJ 08302
Rails to Trails Conservancy
1400 16th Street Northwest, Washington, DC 20036; (202) 797-5400
Rocky Mountain Llama Association
41930 County Road AA, Akron, CO 80720 (for a listing of pack llama
outfitters, contact Dee Goodman)
The Western Horseman Magazine, Inc.
P.O. Box 7980, Colorado Springs, CO 80933; (719) 633-5524 (for a listing of horsepacking vacations, ask to buy a back issue of their Febru-
ary 1995 issue)
Wind River Pack Goats
Route 62, Box 250, Lander, WY 82520; (307) 332-7554 (for information
on goat packing, contact John Mionczynski)

Government Agencies

Bureau of Land Management (BLM), 1849 C Street Northwest, MIB 5600,
Washington, DC, 20240; (202) 208-5717
National Park Service, U. S. Department of the Interior, P.O. Box 37127,
Washington, DC 20013; (202) 343-4747
U. S. Fish and Wildlife Service, Washington, DC 20240; (202) 343-4311
U. S. Forest Service, Technology and Development Program, Missoula, MT
59801 (contact for the free book *Techniques and Equipment for Wilder-
ness Travel with Stock*)

Appendix C:
Suggested Reading

Books

Birkby, Robert. *The Boy Scout Handbook.* Irving, Tex.: Boy Scouts of America, 1990.

Blood-Paterson, Peter, ed. *Rise Up Singing.* Chicago, Ill.: Independent Publishers Group, 1988. (words to 1,200 songs)

Brown, Tom, Jr., and Judy Brown. *Tom Brown's Field Guide to Nature and Survival For Children.* New York: Berkley Books, 1989.

Cook, Charles. *The Essential Guide to Hiking in the United States.* New York: Michael Kesend Publishing, 1991.

———. *The Essential Guide to Wilderness Camping and Backpacking in the United States.* New York: Michael Kesend Publishing, 1994.

Cornall, Joseph Bharat. *Sharing Nature With Children.* Nevada City, Calif.: Dawn Publications, 1979.

Cuthbertson, Tom. *Anybody's Bike Book.* Berkeley, Calif.: Ten Speed Press, 1988.

Doan, Marlyn. *Starting Small in the Wilderness.* San Francisco, Calif.: Sierra Club Books, 1979.

Euser, Barbara J. *Take 'em Along.* Evergreen, Colo.: Cordillera Press, 1987.

Fleming, June. *Staying Found—Complete Map and Compass Handbook.* Seattle, Wash.: The Mountaineers, 1994.

Harrison, David, and Judy Harrison. *Canoe Tripping with Children.* Indiana: ICS Books, 1990.

Herman, M. *Teaching Kids to Love the Earth.* Duluth, Minn.: Pfeifer-Hamilton, 1991.

Hodgson, Michael. *Wilderness With Children.* Harrisburg, Penns.: Stackpole Books, 1992.

Jeffrey, Nan, and Kevin Jeffrey. *Adventuring With Children.* San Francisco, Calif.: Fogreen Press, 1990.

LaChapelle, Edward R. *The ABC of Avalanche Safety.* Seattle, Wash.: The Mountaineers, 1985.

Leccese, Michael, and Arlene Plevin. *The Bicyclist's Sourcebook.* Maryland: Woodbine House, 1991.

Liston, Beverly. *Family Camping Made Simple—Tent and RV Camping with Children.* Chester, Conn.: Globe Pequot, 1989.

Meyers, Carole Terwillinger. *Miles of Smiles—101 Great Car Games and Activities.* Emeryville, Calif.: Publishers Group West, 1989.

Mionczynski, John. *The Pack Goat.* Colo.: Pruett Publishing, 1992.

Moore, Robin. *Awakening the Hidden Storyteller.* New York: Random House, 1991.

Peterson First Guide to Birds. Boston: Houghton Mifflin, 1987.

Peterson First Guide to Mammals. Boston: Houghton Mifflin, 1987.

Peterson First Guide to Wildflowers. Boston: Houghton Mifflin, 1987.

Politano, Colleen. *Lost in the Woods: Child Survival for Parents and Teachers.* Merrillville, Ind.: ICS Books, 1994.

Ross, Cindy and Todd Gladfelter. *A Hiker's Companion.* Seattle, Wash.: The Mountaineers, 1993.

Silverman, Goldie. *Backpacking With Babies and Small Children.* Berkeley, Calif.: Wilderness Press, 1975.

Weaver, Susan. *A Woman's Guide to Cycling.* Berkeley, Calif.: Ten Speed Press, 1991.

Wilkerson, James. *Medicine for Mountaineering.* Seattle, Wash.: The Mountaineers, 1992.

Whitefeather, Willy. *Willy Whitefeather's Outdoor Survival Handbook for Kids.* Tucson, Ariz.: Harbinger, 1990.

Sources for Books and Tapes

Adventurous Traveler Bookstore, P.O. Box 577, Hinesburg, VT 05461; (800) 282-3963 (catalog)

Chinaberry Book Service, 2780 Via Orange Way, Suite B, Spring Valley, CA 91978; (800) 776-2242 (children's tapes and books)

Dover Children's Books, Dover Publications, Inc., 31 East Second Street, Mineola, NY 11501 (catalog)

"A Kid for the Wild," by Walkin' Jim Stoltz, Wild Wind Records, Box 477, Big Sky, MT 59716; (406) 995-4906 (cassette tape and CD)

Music for Little People, P.O. Box 1720, Lawndale, CA 90260; (800) 727-2233 (catalog)

Index

About the Authors

Pennsylvania residents Cindy Ross and Todd Gladfelter are the veterans of thousands of miles of hiking and the authors of several books as well as many articles for outdoor publications, including *Backpacker* magazine. They also teach backpacking classes at a local college.